The European Union and Beyond

ECPR Press

ECPR Press is an imprint of the European Consortium for Political Research. It publishes original research from leading political scientists and the best among early career researchers in the discipline. Its scope extends to all fields of political science, international relations and political thought, without restriction in either approach or regional focus. It is also open to interdisciplinary work with a predominant political dimension.

The European Union and Beyond

Multi-Level Governance, Institutions, and Policy-Making

Edited by Jae-Jae Spoon and Nils Ringe

ecpr
PRESS

Published by the European Consortium for Political Research, Harbour House, 6–8 Hythe Quay, Colchester, CO2 8JF, United Kingdom

British Library Cataloguing in Publication Data
A catalogue record for this book is available from the British Library

ISBN: HB 978-1-7855-2335-9

Library of Congress Cataloging-in-Publication Data Is Available

ISBN   978-1-78552-335-9 (cloth)
ISBN   978-1-5381-5690-2 (pbk)
ISBN   978-1-78552-336-6 (electronic)

ecpr.eu/shop

Contents

Acknowledgments

This project began as a way to honor our colleague, friend, and mentor, Alberta Sbragia. One of us is Professor of Political Science and the Director of the European Studies Center at the University of Pittsburgh. The other was her PhD student at the University of Pittsburgh and is now Professor of Political Science and Director of the Center for European Studies at the University of Wisconsin–Madison. Our careers have both been profoundly affected by the scholarship and the institution-building to which Alberta dedicated her career.

With funding from several sources, including the Erasmus+ program of the European Commission (through a Jean Monnet Center of Excellence grant), the European Union Studies Association, the University of Pittsburgh's Office of the Provost, University Center for International Studies, the Year of Pitt Global funding initiative, Honors College, Graduate School for Public and International Affairs, Global Studies Center, Center for Russian, East European and Eurasian Studies, Center for Latin American Studies, Asian Studies Center, and Department of Political Science, the European Studies Center at Pitt organized an international conference in November 2018, which brought together scholars from around the world to celebrate Alberta's contributions to the study of the European Union. From over forty submissions, half were included in the conference program, and the chapters in this volume were selected from those to demonstrate the depth and breadth of her work. All contributors have a connection to Alberta either personally or through her scholarship (or both). Together, they highlight the impact Alberta has made during her career. They include assistant professors, endowed chairs, those who were trained and work at U.S. universities, and those who were trained and work abroad.

A subsequent book workshop, held in Denver in May 2019, was generously supported by the European Union Studies Association, the European Studies Center at Pitt, and Jean Monnet Grants at the University of Wisconsin–Madison.

Importantly, although this publication was produced with the financial support of the European Union, its contents are the sole responsibility of the authors and do not necessarily reflect the views of the European Union.

A few thank-yous are in order.

First, the initial idea for this entire project was Allyson Delnore's, associate director of the European Studies Center at Pitt. Without her commitment and perseverance to honoring Alberta in the year of her retirement, which also corresponded to the twentieth anniversary of the European Union Center of Excellence programs in the United States, this project would never have gotten off the ground.

Second, Anthony Ocepek, who helped immensely getting the final manuscript into shape, which was no easy task with so many authors.

Third, we thank the editors and reviewers at ECPR Press for their recognition of the importance of this project and willingness to publish it.

Last, but certainly not least, we thank our families and especially our spouses—C. J. Voci and Sarah Halpern-Meekin—for their support as we pursued this project.

Finally, we are indebted to our collaborator on this project, Wade Jacoby, who tragically passed away as this book was being published. Wade was sharp and probing in his scholarship, as well as open, generous, warm, funny, and encouraging as a colleague, mentor, and friend. He was also an institution-builder and enabler of others. His passing is a huge loss to the European studies community. He is dearly missed.

Jae-Jae Spoon
Nils Ringe
August 2019

Foreword

The European Union (EU), in 2019, is quite different from the organization I examined in my 1992 book *Euro-Politics* and from other writing I have published since then. It has developed along lines that were unpredictable and, in some cases, unimaginable. The contributors to this volume have provided a well-informed, clear, and thoughtful commentary on these developments that should be useful for future students of the EU.

More personally, I have been truly touched by the hard work and generosity of both the editors of the volume and the contributors, several of whom are my former students. I am proud of our collaboration and its results. My warmest thanks and best wishes to all of you.

Alberta M. Sbragia

Introduction

Comparative Federalism, Institutional Complexity, and Policy Choice

Jae-Jae Spoon and Nils Ringe

The European Community is "not a political entity that is easily understood. Unique in its institutional structure, it is neither a state nor an international organization."

(Sbragia 1992b, 257)

Alberta Sbragia's scholarship is one of big questions and ideas, as reflected
in the "bumper sticker"[1] above in her conclusion to the seminal book *Euro-
Politics: Institutions and Policymaking in the "New" European Community*.
Over a career of more than forty years, such big questions informed Sbragia's
research and occupied her thinking on the European Union (EU). What is the
EU? Should it be considered an international organization? A state? Is it a (con-)
federation? How does it compare with other regional organizations? What role
should national governments play in its governance and policy-making institutions? Sbragia was less interested in tackling the nuances of what explained certain European Parliament (EP) votes or Commission decisions. Rather, she was
intrigued by the organization itself—which was initially made up of six countries
that came together in the decade following World War II to regulate the production of coal and steel and aid European conciliation and recovery, and which
became the EU, composed of twelve member states, with the coming into force
of the Maastricht Treaty. Today, the EU is made up of twenty-eight countries.

The chapters collected here all build on the big questions to which Sbragia
devoted her research and analysis. Some of the contributions engage them

---

1 Former students of Alberta's will remember her asking for summaries of books, articles, and dis-
sertations that were short and pithy enough to fit a "bumper sticker" and/or the little space dedicated
to a "tabloid"-length article.

directly, while others apply her concepts to more specific empirical questions. Sbragia's work encourages scholars to think about the EU in a comparative politics framework, and several contributors compare governance aspects of the EU to other federal systems, such as the United States and Canada (Brand, Maas) or to regional organizations like the Association of Southeast Asian Nations (ASEAN) (Wong and Irrera). Other chapters tackle narrower empirical questions inspired by her work on the institutional complexities of the EU (Peters) and the role that national governments, institutions, and actors play in the EU's governance structures (Perez, Daniel, Fabbrini). Still others examine the policy implications of EU membership and governance (Salazar-Morales and Hallerberg, Jacoby and Jevtic-Somlai, Piattoni and Notermans). Together, they demonstrate the breadth and depth of the influence that Sbragia's work has had on the field of EU studies during her career.[2]

Through Sbragia's teaching, training, mentoring, and generosity as a colleague, she enabled others to do the kind of original research showcased in this volume. Beyond her scholarship, Sbragia institutionalized this dedication to understanding the complexities of the EU through building a model center for EU studies at the University of Pittsburgh. She worked tirelessly to demonstrate to the European Commission the importance of supporting EU studies in the United States, which resulted in the establishment of the EU Centers of Excellence program in 1998. Each contributor to this volume has been affiliated, or has interacted, with an EU Center at some point in his or her career. Sbragia's legacy is thus embodied in both her scholarship and institution-building.

This project had its inception at an international conference in Pittsburgh, in November 2018, hosted by the European Studies Center, of which one of us is the current director. The conference brought together former students, colleagues, and scholars who were influenced by Sbragia's work to celebrate her contributions to the field of EU studies. The call for proposals generated forty-two submissions—a testament to Sbragia's reputation and recognition as a scholar, colleague, and friend. About half the submissions were included on the conference program, and the chapters in this volume were selected from those to demonstrate the breadth and depth of Sbragia's work. The contributors represent different generations of scholars of different ranks, who have varying backgrounds and experiences. Some were trained and/or work in the United States, while others were trained and/or work abroad. Together the chapters focus on three major themes that infused Sbragia's thinking:

---

2 While the chapters included in this volume reflect much of the breadth of Sbragia's career, they do not touch on everything she researched, analyzed, and commented on.

comparative federalism, the complexity of the EU and its institutions, and policy choice and policy outcomes.

THEMES: FEDERALISM, INSTITUTIONS, AND POLICIES

The concept of multi-level governance, developed by Hooghe and Marks (2001, 2003) around the turn of the twenty-first century, was informed by Sbragia's view, nearly a decade earlier, of the EU in a comparative federalism framework (Sbragia 1992a, 1992b). Since the EU was not, strictly speaking, a constitutionally-defined federal system, Sbragia emphasized governance over government when comparing the EU, implicitly or explicitly, to other federal contexts (e.g., Sbragia 1993, 2004). This conceptualization, as she later described it, highlighted "the (often interdependent) relationship between Brussels, national capitals and (at times) subnational centers in the policy process" (Sbragia 2010b, 267). Furthermore, as the institutions of the EU evolved, typically through the treaty revision process, so did Sbragia's thinking on the EU as a federal (or later an incomplete federal) entity. Ross's chapter carefully tracks Sbragia's understanding of the EU in this framework, and all of the remaining chapters engage the concepts of comparative federalism or multi-level governance in one way or another.

A second theme highlighted by Sbragia early on (1992a, 1992b) is also present in several of the contributions, namely the complexity of the European institutions. This facet of EU governance is familiar to any student or scholar who has attempted to understand the EU. At its simplest, some of the institutions are supranational, while others are intergovernmental, but the nuances of the intra- and inter-workings of the institutions are ever more complex. They have also changed and evolved as the EU has developed and as more competencies have been transferred to the EU from the member states. These complexities are a recurrent topic in several of Sbragia's contributions (see, for example, Sbragia 1992a, 1992b; 2004; 2005); the EU, she emphasized, is not easily understood and cannot be placed into a simple box of a state or an international organization. It is at once much more and much less than either of these polities. In this context, Sbragia often talks of how national governments and the EU are intertwined or enmeshed. The contributors examine these complexities and how they manifest themselves among parliamentarians (Daniel, Perez) and in the executive of the EU (Peters). Fabbrini's penultimate chapter then reflects on the EU institutions more generally and advocates for a reform of the institutions to disentangle the role of the EU from that of the member states.

The chapters by Brand and Maas compare the EU as a federal entity to other federations and consider the complexities of the institutional frameworks governing private international law and citizenship, respectively. But their chapters also engage the focus of some of Sbragia's more recent work, in which she sought to understand the policy choices and outcomes EU membership entails (2008, 2010a)—the third main theme of the contributions in this volume. The challenges of interdependence and external constraints on national policy-making are highlighted by Jacoby and Jevtic-Somlai, for example, who examine the impact of German immigration and macroeconomic policy on the Visegrád states. Piattoni and Notermans similarly look at policy interdependence by exploring the impact of the policies imposed on Italy by the EU as a result of the Euro crisis. Salazar-Morales and Hallerberg apply Sbragia's (2010a) concept of competitive interdependence to explore trade policies between the United States and the EU in the context of China's rise as a major international actor. Finally, using Sbragia's (2008) framework of comparative regionalism, Wong and Irrera compare policy outcomes following crises in the domains of migration and terrorism in the EU with outcomes in the areas of human rights and the environment in ASEAN.

OVERVIEW OF THE BOOK

George Ross (chapter 1) opens this volume by introducing readers to the evolution and breadth of Sbragia's work. He provides an overview of the major themes present throughout her writing, thus previewing some of the major themes on which the other authors focus in subsequent chapters. Beginning with the question that infused much of her thinking—"what kind of sociopolitical animal is the EU?"—Ross describes how Sbragia came to consider the EU as best understood through the lens of comparative federalism. Viewing the EU in this way moved the conversation from past debates about neofunctionalism and intergovernmentalism to how best to understand an organization which at its core comprised both constituent sovereign member states and a central administration. Ross points out, however, that Sbragia was keenly aware that even though one could understand the EU through this federalist lens, there were still "shocks" to the federalist institutions that the EU would face, such as the Maastricht Treaty's intergovernmental pillars of the Common Foreign and Security Policy and Justice and Home Affairs. As the EU evolved, Sbragia's thinking on how best to understand the organization also progressed. In her keynote speech at the European Community Studies Association in 2004, Sbragia argued that both supranational and confederal (or intergovernmental) institutions could exist within a federalist organization, pointing to the expansion of the powers of the Commission president in relation to the rest of the Commission, as outlined in the European Convention following the Nice Intergovernmental Conference. Ross then discusses how Sbragia also began to consider how the EU compared to, and differed from, other regional organizations (see also Wong and Irrera in this volume), concluding that the EU really was quite different and stood alone. In recent years, Sbragia has argued that the EU could increasingly be considered an incomplete federal entity, with both federal and intergovernmental elements. Events such as the Eurozone crisis, Brexit, and democratic backsliding in Hungary and Poland will continue to challenge the institutional complexity that is at the core of the EU.

Diego A. Salazar-Morales and Mark Hallerberg (chapter 2) use Sbragia's (2010a) concept of competitive interdependence as their starting point for investigating the trade policies and relationships of the EU and the United States, with a special eye toward changes therein as a result of China's rise as a global economic giant. Competitive interdependence characterizes how the competitive EU-U.S. relationship in the world economy affects their relations with third markets. Sbragia's article considered these dynamics leading up to its publication date in 2010 and argues that a shift in EU trade policy from focusing on multilateralism to privileging regional trade relationships was in response to the United States actively pursuing free trade agreements (FTAs) to the benefit of American firms. EU trade policy toward third parties was thus driven decisively by efforts to level the playing field for EU relative to the U.S. economic interests. Salazar-Morales and Hallerberg examine what happened since then. They argue that both the EU and the United States have changed their trade policy choices in response to the challenges posed by an evolving and more competitive world, and in particular to the emergence of China as a major trading power, partner, and competitor. In the past decade, the previous bilateral competitive interdependence relationship has thus given way to a trilateral structure in which both EU and United States focus much attention on securing their markets from Chinese competition. The EU has tried to "rebalance" its relationship with China through a strategy that combines using multilateral forums (i.e., the World Trade Organization [WTO]) with competitive "selective bilateralism," including seeking FTAs with countries such as Japan, Canada, and Vietnam. This approach reflects its recognition of China as a partner, competitor, and rival and indicates that the EU has established its own competitive interdependence relationship with China. The United States under President Trump has, meanwhile, left behind both President Bush's "competitive bilateralism" and President Obama's "multilateral pragmatism" in favor of a "strong unilateral" strategy, with sanctions at its core. The Republican administration under President Trump thus imposed a series of tariffs to force China to the negotiation table. The competitive interdependence relationship between the United States and China is characterized by open confrontation, in other words. Competitive interdependence between the EU and the United States, the authors conclude, has been affected by these developments, in that efforts on both sides of the Atlantic are directed at containing China, rather than constraining each other multilaterally through the WTO or bilaterally through FTAs.

Ronald Brand (chapter 3) also focuses on a comparison between the EU and the United States, but in a different policy field. Brand explicitly adopts Sbragia's comparative federalism approach to investigate differences between EU and U.S. approaches to private international law, or the body of conventions, laws, and other documents and instruments that regulate private relationships across borders. It is an area in which the EU, although an international organization composed of sovereign member states, is both more centralized and institutionalized than the United States, where private international law is developed at the state level and very limited at the federal level. The U.S. system is, accordingly, fractured and diffused. A particular focus of the chapter is on the origins and evolution of the EU's regime, which Brand was able to observe as a participant in negotiations at the Hague Conference on Private International Law. He, thus, offers a firsthand scholarly account of the development of EU competence in private international law, a process in which authority has been transferred to the "central government." Brand also considers how this area of law has been influenced by the two different federal arrangements in the EU and United States and, by extension, how they have affected the global development of private international law. While applying a comparative federalism framework to a specific policy area, rather than adopting Sbragia's view of the broader political context for shared levels of governance, Brand's chapter illustrates the utility of Sbragia's approach to a narrower substantive context with important national, European, and international implications.

The same is true of Willem Maas's chapter (chapter 4), which applies Sbragia's comparative federalism lens to questions of citizenship and adds Canada to the EU-U.S. comparison. Maas argues that political and social tensions associated with borders may be particularly pronounced in the EU—where the importance of national governments for shaping political power and economic wealth can hardly be overestimated (Sbragia 1992a)—but they are also present in federal *states* like the United States and Canada. Hence, one can usefully compare the EU with those two cases in an effort to gauge the trajectory of strengthening ties across boundaries and territories in Europe, as the EU continues to grapple not only with the economic logic associated with free movement but increasingly also with political considerations and their implications. The freedom of movement in today's EU is no longer about workers moving across borders within the single market, it is about EU citizens moving throughout the territory of the EU as a political entity with a deep and complex form of "shared rule" across multiple levels of governance. At the same time, questions related to EU citizenship and the rights associated with it are particularly tricky and politically sensitive, given the key role of national governments within the EU's confederal structure, which means that decisions about citizenship are not exercised solely by a central authority. Citizenship in the EU is, thus, best understood as a multi-level phenomenon, as it is governed by multiple institutional actors across multiple levels. The "Europeanization" of citizenship and free movement evolves within this multi-level context, making it a function of the role of national governments, the dynamics of the joint processes of economic and political integration, and changing conceptions of who is part of the political "people." In sum, Maas sheds light on the complex question of EU citizenship by engaging Sbragia's comparative federalism approach focused on governance, rather than strictly on government, and on confederal models of governance, in particular (Sbragia 2004), and through careful comparative analysis of questions of citizenship and the free movement of people within shared political spaces.

William T. Daniel (chapter 5) moves our attention toward the EU and its member states and from legal to political institutions. He takes as a starting point Sbragia's emphasis on the institutional complexity of the EU, which meshes national institutions and leaders with European ones (Sbragia 1992a). Investigating the interconnections and mutual influences of national and EU politics has been the subject of much research over the past two decades, especially as part of the "comparativist turn" in EU studies described in Ross's contribution. Daniel's chapter adds to a broader research program on career paths in EU politics, in particular of elected politicians in the EP, which offers important insights into the development and realities of multi-level governance in the EU. Specifically, it sheds light on how the EU's multi-level political space influences party careers that used to be contained in the member states. Daniel investigates the career trajectories of the 106 members of the European Parliament (MEPs) who gave up their EP mandates early during the 2014–2019 legislative term. Using carefully assembled original data, he finds that departing MEPs from federal or decentralized counties are more likely to drop out for nonpolitical reasons, likely because they are more likely to display static ambition (for advancement within the EP) as opposed to progressive ambition (toward higher office in national politics); that MEPs from fringe parties are more likely to leave for national legislatures or key local and regional offices, which they use to build an electoral base for the future; that MEPs from mainstream parties depart to assume high-level political jobs at the national level, such as positions in the national cabinet; and that the same is true for MEPs from Central and Eastern Europe (CEE), who are also more likely to move on to positions in other EU institutions such as the Commission or the Court of Justice. The chapter contributes

to our understanding of the role of the EP not only as an increasingly important and institutional legislature in its own right but also as a chamber used as
an incubator for cultivating political talent for national politics. By extension,
it adds to what we know about the political fortunes of national political parties that participate in and use the EU as an arena to advance their electoral
ambitions and political influence at the national level.

Lauren K. Perez (chapter 6) similarly considers institutional dynamics at
the intersection of EU- and national-level politics. One of the key challenges
of studying EU politics is that the EU is a moving target, a multi-level polity that is consistently evolving, with an ever-changing set of institutions
and institutional arrangements (Sbragia 1992b, 257). Perez explores these
changes through the increased involvement of national parliaments in the
EP's legislative process. Interviews with individual national legislators in
Belgium, Denmark, Germany, Poland, and the United Kingdom allow her
to examine variations in parliamentarians' views of their role in the EU. She
argues that there are two main dimensions along which legislators' opinions
differ. First, how interested is a legislator in involvement in European affairs?
And second, how optimistic or pessimistic is he or she about the practicality of
this involvement? Using these two dimensions, Perez then derives a typology
of four types of legislators: disinterested pessimists, disinterested optimists,
interested pessimists, and interested optimists. Although there are many disinterested legislators, she concludes that there is evidence of increased interest in the EU among many legislators, as this is a way to increase democratic
representation of their constituents in the EU. Moreover, those who are more
interested and more involved tend to be more optimistic. Perez concludes that
national parliamentarians will have overall a more positive outlook on the EU
as they become more interested in what happens at the European level. This
offers one potential way to counter increasing Eurosceptic tendencies among
some national legislators and in some national parliaments.

Turning to an examination of public administration styles, Guy Peters
(chapter 7) shares the institutional focus of the two preceding chapters by
Daniel and Perez. He asks whether there is a single administrative style in the
European Commission and argues that while administrative styles and traditions have their roots in the past, they continue to influence contemporary public administration. The universal phenomenon of New Public Management,
which emphasizes efficiency over probity and effectiveness, for example, was
accepted and implemented differently across national settings. Peters then
develops four different patterns of administration characterized by six dimensions: law versus management in defining the roles of public servants; distinctiveness of the civil servant career; the relationship between state and society;
expectations of uniformity among different administrative dimensions across
European countries; the relationship between politics and administration;

and holding bureaucracies accountable. These four traditions are thus: Anglo-American; Germanic; Napoleonic, and Scandinavian. Peters then applies these different administrative traditions to understanding the Commission as the locus of public administration within the EU. He finds that there are some elements of all four traditions within the Commission and considers the administrative system to be a hybrid, which arguably reflects the development of the Commission and other EU institutions over time. This, in turn, reflects the balancing act involved in accommodating competing demands for uniformity and diversity in federal governance, as highlighted by Sbragia (1993). Moreover, Peters's finding supports Sbragia's (1992a, 2) assessment that EU governance is best understood as a "meshing between" national and European institutional leaders, which is echoed in other chapters as well (e.g., Fabbrini, Daniel, Perez). Importantly, however, Peters recognizes that even though we can see elements of national administrative traditions in how the Commission's administrative system operates, to some extent, it is *sui generis*, as Sbragia stated in the quote at the beginning of this chapter. The Commission is also not a unitary actor, since individual Directorates General and agencies have their own administrative patterns. Hence, to understand its administrative style, according to Peters, is to consider national traditions, the uniqueness of the institution, and internal differences. Together, these provide a more nuanced view of the role that public bureaucracy plays in EU policy-making.

Wade Jacoby and Elizabeta Jevtic-Somlai (chapter 8) shift our focus from institutions to policies and policy-making in the EU's multi-level system, which involve not only vertical interdependencies across levels but also horizontal interdependencies between politics at the national levels of the EU member states. The chapter revisits a key issue raised by Sbragia (2000b) two decades ago about clashes of regulation between rich and poor member states, especially in the context of the looming EU enlargement to CEE. Jacoby and Jevtic-Somlai consider how the policy choices of one EU member state can critically affect politics in others, especially if the member state is as rich and powerful as Germany. Jacoby and Jevtic-Somlai investigate the impact of German macroeconomic and immigration policy in the Visegrád states of Poland, Hungary, the Czech Republic, and Slovakia. Germany's policy choices, they argue, have deep and challenging effects in the poorer Visegrád countries. They have forced painful adjustment and thus contributed to the rise of populism in the region. Concerning macroeconomic policy choice, the authors point to the persistent imbalance between Germany's surging production and lagging domestic consumption and investment, leading to increased national savings that flow to other countries as foreign capital. That foreign capital, however, while initially spurring economic activity and growth, ultimately entailed malinvestment, consumption bubbles, increased debt, and unemployment in the Visegrád countries—but it could not be refused under Single Market rules. Germany's current account surplus, thus, had highly disruptive consequences for consumption and investment outside its borders and, when liquidity dried up after 2007, led to a painful mix of internal and currency depreciation. In the absence of robust welfare states to cushion the blow, the political beneficiaries were populist parties, while those in the mainstream became associated and tainted by economic dynamics outside their immediate control and difficult for regular voters to appreciate. Those parties also benefited from a backlash against another German policy choice, namely its open borders approach during the so-called immigration crisis. Germany's unilateral shift toward a liberal immigration policy in 2015 was interpreted as evidence that countries in CEE were expected to bow down and accept externally imposed policies, even if they entailed both real and perceived financial and cultural adjustment costs—which in turn were exacerbated by the aforementioned negative economic externalities. Public opinion and populist sentiment were thus inflamed in the Visegrád countries and exploited to justify populist and even illiberal policy actions. The chapter illustrates Sbragia's important insight that relations between EU member states not only are a function of one-time high-level bargains but also reflect enduring and politically pertinent "tradeoffs" (Sbragia 2000b)—in the context of enlargement and beyond.

Simona Piattoni and Ton Notermans (chapter 9) ask a similar question as the previous chapter about the constraining effects of EU and Eurozone membership, and the policy interdependence this entails, on national policy choice. They examine the impact of policy approaches imposed on Italy as a result of the Euro crisis and their economic and political implications. The chapter traces Italy's public debt to the 1970s and early 1980s, a period of social and political polarization and escalating debt service. While spending was brought under control in the run-up to Economic and Monetary Union (EMU), in part through politically and economically painful microeconomic structural reforms as envisioned by the economic philosophy behind EMU rules, that debt remained a structural burden and exposed Italy to contagion effects after the Euro came under threat in 2009. Under the leadership of Germany, in particular, the EU's response to the crisis prescribed fiscal austerity and a focus on structural reforms, including labor and product market liberalization. These conditions only intensified the debt problem, however, as they depressed gross domestic product (GDP) growth in Italy (and elsewhere). Piattoni and Notermans identify as a key problem that the "German model"—combining monetary stability, structural reforms, and current account surpluses—was inappropriately generalized to and imposed on countries where it did more harm than good. Even when burdened with high public deficits and debts, Germany could rely on its reputation of creditworthiness, lower interest rates, and a generous and functioning welfare state when reforming its labor market and regaining its competitiveness after reunification. The conditions in other countries were far different. In Italy, trying to apply the German model led to rising debt-to-GDP ratios despite primary surpluses, as it compelled the country to try and solve a macroeconomic crisis using microeconomic means. The authors not only conclude that the assumptions underlying EMU are problematic, as they focus on constraining politics to insulate the market from interference with the disciplining force of market integration, but also point to the political costs of forcing this approach onto "lower" levels of governance. As evidenced in Italy, the policy recipes imposed on Italy have contributed to the transformation of what Sbragia (2000a) called a "fundamentally European" country into one that elected the first populist, Eurosceptic coalition government in the EU.

In the final chapter with a focus on policy and policy-making, Reuben Wong and Daniela Irrera (chapter 10) examine regional integration from a comparative perspective. They highlight the importance of comparing the EU to other regional organizations to understand regional variations. Their chapter asks what the EU can learn from other regions, particularly as it relates to crisis, which they define as an immediate and ongoing situation of disorder that threatens the high-priority goals of more than one member of a regional integration project, in which the amount of time available for an urgent response is highly restricted, and where its occurrence is previously unanticipated. In particular, they compare the relationship between crisis and integration in the EU and in ASEAN. Wong and Irrera examine four policy domains: migration and counterterrorism in the EU and the advancement of a human rights regime and the development of the Transboundary Haze Agreement following the 1997 environment crisis in Asia as addressed by ASEAN. The authors argue that both the EU and Association of ASEAN see regional integration as a means to an end; however, understanding how the different organizations approached these crises is much more complex and nuanced. In the EU, they argue that the process can be explained by the political will of the member states and their ability to adapt to, and manage, crises, whereas in ASEAN the process of regional integration is focused on assuaging differences between its member states. In sum, the chapter finds that crisis continues to be a major underlying force in the process of supranational integration, but as Sbragia (2008) argued, that particular regional factors are an important mediator.

In the last substantive chapter of this volume (chapter 11), Sergio Fabbrini takes up the question that Sbragia (1992b, 257) asked in her conclusion to *Euro-Politics*: "how much should national governments shape Community policy-making?" by investigating post-Maastricht governance in the EU. He first discusses the differentiated governance regime in the EU, which includes the Council, Commission, and EP. He then identifies two models of governance found in the extant literature: the club governance model, which interprets the EU as a quasi-international organization, and the state governance model, which interprets the EU as a quasi-state organization. Coming to the conclusion that neither sufficiently explains policy-making in the EU, Fabbrini argues that the role national governments should play in the EU is best understood through the lens of comparative federalism. Using a normative-deductive approach, he then posits that it would be through a separation of powers strategy that we could use the experience of federal unions to understand the decision-making role of national governments in the EU. This, however, would require certain reforms to the existing governance structures, including both separating the supranational institutions from the national institutions of government and separating the institutions involved in the decision-making process itself. An example of the later would be the creation of a dual executive. This would involve, first, reforming the Commission president. The president of the Commission would no longer be the *spitzenkandidat* but would instead be an official "enjoying the 'advice and consent' of the EP," without relying on the confidence of the EP. Second, there would be an elected EU president selected by national electoral colleges. These two executives would be separate and independent from both the European Council and the EP. According to Fabbrini, it would be through these reforms that the EU would be able to overcome the challenge raised by Sbragia, while at the same time not becoming an "undemocratic federation of national executives."

CONCLUSION

Alberta Sbragia's work, both scholarly and institutionally, has been genuinely foundational for the field of EU studies. Her analysis of what the EU is and is not was never part of any one "paradigm" or school of thought; in part because of this, her writing foreshadowed much of what is now commonly accepted among most EU scholars. At the height of the debate between supranationalists (Sandholtz and Zysman 1989; Sandholtz and Stone Sweet 1998) and intergovernmentalists (Moravcsik 1993, 1998), she recognized both the substantial contributions and important limitations of each approach. Before the concept of multi-level governance was formally introduced and became an important reference point for our understanding of EU politics (Hooghe and Marks 2001, 2003), Sbragia emphasized the multi-level nature of EU governance. Before the "comparativist turn" in EU studies (Hix 1994), she emphasized the importance and utility of comparing the EU as a political system to others, eschewed the strictly *sui generis* view of the EU, and motivated others to do the same. The substantive breadth and variety of the chapters in this volume attest to this.

On all accounts, Sbragia thinking and analysis were ahead of her time, reflecting what are today mainstream views of EU politics and in the field of EU studies, and informing the numerous and substantial contributions of her peers and students. Aside from the sheer intellectual merit of her work, among the important contributors to her success are Sbragia's collegiality, modesty, helpfulness, and encouragement of others. She is a model for how to be a scholar and help others become the best scholars they can be, as is evident in her influence on the contributors to this volume.

BIBLIOGRAPHY

Hix, Simon. 1994. "The Study of the European Community: The Challenge to Comparative Politics." *West European Politics*, 17.1: 1–30.

Hooghe, Liesbet and Gary Marks. 2001. *Multi-Level Governance and European Integration*. Lanham, MD: Rowman & Littlefield.

Hooghe, Liesbet and Gary Marks. 2003. "Unraveling the Central State, But How? Types of Multi-Level Governance." *American Political Science Review*, 97.2: 233–243.

Moravcsik, Andrew. 1993. "Preferences and Power in the European Community: A Liberal Intergovernmental Approach." *Journal of Common Market Studies*, 31.4: 473–524.

Moravcsik, Andrew. 1998. *The Choice for Europe: Social Purpose and State Power from Messina to Maastricht*. Ithaca, NY: Cornell University Press.

Sandholtz, Wayne and Alec Stone Sweet, eds. 1998. *European Integration and Supranational Governance*. Oxford: Oxford University Press.

Sandholtz, Wayne and John Zysman. 1989. "Recasting the European Bargain." *World Politics*, 41.1: 45–78.

Sbragia, Alberta M. 1992a. "Introduction." In *Euro-Politics: Institutions and Policymaking in the "New" European Community*, edited by Alberta M. Sbragia, 1–22. Washington, DC: The Brookings Institution.

Sbragia, Alberta M. 1992b. "Thinking about the European Future: The Uses of Comparison." In *Euro-Politics: Institutions and Policymaking in the "New" European Community*, edited by Alberta M. Sbragia, 257–291. Washington, DC: The Brookings Institution.

Sbragia, Alberta M. 1993. "The European Community: A Balancing Act." *Publius: The Journal of Federalism*, 23.3: 23–38.

Sbragia, Alberta M. 2000a. "Italy Pays for Europe: Political Leadership, Political Choice, and Institutional Adaptation." In *Transforming Europe: Europeanization and Domestic Change*, edited by Maria Green Cowles, James A. Caporaso, and Thomas Risse, 79–96. Ithaca, NY: Cornell University Press.

Sbragia, Alberta M. 2000b. " 'Trade-Offs Rather than Bargains in Europe?' Symposium on Governing in Europe: Effective and Democratic?" *Journal of European Public Policy*, 7.2: 316–321.

Sbragia, Alberta M. 2004. "The Future of Federalism in the European Union." Key-note Address delivered at the European Community Studies Association Canada Biennial Conference, Montreal, Canada.

Sbragia, Alberta M. 2005. "Territory, Electorates and Markets in the US: The Con-struction of Democratic Federalism and Its Implications for the EU." In *Democracy and Federalism in the European Union and the United States: Exploring Post-National Governance*, edited by Sergio Fabbrini, 93–103. London: Routledge.

Sbragia, Alberta M. 2008. "Review Article: Comparative Regionalism: What Might It Be? *Journal of Common Market Studies*, 46: 29–49.

Sbragia, Alberta M. 2010a. "The EU, the US, and Trade Policy: Competitive Inter-dependence in the Management of Globalization." *Journal of European Public Policy*, 17.3: 368–382.

Sbragia, Alberta M. 2010b. "Multi-Level Governance and Comparative Regional-ism." In *Handbook on Multi-Level Governance*, edited by Henrik Enderlein, Sonja Wälti, and Michael Zürn, 267–278. Cheltenham: Edward Elgar.

Chapter 1

Stalking an Unidentified European Political Object

Alberta Sbragia at Work

George Ross

Transnational comparison began early for Alberta Sbragia. As an Italian-speaking child of U.S. immigrants, she grew up in Nevada at a time when the U.S. federal government controlled most of the state's land. She then became attentive to the issues and meanings of federalism. As a student in Paris during the 1968 "May Events," she acquired a vivid sense of comparative political differences and the uncertainties of democratic politics. Her dissertation in political science at the University of Wisconsin–Madison (1974) analyzed innovative public housing programs in Milan, Italy, where good politics and intelligent public policies had successfully lodged a flood of immigrants from the Italian south. Sbragia's question was, "How did Milanese creativity emerge from Italy's relatively stagnant centralization?" (Sbragia 1979).[1] After she left the University of Wisconsin–Madison for the University of Pittsburgh, she added British data to her work on comparative central-local financial matters (Sbragia 1981, 1985). Her dissertation may have reinforced her interest in European politics, but her first book dealt with the complex funding strategies and dealings between local and federal levels during the Reagan years in the United States, when Washington sought to reduce government spending at all levels and with significant consequences for local and municipal finances (Sbragia 1983, 1996). Soon the European Union (EU) became her major research concern. Focusing on one country's politics was for a long time the bulk of research in political science, with comparative politics and international relations constituting much of the rest. For many decades, comparative work observed the institutional systems and political processes of different national states in ways that demanded deep knowledge

---

1 Sbragia's doctoral adviser was Matt Holden, primarily an Americanist who would later be the President of the American Political Science Association.

of, and familiarity with, the countries studied. By the time of Sbragia's doctoral work, however, comparative politics was evolving. Beyond looking at political systems as a whole, comparativists began to look more closely at the distinct dimensions of roughly similar systems such as voting, parties, interest groups, social movements and other methods of representation, citizen attitudes, and distinct public policy areas. They also examined dissimilar systems, for example, democratic and nondemocratic ones. Then, in the optimistic afterglow of the end of the Cold War, they reconsidered large historical issues such as processes of democratization. With these shifts, comparative politics, along with the rest of political science, became much more sophisticated conceptually and methodologically, placing new emphasis on theory-building and systematic data-gathering and expanding its geographical scope.

Phenomena that were neither national nor international, European integration prominent among them, did not easily fit most comparative frameworks. In the EU's Common Market years, many comparativists, including some eager for evidence that the nation state and the Westphalian state system could be transcended, claimed that the EU was *sui generis*, "an unidentified political object" perhaps moving toward an eventual United States of Europe. The European Economic Community (EEC) that followed the European Coal and Steel Community of 1950 was a treaty-based multinational system built around market-building and pooling national economic sovereignty, while initially leaving other dimensions of sovereignty in national hands. In the EEC's market-building areas, formal proposals of law came from a transnational executive, the European Commission, charged with promoting the common economic success of the original six EEC members and with some enforcement powers. After vetting by a transnational European Court of Justice, this process sometimes led to the perception that the accumulated laws were "judge made." The Commission thus had to always anticipate that its ideas and proposals had sufficient member state support. Beginning in the mid-1970s, a European Council, composed of the heads of state and government of member states, slowly became the EEC's general strategist and decision-shaper.

Early theorizing, including that of Jean Monnet, argued that European integration was about building European peace. The assumption was that market integration would remove major sources of conflict among European nations. In the immediate aftermath of World War II, this was good politics because integration confronted Europe's "German problem" by binding Germany with France and others economically. The EU's institutions and the emphasis on market integration were also meant to allow EU laws to fly under the radars of European citizens to avoid exciting nationalist reflexes. In these early days many scholars and practitioners argued optimistically that market integration would "spill over" into other, more political, areas, anticipating movement toward the "ever closer union" announced in the 1957 Rome Treaty. Such "neo-functionalism" had its detractors, however. Some doubted the automaticity of spillover. Others claimed that European integration would be carefully confined to economic matters because the power of national interests and identities would lead some member to refuse movement into "high political" areas such as foreign relations, defense, and justice (Hoffman 1966).

Debate about whether the EU was *sui generis* died down after the initial pace of integration slowed. Once the first Common Market rules were in place, member states were wary of anything more ambitious. Many even sought to navigate around these first rules by using nontariff trade barriers, especially once the post-war decades of reconstruction and growth began to give way to new problems. The relative stagnation that followed led some scholars (and some citizens) toward disdainful views of the EU as a "Brussels bureaucracy" that counted carrots, subsidized farmers, and talked to itself technocratically. The stalemate ended in mid-1980s, however, when the Delors Commission, backed by France and Germany, proposed a Single Market with free movement of goods, capital, and people. Treaty changes, an expansion of EU prerogatives and institutional reconfiguration in the 1985 Single European Act and thereafter, ostensibly in response to large new economic problems, regenerated the European project. Scholarly responses to this—unexpected—new vitality included a rebirth of confrontation between neofunctionalist hopes and counterarguments anticipating national resistance to ambitious new integration (Keohane and Hoffman 1991; Moravcsik 1998; Sandholtz and Zysman 1989).

These circumstances and the return of classical debates led some, including Sbragia, again to seek answers to the question of "what kind of sociopolitical animal is the EU?" In her work, she began to document that *sui generis* arguments that the EU was an "N of one" were not theoretically sustainable. Neofunctionalist arguments were overly optimistic and normatively based. Claims drawn from international relations that the EU was some kind of muscular international organization where only member states counted minimized the EU's institutional novelty. Might not thinking of European integration as a variety of federalism provide a useful analytical framework to understand the EU?

IDENTIFYING THE UNKNOWN OBJECT

Understanding the Single Market—the "1992" period—called for new approaches because of the magnitude of changes the Maastricht Treaty and subsequent agreements brought: qualified majority voting in the Council of

Ministers; amending power for a European Parliament (EP) that had been directly elected for the first time in 1979; measures to eliminate the nontariff barriers that had stymied the Common Market; enlargement to Spain and Portugal; mutual recognition of product standards; increased and redesigned regional development funding (the structural funds); new social policy initiatives (Europeanized health and safety regulation, a "social charter," and encouragement of European-level trade unionism); an increase in the Commission's agenda-setting influence; and, last but not least, processes leading member states toward a new Economic and Monetary Union (EMU) and eventually the Euro. Given the ambition of the program, it was no accident that when the Brookings Institution commissioned a book on the "new" EU, it wisely judged that intellectual fresh air about European integration was needed. Its choice of Alberta Sbragia to organize the volume and her assembly of a group of talented political scientists to contribute were both very fortunate (Sbragia 1992).[2]

In her introduction and conclusion chapters of *Euro-Politics*, Sbragia sought new categories to shed better analytical light on what the EU was becoming. Her conclusion was that the EU was best understood through the lens of comparative federalism. Existing federalist systems sought solutions to the problems generated by deep differences, particularly ones that were territorially grounded, by allowing cooperation within a single political framework. Sbragia drew particularly on the American, Canadian, and German examples. The EU was not a classical federal system because it had no permanent political "center," she noted. In addition, it lacked a stable constitutionalized division of powers, political labor, and policy tasks. In part, this was because the EU had no permanent constitution but was "treaty-based." The EU treaties had recently been reconfigured by the Single European Act and Maastricht, and they were likely to be reconsidered again, she thought. This did not mean that efforts at treaty renegotiation would always be successful, however, because negotiations could sometimes fail because of clashing national preferences. Even when there was agreement, it had to be the product of complicated compromises among different national preferences and might point the EU in unpromising new directions.

The specific organization of the EU's territorially grounded differences was very important. The Council of Ministers, and from the mid-1970s onward the European Council, promoted and decided significant changes through diplomatic negotiations that had to recognize both the centrality of EU's internal boundaries and large differences in national cultures and

---

2 The chapter authors were David R. Cameron on "1992," B. Guy Peters on bureaucratic politics and EU institutions, Martin Shapiro on the European Court of Justice, John Wooley on European monetary institutions, and Gary Marks on the structural funds.

identities. These particularities made transnational political, as opposed to economic, links across EU territories relatively weak. In the Union, democratic representation did not focus on a strong "center." Instead, citizens' political attention focused mainly at the national level. Europeans connected with European integration primarily in indirect ways, mainly through elected national governments. This remained the case even after the institution of direct elections to the EP in 1979 that were quickly characterized as "second order" national elections because they were contested within national boundaries by national political parties and conditioned by specifically national concerns. Europeans, thus, continued to live primarily within their national political communities, languages, and media. When making European-level decisions, leaders thus had to represent national citizens as much, or more, than the interests of Europe as a whole. It also implied that member states with the largest populations, strongest economies, and best strategic locations would have more negotiating powers than those lesser endowed. Moreover, the supranational EU Commission was an institution that had no parallel in federal regimes, being simultaneously a stealthy agitator for "more Europe" and an administration that could easily be regarded by some national citizens as encroaching on their sovereignty.

Sbragia's arguments in *Euro-Politics* were predominantly institutional, rather than speculating about the economic, geostrategic, public opinion, and national political concerns that might have prompted change in the first instance. When, at that point, she did address such questions, her focus was mainly on the potentially disruptive effects of the Maastricht Treaty on EU prerogatives and on the perturbations that additional EU treaty changes could bring. When she dealt with the ending of the Cold War, for example, her main concerns were how the EU would integrate formerly communist European countries and what this might mean for its functioning. She was also apprehensive about the implications of Maastricht's two new "intergovernmental" pillars, foreign and security policy and justice and home affairs, both implying significant new EU involvement in central areas of national sovereignty. Would this intergovernmentalism last, would it be effective, and what would it mean for the EU more broadly? Maastricht's biggest open question, however, was what EMU might bring. In short, she was aware that however unique the EU's specific federalist structures, they were unlikely to shield the EU from the shocks that other federalist arrangements had periodically faced.

REFINING

The European Commission, the lodestar of neofunctionalists, needed further consideration, leading Sbragia to examine carefully the Commission's 2001

White Paper on European Governance (European Commission 2001). Written in the midst of one of the worst scandals in Commission history, the White Paper sought ways to redeem the Commission's position and regenerate its dynamism. It proposed some classical ideas for deepening the "Community Method" but, more importantly, suggested new routes to more collaborative relationships with regional and local governments and civil society. Sbragia (2002b) read the White Paper's arguments as recognition by the Commission that it needed to work creatively to persuade member state citizens that EU law was neither "foreign," because it came from outside national cultures and systems, nor technocratic. It was, in other words, addressing basic and chronic concerns about the Commission's reputation and the EU's "democratic deficit." The White Paper acknowledged that the Commission's interaction with member state citizens' national identity was insufficient and that this obliged a rethinking of Commission's assumptions about the EU Europe that it sought. The White Paper sometimes repeated optimistic, often neofunctionalist, claims about the Commission's role, despite the fact, as she wrote, that "the Commission works without the benefit of an elected government but co-exists with a set of national governments which have far deeper roots in national societies than does the EU" (Sbragia 2002b, 12). Sbragia's broader discussion contextualized the White Paper within the "governance" debate among scholars and politicians attracted by the "new public management" school which, however, was based on the existence of a legitimate central government that already incorporated civil society via elections, parties, and other mechanisms around a shared identity. She noted that "the Commission . . . was created precisely because none of (these) characteristics . . . existed at the European level—and they still do not exist" (ibid., 1–2).

Sbragia described the Commission as a "key member of the core executive" of the EU but a core quite unlike those in national governments (ibid., 2). Could the Commission actually benefit from the White Paper's proposals? Its legislative propositional role and administrative capacities allowed it to set the EU's legislative agenda, but, beyond its enforcement powers, it had limited political resources to help its proposals succeed, in particular by reaching out to EU citizens. It could, and did, try to influence the EP, whose powers had been increasing and which, given its new importance to the Community Method, made it a likely ally of the Commission. The EU Council of Ministers had greater strategic power, however, because of its "co-decision" relationships with the EP, and no matter how "European" the Council's members were, in the last analysis, they had to prioritize their national situations. Thus, the Commission was "more powerful than a traditional civil service, less powerful than an elected executive . . . and more exposed to political attack from both national governments and the public" (ibid., 3). It had influence and visibility, in other words, but it could not easily tap national identities. Ultimately, as she had concluded earlier, the Commission had far greater "steering" power and independence than national administrations but had considerable difficulty playing its dual roles of "coxswain" and civil service (Sbragia 2000). She thus argued that the more systematic outreach to member state citizens and civil societies that the White Paper advocated was a good idea, but it was unlikely to help clarify the Commission's roles, which would remain difficult for ordinary citizens to understand.

Sbragia pursued these reflections in several articles comparing the EU's development with that of the United States (Sbragia 2005, 2006b). Her starting point was the difficulty Americans had in understanding the EU, caused by the differences between United States and European institutional development. The EU had great power over member state economic matters but lacked the U.S. federal control over external sovereignty, a prerogative largely retained by EU member states, even if there were exceptions for market-related international areas like competition and trade policy. The U.S. federal center, originally with weak influence over the policies of states, quickly acquired great power vis-à-vis other countries. The EU's complicated center had begun in transnational market-building and -regulating and not foreign affairs. Americans, thus, saw the EU as unable to "get its act together," because it lacked foreign policy strategies and tools. At the same time the EU could levy huge fines on Microsoft for anticompetitive behavior, block mergers between American corporate giants, negotiate a vast range of trading arrangements, and regulate its members' product standards in ways that had significant consequences both within Europe and internationally.

Further consideration of these two *sui generis* systems provided greater detail. The United States was a nation state and the EU was a complicated, nonstate form of regionalism, even if both had avoided the institutional concentration of political power of parliamentary systems by dispersing authority at both federal and state levels. The United States had a complex arrangement of separated powers and the EU had its confederal strategic leadership and its supranational "Community Method" in market and economic matters. But the dynamics of each system were very different. In the United States, the federal center and its institutions had diminished state prerogatives and powers over time, while in the EU national leaders in the Council of Ministers, European Council, and Eurogroup dominated the confederal center, constraining any expansion of the federalizing "Community Method." Similarly, the U.S. federal budget had exploded over time, while EU member states had managed to keep the EU budget very low. Finally, in the United States, political parties covered the whole country at both central and state levels, while in the EU territorially differentiated parties had been sustained, perhaps even accentuated.

Continuing her reflection on EU development, Sbragia was aware that because of the challenges from globalization, the end of the Cold War, and unfinished issues from the Maastricht Treaty, new EU treaty changes were inevitable. This led her to monitor and reflect upon new treaty deliberations carefully, mainly by analyzing the key intergovernmental conferences (IGCs) in the new century. Maastricht had consolidated and elaborated the Single Market and launched the EMU plus new intergovernmental "pillars" in foreign and security policy and justice and home affairs. The Amsterdam Treaty, called to review and complete these initiatives, adopted the EMU's Stability and Growth Pact and began movement toward enlargement to Central and Eastern countries. Sbragia's first IGC commentary, thus, focused on the 2001 Treaty of Nice, convened to devise the institutional changes needed for EU enlargement from fifteen to twenty-seven members and others followed with updates over the years (Sbragia 2002a, 2006a, 2007, 2012).

The Nice IGC was a delicate process because it put the relative EU power of individual member states into play. Several factors, moreover, increased the delicacy. The Commission's negotiating and deal-brokering influence had been in decline since the Delors' years, and its position had been further weakened by the Santer Commission's scandal and by the fact that France, which presided in Nice, had disdain for the Commission. These facts enhanced the negotiating influence of the Council of Ministers Secretariat, a member state stronghold. The French presidency was also likely to be turbulent because it would happen during a moment of political "cohabitation" between Gaullist president Jacques Chirac, with a strong "realist" sense of French national interests, and Socialist prime minister Lionel Jospin, who had quite different views, and just as the next French presidential campaign, when the two would run against each another, was beginning.

The easiest bit at Nice was allowing ten candidate members to join in 2004, followed by Bulgaria and Romania in 2007. This decision calmed the fears of applicant countries that they would be kept outside longer. The rest of the agenda, however, caused fierce arguments.

The issue of the post-enlargement number of votes that each member state would have in qualified majority decision-making in the Council of Ministers was highly contentious. Newly unified Germany initially sought more votes than others. This was successfully opposed tooth and nail by France. As compensation, Germany was given more seats than others in a bloated future EP (751 seats). Spain and Poland fought to a draw about their own future voting strengths. The smaller EU-15 member states, struggling to maintain their prior relative over-representation, eventually got more Council votes than the smaller eastern candidate countries. The formula for Council-qualified majority in the Council was set at 74 percent of votes, but Germany insisted that member states could also demand that qualified majority voting also include at least 62 percent of the EU's total population, a significant introduction of demographic matters into EU decision-making rules. The Commission had to be reconfigured as well. Larger member states wanted to downsize it to seventeen members appointed by rotation among all members, but here smaller members prevailed over larger ones, leading to a final compromise in which each member state would get one Commissioner (formerly, larger members had two), ensuring that future Commissions would have more members than important jobs for them to fill. The Nice Treaty came into force in 2003, but not before the Irish had turned it down in a referendum and were then persuaded to accept it by new commitments to Irish military neutrality.

Sbragia later summarized the Nice episode in historical terms. The "conflicts associated . . . reflected the stresses of a particular period in post-war European integration. The role of France and Germany, of the applicant states, and the small member states, were indicative of a European order . . . still very much divided between 'Western' and 'Eastern' Europe" (Sbragia 2012, 160). It may be that this summary underplayed EU's adjustment difficulties, however, because the "conflicts" would continue for some time in different forums. More importantly, Nice gathered such bad press that the successor to the French Council presidency called a "European Convention" to reflect further on treaty changes. The Convention, which invited representatives of EU civil society to contribute to its deliberations in an effort to repair Nice's damages, would then propose a new EU "constitutional treaty." It would not be enough, however, to carry the day.

Sbragia closely followed the Convention's debates and, in an important 2004 speech, gave her clearest statement to date on the EU and comparative federalism (Sbragia 2004). After acknowledging the difficulties in characterizing something that was confusing and, to many observers, also seemed confused, she continued to state that "for analysts interested in emphasizing the federal-like characteristics of the union . . . such problems are . . . indicative of the fact that the Union is a semi-polity which has not yet transformed itself into a complete polity. . . [but] . . . in spite of its deficits, the current state of the European Union can be viewed as exhibiting very significant federal type arrangements" (2004, 2). Then, citing Daniel Elazar, the renowned American expert on federalism, she argued that both confederal and supranational institutions could coexist in a federalist whole. Elazar had understood federalism writ large as an institutionalized combination of "self-rule and shared rule." Sbragia proposed that if "applied to the EU, such a definition would not necessarily make a major distinction between shared rule arrived at via the Community Method and the intergovernmental method. . . . Shared rule is shared rule—it can be accomplished either through a supranational arrangement . . . or a much more confederal arrangement . . . in which governments would collectively rule each other" (Sbragia 2004, 3). She went on to note that the European Convention was "designed to expand the range of shared rule . . . a turning point . . . because it changes the nature of the 'balancing act' between supranational and confederal by expanding the role of the European Council over the Commission," continuing a process underway since Maastricht (Sbragia 2004, 4). Creating a powerful president of the European Council, granting the EU an independent legal personality, and increasing the EP's budgetary and codecision powers were all dimensions of this. The Convention went further, however, to propose a new Minister for Foreign Affairs appointed by the European Council who would chair the Foreign Affairs Council, be a Vice President of the Commission, and oversee a new External Action Service recruited from both Council and Commission. Sbragia's conclusion was that these, and other, changes would deepen and extend the reach of EU federalism. As important, changes to the European Council were likely to push national representatives to expand their responsibilities, leading member states to become differently engaged and more committed to collective Union interests as opposed to national ones. At the same time, the Union's supranational dimensions would be more responsive to the confederal side, particularly because the powers of the Commission President vis-à-vis the rest of the Commission would be enhanced. To Sbragia, therefore, the Convention's inclinations were likely to promote "a deeper and more sophisticated form of shared rule" (Sbragia 2004, 5).

In the spring of 2005, the Convention's proposal for a constitutional treaty was rejected by French and Dutch voters in national referendums. Much of France had been incensed by the recent EU Services Directive, the Socialist Party had divided over the Convention's proposals, the government carried out an informational campaign—sending copies of the Convention proposals plus the EU treaties to all citizens—which exposed the French even more to the EU's complex nature. Many disliked what they read. In general, there was anxiety about losses of sovereignty, President Chirac was unusually ineffective at making the "yes" case, and, in the background, there were growing anxieties about immigration, represented in the term "Polish Plumber." The Dutch, inexperienced with referendums, mobilized against the constitutional treaty in similar ways, with much talk about a European "super state," discontent about domestic social policy changes, and a growing hostility to immigration. The "constitution" thus officially died. After a three-year "reflection period," however, most of the changes the constitutional treaty had proposed, minus the constitutional rhetoric, were included in the 2009 Lisbon Treaty. On the supranational (market-building and regulating) side of the EU, the Commission's power of legislative proposition was strengthened, with the European Council standing behind it as the EU's designated strategist. So too was the EP's role enhanced, at least potentially through the 2014 *spitzenkandidat* system in which the president of the Commission was named by the party bloc with the largest vote in elections to the EP, with the aim being to strengthen the EP in codecision. On the intergovernmental (or confederal) side, the European Council acquired a new President and new power and influence over EU decisions, in particular those needed in crisis situations, along with the Council of Ministers, in those areas that went beyond market-building, in particular foreign and defense and justice and home affairs policies, where important member state interests needed to be considered (Sbragia 2007).

Sbragia proposed the lens of comparative federalism as the most promising way to understand the EU but, like all good comparativists, she also considered other plausible approaches. Comparative regionalism was a likely candidate. The EU had grown in the same period as a range of other regional associations, almost all responding to economic changes and challenges from international trade by seeking some protection from more powerful neighbors and globalization. There had developed many trading areas, "communities," postcolonial arrangements, and other types of regional organizations. Sbragia once commented that the "European Union (EU) is the 'poster-child' of regionalism" (Sbragia 2011) but questioned whether European integration was a good fit in the academic field of comparative regionalism. Did all of these new forms resemble each other enough to consider a common analytical framework different from comparative federalism? She reviewed the burgeoning literature, particularly on non-European developments, finding an abundance of research and a multiplicity of different approaches. Economic analysis was mainly concerned with trade promotion and distortion. The "rise of Asia" had led to work on nascent Asian regional arrangements, particularly the Association of Southeast Asian Nations. International political economy and international relations security specialists considered new regionalization because of its implications for changing power balances, and area studies scholars carved out their own pieces of the "new regionalism." Sbragia's overall conclusion, however, was that comparative regionalism, as an academic field, was vast and "loose limbed" (Sbragia 2008, 33). More importantly, however many new regional arrangements there were, few had anything like the EU's degree of institutionalization, scope, complexity, and coherence. In the crowded but diverse world of new regions, the EU still looked to be one of a kind.

MOVING FORWARD

There have been many sides to Alberta Sbragia's career. She was a central participant in U.S. scholarly associations focused on Europe from early on. In the 1980s, she served on the executive board of the Council for European

Studies. Then, as European integration re-energized, she grew interested in
the U.S.-based European Community Studies Association (ECSA), which
was then a relatively small group of scholars, many having focused on the EU
from its beginnings. In the Single Act-Maastricht years, she was a leader in
transforming ECSA into EUSA (the European Union Studies Association), a
change that opened new and different perspectives. She founded and directed
a Center for European Studies at the University of Pittsburgh that became a
model for the EU Commission when it decided to support EU Centers in the
United States and elsewhere.[3] Throughout these years she also helped build
the University of Pittsburgh's political science department, trained many
doctoral students, and in 2010 was recruited into the broader governance of
the university as Vice Provost for Graduate Studies.

Sbragia's research and her organizational contributions both stand out
because of the large questions she asked and answered. Identifying Europe's
unidentified political object, to her, meant elaborating a plausible category
of political objects within which the EU fit. In time, the EU had become a
particular form of incomplete federalism, she argued, whose supranational
(federal) elements lay in market-building done by the "Community Method,"
while much of the rest of European-level politics had begun to encroach
upon the "regalian" dimensions of national sovereignty, areas where the EU
remained intergovernmental. If the EU's "shared rule" dimension had most
often been balanced by the confederal, there had, in recent years, been "rebalancing" toward the latter. The EU's confederal side allowed member states to
prioritize European problem-solving as needed, while allowing the representation of the preferences of member state citizens and encouraging the emergence of "member" states with increasing transnational EU loyalties beyond
the exclusively national. In a 2006 article on the referendum defeat of the
European Constitutional Treaty, meant for the consideration of professional
political scientists, Sbragia argued that the EU's long-term development had
been driven by elite rather than public opinion and that, despite the constitutional treaty's defeat, this form of elite-driven development was likely to
continue. Many of the "constitution's" proposals were meant to strengthen
the EU's intergovernmental side to allow new EU international efforts in the
face of new global challenges. In time, this would prod the EU to sharpen its
strategies and practices in support of further work building the multilateral
trading and legal order that it had long desired (Sbragia 2006a). The relatively
uneventful adoption of almost all of the constitutional treaty's proposals a
few years later in the Lisbon Treaty confirmed this line of thought.[4]

---

3 Sbragia became a lifetime *ad personam* Jean Monnet Chair in 2005, one of the EU's most
prestigious honors for academics. She was awarded EUSA's Lifetime Achievement Award in 2013.

4 The Irish rejected Lisbon in a referendum, but, given a few concessions and a persuasive campaign by the Irish political elite, voters then accepted it in a second referendum, indicating, among

Unfortunately, however, an unforeseen and misunderstood international challenge then presented itself and drained much of the EU's energy for nearly a decade. The implosion of the global financial sector, including its complicit European elements, led first to the Great Recession and then to the Eurozone crisis in 2008 and after. Fighting very large financial fires, rather than building up an international rules-based liberal order, would then preoccupy the EU for years. Sbragia's discussion of the EU's quasi-federalism had also acknowledged that most of the examples of "shared rule" that she discussed had been prone to distressing and disorienting crises. American federalism has faced many difficult moments in its history, often because of conflicts of interest between different regions, including one of the bloodiest civil wars ever fought. Canadian federalism had its own share of difficulties, also mainly between regions, as exemplified in bitter ongoing struggles around the demands of francophone Quebec for greater recognition either within or outside the federation. Germany's internal differences had had a grim past, even if the Bundesrepublik's delicate position within broader Cold War struggles had improved its record. "Shared rule" has not always been a guarantee, therefore, of stability and mutual toleration.

Recent EU history has confirmed these cautious, and realistic, views. The federal side of Sbragia's comparative federalist EU equation has changed historically in large ways. The Commission has recently been "normalized" by key member states in the aftermath of the hyperactive, ambitious Delors' years. This was begun by appointing weak Commission presidents. Then the aftermath of the Santer Commission scandal and the further reforms in the early 1980s partially reconfigured the Commission's internal workings, in ways that tamed the ambitions of Commission civil servants. The Barroso presidency (from 2005 to 2014) changed the Commission's internal rules again, while also enhancing the power of the Commission Secretary-General to create greater presidential authority and undercut the chronic and conflictual "siloing" of internal Commission workings. Barroso himself, a former Conservative Portuguese Prime Minister, could not have been more deferential toward key member states. In all, the Commission lost much of its "functionalist" zeal in two decades. The Lisbon Treaty in time then further strengthened member state powers over large policy decisions against a threatening background of rising Eurosceptical "populisms," nationalisms, and nativism.

In recent years, beginning with the international financial meltdown, EU responses to large crises have repeatedly called its effectiveness into question in many ways. The Eurozone crisis led to emergency interventions to save

---

other things, that EU confederal elites were determined to get what they had wanted out of the Convention, with only a relatively small delay.

EMU. Most importantly, the confederal Eurogroup, backed by intransigent insistence from key member states, imposed punishing austerity on some EU members to oblige them to change their economic policy practices. Major reforms were also proposed to make EMU more risk-averse. Some were adopted, others were not, depending on what key member states were willing to accept. The damage to EU credibility that followed, fed by lower growth, higher unemployment, and greater misery, particularly for those most severely punished, may be repairable. It has been, however, great. The refugee crisis, fed by massive human flight from Middle Eastern conflicts and sub-Saharan poverty, then followed. The EU, challenged to respond by beefing up its weak external border controls, redesigning asylum regulations, and, most importantly, finding ways to distribute and better integrate migrants, failed badly once again. This time the primary reason was its inability to find—or, more precisely, to negotiate—serious solutions. Underlying this failure were deep divisions among member states about the desirability of immigration, in particular opposition to reforms from some of the most recent members of the EU whose citizens were most adamantly opposed, plus others who feared anti-immigrant political and electoral surges among their citizens. The consequences of this crisis were also politically costly, particularly for member states like Greece and Italy that had already borne the brunt of the Eurozone crisis. During the same period, some of the new central and eastern member states, Hungary and Poland in the forefront, embraced illiberal political outlooks that were distinctly at odds with the EU's claim to be a "community of values." These challenges elicited only the weakest of responses from the EU, once again because of deep divisions among member states. Brexit has obviously been a pressing issue. The possibility that ineffective EU responses to it could prod other unhappy member states to imitate the British has so far prompted better responses, even if the story is not yet over. How to respond in clear ways to the Trump administration's expressed disdain for the EU, European trade practices, North Atlantic Treaty Organization, and its general desire to rollback multilateral international organizations and practices that the EU has always supported is presenting new challenges that are as of yet not answered.

Underneath these challenges lay unresolved institutional issues, including fault lines in the EU's institutional development, many connected with the EU's "shared power." The EU has always had problems combining market-opening federalism with confederal strategizing and decision-making. Since the beginning of the Eurozone crisis in 2008–2009, however, it has faced several large events that have severely challenged this institutional setup. In each, the EU's confederal side, mainly the European Council and the Eurogroup, has been called upon to respond. These responses have worked relatively well so far on Brexit. In some other cases, like the Eurozone crisis, member state decisions were made by the EU's larger, richer, and more powerful members even if they brought large economic and political costs to others. Then in the refugee crisis and the emergence of "illiberal democracy" these more powerful members have been unable and/or unwilling to make large choices at all, either because they could not agree or because they believed that the results of making hard choices could be dangerous to the EU as a whole. Here it is evident that weak decisions, or even nondecisions, have had real costs as well: responses to foreign and economic policy shifts in the Trump administration's United States and the more general decay of the "rules based liberal international system" within which the EU has lived most of its life are pending.

It may be that recent years have been exceptional in producing "events" that have challenged the EU's confederal side to respond. It is possible, however, that confronting such "events" intergovernmentally will be a recurring part of the EU's future. The most important question, however, is whether the institutionalization of confederal responses to such events is politically sustainable. Complex "shared power" systems are common in the world of comparative federalism. It is also not unusual for the methods of "sharing" to change over time. As Sbragia has discussed, the EU's confederal side has gained power since the 1980s at the expense of the "Community Method." The European Council now has very large responsibilities in responding to large crises. Divisions among EU members in an enlarged, more regionally, economically, and politically differentiated EU have made it more difficult to respond satisfactorily, however. The idea, floated by Sbragia and others, that EU nations might be becoming "member states" willing to be more responsibly European, as opposed to responding primarily to their national duties, has been circulating for some time. Some see confederal crisis decision-making to such "events" as a manageable "new frontier" for today's EU.[5] Whether this will turn out to be accurate is unclear. Others find it difficult to envisage that becoming a "member state" will be sufficient to limit the negative reactions to the often highly distributive costs of conflict resolution imposed by the more on the less powerful. They, thus, worry that future events could test the EU's ability to continue successfully.[6] Sbragia's comparative federalist analyses of the EU are important in helping to make sense of these dilemmas. They do not, however, resolve them. It thus falls on the students and colleagues persuaded by Sbragia's comparative federalist approach to tell us what all this now means and how the institutional puzzles might be resolved.

---

5 See Van Middelaar (2018) for a strong argument in this direction.
6 For such worries, well argued, see Fabbrini (2019).

BIBLIOGRAPHY

European Commission. 2001. "European Governance: A White Paper." Brussels: European Commission. https://ec.Europa.eu/Europeaid/European-governance-white-
paper_en.

Fabbrini, Sergio. 2019. *Europe's Futures*. Oxford: Oxford University Press.

Hoffman, Stanley. 1966. "Obstinate or Obsolete? The Fate of the Nation-State and the
Case of Western Europe." *Daedelus*, 95.3: 862–915.

Keohane, Robert and Stanley Hoffman, eds. 1991. *The New European Community:
Decision- Making and Institutional Change*. Boulder, CO: Westview Press.

Moravscik, Andrew. 1998. *The Choice for Europe*. Ithaca, NY: Cornell University
Press.

Sandholtz, Wayne and John Zysman. 1989. "1992: Recasting the European Bargain."
World Politics, 42.1: 95–128.

Sbragia, Alberta M. 1979. "Not All Roads Lead to Rome: Local Housing Policy in the
Unitary Italian State." *British Journal of Political Science*, 9.3: 315–339.

Sbragia, Alberta M. 1981. "Cities, Capital and Banks: The Politics of Debt in the
United States, Great Britain, and France." In *Urban Political Economy*, edited by
Kenneth Newton, 200–220. London: Frances Pinter (Publishers) Limited.

Sbragia, Albert M., ed. 1983. *The Municipal Money Chase: The Politics of Local
Government Finance*. Boulder, CO: Westview Press.

Sbragia, Alberta M. 1985. "The Politics of Public Investment: An Anglo-American
Comparison." *Studies in Public Policy*, no. 109. Glasgow: Centre for the Study of
Public Policy, University of Strathclyde.

Sbragia, Alberta M., ed. 1992. *Euro-Politics: Institutions and Policymaking in the
"New" European Community*. Washington, DC: The Brookings Institution.

Sbragia, Alberta M. 1996. *Debt Wish: Entrepreneurial Cities, US Federalism and
Economic Development*. Pittsburgh, PA: University of Pittsburgh Press.

Sbragia, Alberta M. 2000. "The European Union as Coxswain: Governance by Steering." In *Debating: Governance, Authority, Democracy and Steering*, edited by Jon
Pierre, 219–240. Oxford: Oxford University Press.

Sbragia, Alberta M. 2002a. "Conclusion to Special Issue on the Institutional Balance
and the Future of EU Governance: The Treaty of Nice, Institutional Balance, and
Uncertainty." *Governance*, 15.3: 393–412.

Sbragia, Alberta M. 2002b. "The Dilemma of Governance with Government." The
Jean Monnet Program—European Union Jean Monnet Chair, paper 3/02. New
York: New York University School of Law. Accessed July 21, 2019. https://jean-
monnetprogram.org/archive/papers/02/020301.rtf.

Sbragia, Alberta M. 2004. "The Future of Federalism in the European Union." Keynote Address delivered at the European Community Studies Association Canada
(ECSA-C) 2004 Biennial Conference "A Constitution for Europe? Governance and
Policy Making in the European Union," May 27–29, 2004. Accessed July 21, 2019.
aei.pitt.edu/1877/2/Sbragia_ECSA-Canada_keynote_address_May_2004.rtf.

Sbragia, Alberta M. 2005. "Seeing the European Union through American Eyes: The EU
as a Reflection of the American Experience." *European Political Science*, 4.2: 179–187.

Sbragia, Alberta M. 2006a. "Introduction—the EU and Its 'Constitution': Public Opinion, Political Elites, and Their International Context." *PS: Political Science and Politics*, 39.2: 237–240.

Sbragia, Alberta M. 2006b. "The United States and the European Union: Comparing Two *sui generis* Systems." In *Comparative Federalism: The European Union and the United States in Comparative Perspective*, edited by Anand Menon and Martin Schain, 15–34. Oxford: Oxford University Press.

Sbragia, Alberta M. 2007. "An American Perspective on the EU's Constitutional Treaty." *Politics*, 27.1: 2–7.

Sbragia, Alberta M. 2008. "Review Article: Comparative Regionalism: What Might It Be?" In *The JCMS Annual Review of the European Union in 2007*, edited by Ulrich Sedelmeier and Alasdair R. Young, 29–49. Oxford: Wiley-Blackwell.

Sbragia, Alberta M. 2011. "The European Union: A New Form of Governance." In *The Ashgate Research Companion to Regionalisms*, edited by Timothy M. Shaw, J. Andrew Grant, and Scarlett Cornellison, 91–112. London: Ashgate Publishing.

Sbragia, Alberta M. 2012. "The Treaty of Nice." In *The Oxford Handbook of the European Union*, edited by Erik Jones, Anand Menon, and Stephen Weatherill, 149–162. Oxford: Oxford University Press.

Van Middelaar, Luuk. 2018. *Quand l'Europe Improvise: Dix ans de crises politiques*. Paris: Gallimard.

Chapter 2

Trilateral Competitive Independence

European and American Trade Policy Choices and the Rise of China

Diego A. Salazar-Morales and Mark Hallerberg

Since the establishment of the World Trade Organization (WTO) in 1994, important international actors such as the United States and the European Union (EU) have engaged in a process known as 'competitive interdependence' (CI). Alberta Sbragia (2010) used this term to refer to EU-U.S. structural competition. Each actor sought to advance its economic interests in relation to third country's markets. In doing so, each can adopt different strategies. One might seek a multilateral deal, which involves many countries. The General Agreement on Tariffs and Trade (GATT) rounds are examples. One or both may focus on bilateral deals, which eventually conclude in free trade agreements (FTAs). Also, some other countries might adopt a unilateral stance to attract foreign chain production to their shores.

CI between the EU and the United States was predominant between 1995 and 2009. Initially, competition pressured the United States to first secure their investors' access to third markets by signing FTAs. Under the Bush administration, the United States used FTAs to gain first advantage. Robert Zoellick, the U.S. trade representative (USTR), from 2000 to 2005, helped create a sense of urgency about the necessity of FTAs. He argued that the United States was 'lagging behind' in terms of trade. At the end of the Bush era, the number of FTAs rose from three to sixteen.

The EU responded to the initial U.S. advantage by transforming its pure multilateral approach to a more pragmatic-oriented one. Initially, under the 'Managed Globalisation' strategy, Trade Commissioner Pascal Lamy (1999–2004) committed to a 'pure multilateral' approach. The EU sought not only to expand its commercial interests but to export its model. In more recent trade strategies, the EU has pledged bilateralism as its preferred policy choice. The current 'Trade for All' strategy of Trade Commissioner Cecilia Malmström

(2014–) has been presented as a response to U.S. 'first advantage' moves. It explicitly argues that FTAs should cover at least 'two thirds' of EU's trade, while it prioritises the ongoing negotiations with Japan (started in 2013 and signed in 2017), Canada (started in 2009 and signed in 2017), Vietnam (ongoing since 2009) and the new upcoming ones with Australia and New Zealand (European Commission 2015, 2).

In the past decade, both EU's and U.S. CI has changed. Pressured by the growing role of China in the international trade arena, and the pace of technological advancements, they have opted for more bilaterally oriented strategies as their preferred policy choices, while also they selectively used multilateral forums (WTO) to advance their commercial interests. Drawing on recent scholarship, we argue that prior CI between the EU and the United States has shifted towards China, thus veering off towards a trilateral cooperation and competition relationship (Sbragia 2010; Heron and Siles-Brugge 2012; Irwin 2018). In that sense, the United States and the EU have responded distinctively to China's rise. In August 2018, President Trump announced a set of progressive tariffs worth US$250 billion, while in his 2018 Trade Policy Agenda he withdrew from various multilateral treaties by claiming that they are damaging to U.S. trade policy. He also criticised the WTO's dispute settlement – especially the Appellate Body – because it does not rapidly translate the changes in law or practice, thus damaging U.S. trade policy sovereignty. He declared then that the United States has no obligation to follow the WTO's ruling (USTR 2017, 2).

Different from the United States, the EU seeks to 'rebalance' its relationship with China through both multilateral and bilateral strategies by deepening their commercial links, pursuing robust reciprocal policies, and strengthening European investments in the Asian country. The recently released 'EU-China—a Strategic Outlook' strategy considers China both a partner and a competitor in the trade arena, thus regarding as crucial the negotiations for a balanced playground for both actors' investors.

This chapter presents its arguments in three stages. First, based on a brief review of previous scholarship concerning trade relations between the EU and the United States, we present a typology of their most common existing trade policy strategies (unilateral, pure multilateral, competitive liberalising and pragmatic multilateral). In the second stage, this framework is used as a reference point for the analysis of both actors' trade policies changes in relation to China's emergence as a trade power. In this section, we argue that China's growing relevance in the trade arena in the past decade might underlie both EU's selective bilateralism and U.S. novel unilateralism, trade policies. Finally, we summarise the findings and its implications.

THEORETICAL STANDPOINT

This section presents a typology of the most common trade policies employed by both the EU and the United States. This typology is based on two axes. One concerns whether the trade policy is multilateral, and the other focuses on whether it is cooperative. This classification is important to further understand how they have been interchangeably used in the context of EU-U.S. relationships with China.

The Trade Policy Choice Set

The international trade system is governed by state (and non-state actors), rules and competition strategies (Hudec 1975; Cass 2005; Irwin 2018). Based on these elements, a trade actor – being a country and/or a bloc such as the EU – chooses the type of relationship it seeks to establish with others.[1] These relationships can be unilateral, bilateral or multilateral (Corbet 1970; Sally 2007; De Ville and Siles Brügge 2018).

To decide which policy option to employ, a trade actor weighs a set of elements: the international economic circumstances, its relative power position in the international community and its potential competitors' actions (Corbet 1970; Sally 2007, 2008). As a result, an actor might either aim to promote a system of values (i.e. searching for the promotion of democracy and strengthening international forums) or aim to focus on purely commercial interests. In general terms, actors seeking value-oriented trade are likely to opt for a 'multilateral' policy, while those searching to only advance purely commercial interests are likely to choose the unilateral – or also bilateral policies (Rodrik 1995, 1459). Other factors such as a country's size, and its relative trade power position in the world, might influence its choices for cooperation and degree of multilateralism.

In short, the relationship between the 'values' pursued in a determined trade strategy, and how many others it involves (how multilateral it is), can be classified in a fourfold category. Table 2.1 summarises them, while also including a distinction between 'pragmatic' and 'pure' typologies within the 'multilateral' category.

To further clarify the implications of each trade policy choice, a brief description is in order.

---

1 This chapter considers a strategy as a series of internally defined norms deemed to promote countries' interests through opening markets in a competitive international system. Also, note that we employ the terms 'trade policies' and 'trade strategies' interchangeably (see Corbet 1970; Bhagwati 1988).

Table 2.1.   A Typology of Trade Policy Choices

		Commercial interests only	*System of values*
Degree of multilateralism	–	Unilateral liberalisation	Bilateral competitive liberalisation
	+	Pragmatic multilateralism	Pure multilateral

Source: Authors' elaboration based on Sally (2007, 2008), Corbet (1970), Baldwin (2010) and Irwin (2018).

Unilateral Liberalisation

Unilateral liberalisation refers to the action taken by a country (or trade bloc) without a previous negotiation or expecting a reciprocal partner response. For instance, Sally (2007), Baldwin (2010) and Baldwin and Forslid (2016) stress that through this strategy trade actors can (1) attract foreign decentralised production to their shores, while (2) also incentivise their local economies.

This policy has largely been used by developing countries during the 1980s to capture value-chain enterprises which can produce at short labour prices in their shores, thus providing them with competitive advantages (Campos Filho 1998). The World Bank reports that between 1983 and 2003, developing nations unilaterally lowered their tariffs by 14 per cent. This means that almost 65 per cent of developing countries' tariff liberalisation have been unilaterally decided (Baldwin 2010, 10–15).

Among the best examples of this trade policy are Chile (1974–1990s) (see Edwards and Lederman 1998); China before its accession to WTO (Sally 2007, 37) and the United States, which through its 1994 Trade Act created a 'Generalised System of Preferences' to open commercial opportunities for developing countries (USTR 2018). Moreover, the WTO recognises this type trade policy under the label of preferential trade agreement (PTA) through which 'countries grant non-reciprocal preferential schemes' to other nations. To date, the WTO reports thirty-four PTAs (WTO 2019).

Pure Multilateralism

The idea of a negotiated multilateral system emerged as a reciprocal way for countries (or trade blocs) to obtain non-discriminatory tariffs and rules. Initially, many countries supported the creation of multilateral organisations that were thought to bring order to a chaotic international structure. This idea, in 1945, evolved into a proposal to create the International Trade Organisation (ITO), which was later ratified in 1948 by fifty-six countries in the United Nations Conference on Trade and Employment held in La Havana, Cuba. Although the U.S. Congress did not ratify the agreement, twenty-three countries still adopted a revised version of the ITO, known as the GATT (see Irwin 1994, 133), which survived until 1994, when the WTO was created.

In the past, the United States has opted for pure multilateralism. In 1943, when the United Kingdom proposed a 'Commercial Union', the United States responded with a more enthusiastic 'Multilateral Convention on Commercial Policy'. This institution sought to institutionalise clear trade rules among post-war allies, so that they avoid the usual commercial wars of the pre–World War II era (Irwin 1994, 133).

Moreover, some countries have committed to multilateralism as the only orderly way to trade and resolve commercial disputes. Sbragia (2010) and Heron and Siles-Brugge (2012) cite the approach of Pascal Lamy, who served as European Trade Commissioner (1999–2004), as an example of 'multilateral' approach. His self-imposed moratorium to pursue FTA deals, which he deemed detrimental to the multilateral forum (WTO), was precisely one of the main characteristics of his administration.

Pragmatic Multilateralism

Another version of multilateralism adopts a more pragmatic stance. It is less concerned with strengthening international rules or the promotion of democratic values but more pragmatic to advance the trade actors' interests. The U.S. trade policy under President Obama's administration fits this category. In his 2010 Trade Policy Agenda, he explicitly mentions that his administration would enforce WTO rules as a way of settling multilateral disputes, while also aggressively seeking to open international markets. His policy agenda mentions: 'If America sits on the side-line while other nations sign trade deals, we will lose the chance to create jobs in our shores' (USTR 2010, 1–3). His administration, thus, coined the term 'pragmatic multilateralism' as a third way – a mixed approach that combines the multilateral – mentioned in the documents as 'multifaceted economic relationships' – and the bilateral. The document notes further: 'The WTO remains the critical forum for strengthening the multilateral rules-based trading system, enforcing global trade rules, and serving as an important bulwark against protectionism', yet he also highlighted that '[the United States] cannot sit on the side-line while other nations sign trade deals' (USTR 2016, 26). Obama's approach sought to integrate both ways of participating in the international trade system, in line with the similarly pragmatic stance of countries, such as China, and blocs, such as the EU (see Zhao 2016).

Bilateral Competitive Liberalisation

While multilateral trade policies require commitment and disposition to align competing countries' interests, they also usually involve a long-term negotiation process, which is largely overcome by the pace of the economic and technological advancements (Sally 2008). In consequence, some countries seek 'fast-track' agreements, which can shorten strenuous multilateral negotiations. This type of trade policy receives the name of bilateral 'competitive liberalisation' (Baldwin 1997; Chorev 2009; Sbragia 2010).

This term describes a trade actor's willingness to promote bilateral agreements to advance its interests and gain 'first entry advantage' (Heron and Siles-Brugge 2012). It is characterised by the aggressive employment of one-to-one provisions to ensure economic partnerships (namely FTA, economic partnership agreements, among others).

A bilateral competitive approach considers trade agreements as an end in themselves, and they are not espoused to 'value creation' or strengthening international institutions. One of the most referred examples is the case of the United States under Bush's administration (2001–2009), who raised the number of FTAs from three to sixteen.

Other countries have also followed the U.S. example, thus negotiating bilateral agreements. China, for instance, has already concluded FTAs with Chile (2006), Costa Rica (2010), Peru (2010), Switzerland (2014) and Australia (2015). Bilateral agreements have also gained importance in the EU, which has recently concluded negotiations with Japan (2017) – labelled as the most ambitious and comprehensive to date – and with Canada (CETA in 2017) (European Commission 2019c).

In sum, a variety of trade policies have been traditionally employed at different times and under different circumstances. The next section analyses the patterns that the EU and the United States have followed to champion trade agreements in a more competitive and chaotic environment marked by growing trade relevance of China.

U.S. AND EU TRADE POLICY CHOICES

In this section, considering our policy choice set, we briefly address Sbragia's (2010) claim that the EU and United States have engaged in a CI relationship between 1995 and 2009. We explain how China has changed the international trade scenario and pressured both actors to change their policy choices: in the U.S. case, towards a novel unilateral stance and, in the case of the EU, to a selective bilateralism.

A Brief Revision of EU-U.S. Competitive Interdependence (1995–2009)

Sbragia (2010) refers to CI as the structural competition between the United States and the EU where both seek to advance their commercial interests. In this context, the world is seen as a chess game scenario defined by the steps made by one trade actor to secure its deals. The logics underpinning the application of CI, Sbragia (quoting Jacoby and Meunier 2010) mentions, are twofold: multilateral forums (WTO) and bilateral trade agreements. Trade actors use them to advance their interests.

Sbragia also argues that the CI involves the establishment of trade institutions that set the playground for trade relationships. A CI logic seeks to implement rules with trading partners, which cannot be monopolised by one actor only, therefore limiting the access of third actors to those markets with existing agreements.

In this context, the EU-U.S. relationship has been shaped by the dynamic of cooperation and competition within WTO rules. While the EU tried to constrain the United States through WTO pacts, the United States opted for a more bilateral approach, thus actively recurring to FTA's effectively gaining a first advantage.

However, competition has not been limited to EU-U.S. interaction in the WTO. It also demands the conscious choice of their preferred trade policies to promote their interests and challenge the other. Sbragia describes these choices in detail while also identifying the dynamics of competition and contention of both trade powers in three stages. Initially, the EU challenged the United States through its 'managed globalisation strategy'. This provoked a U.S. response through rapidly securing bilateral competitive policies (FTAs). Finally, the EU retaliated by renewing its expansion to Latin America and Asian countries through a more pragmatic approach.

Sbragia's analysis extends until 2009, when she foresees a further convergence in both trade actors' policy choices in favour of bilateralism. Posterior publications have confirmed this trend. De Ville and Siles-Brugge (2018), for instance, claim that EU trade policies have adopted a clear competitive bilateral stance – more in line with U.S. standards. Others also argue that Europe's change to bilateralism has only happened recently under EU Trade Commissioner Cecilia Malmström (2014–).

Although authors have divergent opinions about when Europe transited to a more bilaterally oriented trade policy, it is still evident that this has been the case in the latest decade. In the case of the United States, the trend is clearer. Since the Obama administration, the United States has transited to a more unilateral stance characterised by the imposition of tariffs, the withdrawal from multilateral initiatives and the preference for one-to-one negotiations.

The following section discusses the European and American policy choices after Sbragia's CI (2010–2018).

The EU, the United States and the China Factor (2009–2018)

The EU-U.S. trade policy choices changed amid China's rise in the international trade arena. Since 2001, China's exports have grown from 5 per cent to 10 per cent of the total world's exports. China's growth in the trade international arena has also impacted in the commercial position of both the EU and the United States. Also, since 2001, EU's global market share has decline 1 per cent point to 15. The reduction is more serious in the U.S. case; its share has declined four times in relative terms more than the EU to 11 per cent (European Commission 2015, 9).

Commercial deficits have also soared. The U.S. Census Bureau (2019) reports that the commercial balance deficit with China reached $429 billion in 2018. This is five times increase since China inclusion in the WTO in 2001. In the case of the EU, the deficit is €180 billion; this is a relatively small decline since 2007, when the deficit reached €179 billion (Eurostat 2019).

The role of China has been crucial in pressuring both American and European policy choices, ultimately making the CI relationship between them shift towards securing their market shares in third countries from Chinese competition. The economic development of China has led to a trilateral CI.

EUROPEAN UNION

In terms of trade policy choices, the EU has gradually changed its position towards FTAs. Under the Trade Commissioner Pascal Lamy (1999–2004), the EU championed a 'pure multilateral' stance that sought to contain the United States through WTO multilateral agreements (Sbragia 2010, 369). This strategy, however, evolved due to U.S. competitive liberalisation, which dramatically increased the number of FTAs. More recently, the EU has eased its commitment to pure multilateralism, also recurring to bilateral agreements. Its trade strategies, especially the 'Global Europe Competing in the World' and the 'Trade for All', reflect these changes. They adopted different policy choices in relation to both the United States and China.

Pragmatic Multilateralism

The failure to reach agreements in WTO conferences pushed the EU to reconsider its 'Managed Globalisation' approach, championed under Trade Commissioner Pascal Lamy (1994–2004). In his words, 'There [was] no way to structure and steer discussions among 146 members in a manner conducive to consensus' (Jaura 2003).

Through its new policy, 'Global Europe Competing in the World' released in 2006, the bloc aimed to (1) promote 'right' internal European policies responsive to external competitive challenges, (2) ensure EU market openness[2] and (3) adopt FTAs as a 'faster and effective' previous step towards a posterior multilateral outcome (European Commission 2006a).

This strategy set the criteria for Europe to establish future commercial relationships: a country's economic size, growth and the level of protection to EU export interests (tariffs and non-tariff barriers) (European Commission 2006a, 11).

Although the EU started to search for bilateral relationships, the 'Global Europe' approach was still considered complementary – and not a replacement – of multilateral efforts. In fact, the new Trade Commissioner Peter Mandelson (2004–2008) mentioned that 'no European retreat from multilateralism' will occur (European Commission 2006b). He claimed that his new trade policy sought to promote European involvement in the WTO as an additional platform to pursue agreements – only if they were in line with European interests. It was an optional arena to fight third countries' tariffs and limitations to trade. It was at its core – following our typology – a pragmatic stance.

Applied to China, the EU's pragmatic multilateralism opted for ensuring the implementation of China's commitments made in their accession to the WTO.[3] Seven years after China's inclusion in the WTO, the country failed to comply with its commitments in relation to the respect of intellectual property and subsidies to its industries. Moreover, the EU was especially concerned about China's internal trade barriers to European investors: China requires that 51 per cent of a total joint venture in the automaker and communication industries should be controlled by a local (Chinese) partner (European Parliament 2011, 21). The EU considered this requirement particularly damaging to its investors. Peter Mandelson worried that China could gain 'market economy status' by 2016 (as its accession protocol suggests) before having fully implemented their WTO commitments, although his preoccupation did not translate – unlike the United States (which set a Congressional Executive Commission on China) – into a specific task force to monitor the implementation of Chinese WTO commitments.

---

2 They refer to emerging markets as Brazil, India and China that combines economic growth with higher barriers to EU products: 'The EU is open to exports from developing countries yet its ready to go further'. In addition, they not only go beyond simply market but also aim to build a focus in promoting some areas: (1) non-tariff barriers, (2) access to resources, (3) services (which at the time represented 77 per cent of gross domestic product [GDP]) and (4) public procurement (European Commission 2006a, 8).

3 The commitments include reduction in tariffs to an average of 10 per cent by 2005; a quota to bring agricultural tariffs close to 0; elimination of quotas and licences in relation to imports; reduced participation of the state in the economy; opening of critical sectors, such as communications, banking, insurance and asset management. Also, the protocol includes commitments in relation to the respect of intellectual property (see Lardy 2001).

Apart from the external limitations posed by China, the EU also faced internal divergent voices. One of the major challenges for the determination of a coherent trade policy to address China relies on the EU capacity to convey a unitary perspective. An evaluation conducted by the EU to its relationship with China – EU-China Trade Relationships (European Parliament 2011, 21) – stresses that 'without a strong consensus of member states to back European Commission in its efforts to achieve reciprocal market access, the balance of power will remain overwhelmingly with China. . . . The commission does not possess the same political and economic power of an authoritarian and centralised state as China.'

In 2008, following the resignation of Peter Mandelson as Trade Commissioner, the 'Global Europe' strategy was replaced by the 'Trade, Growth and World Affairs'. This new trade policy, presented by the Trade Commissioner Karel de Gucht (2010–2014), pledged continuity to its predecessor; yet it also recognises China's growing trade power as Europe's main capacity test.

In his relationship with China, de Gucht argued to reopen previously cancelled Association of Southeast Asian Nations (ASEAN) region-to-region agreements, although in a bilateral format (European Commission 2010). He thought that engaging in FTAs at a faster rate in the ASEAN region will help to secure European interests from China. He further mentioned that '[the EU] must deliver the multilateral and bilateral trade deals already underway or on the starting bloc' (European Commission 2010, 1).[4] He also set a vis-à-vis policy with China, which focused on three priorities: (1) the dismantlement of trade barriers that prevent EU exports, (2) the promotion of European companies in China and (3) an underlying multilateral engagement. Through this strategy the EU also sought to establish institutional channels of cooperation and communication with China. Among them are annual summits at the level of the Head of State (celebrated in either Beijing or Brussels), executive meetings (at the level of the European Commission President and the Chinese Premier), regular meetings with EU High Representative for Foreign and Security Policy and the Chinese counterpart and regular annual meetings with other minor directorates (Political Directors and Asia Pacific Affairs).

In sum, European pragmatic multilateralism set the initial priorities for its future relationship with China. During this period, EU relationship with China was primordially multilateral; yet in the following years, European

---

4 As they mentioned:

> Getting EU exporters better access to the ASEAN market is a priority for the EU. Negotiations for a region-to-region trade and investment agreement between the EU and ASEAN were launched in 2007. These talks were then paused by mutual agreement in 2009 to give way to a bilateral format of negotiations. These bilateral trade and investment agreements were conceived as building blocs towards a future region-to-region agreement. (European Commission 2019a)

pragmatic stance changed towards a more – although still selective – bilateral-oriented relationship.

Bilateral Competitive Liberalisation

Towards the end of the de Gucht period in 2014, the EU's trade policy gradually shifted to a clearer bilateral stance. Important to mention is that scholars still disagree on whether European transition to a more bilateral-oriented trade policy occurred during de Gucht administration or right after he resigned from office.

Heron and Siles-Brugge (2012) argues that European trade policy, during the Mandelson era (2004–2008), did already embrace a bilateral 'competitive' tendency. Similarly, De Ville and Siles-Brugge (2018, 249) contend that while the 'Global Europe' strategy still presented a multilateral focus, the 'Trade, Growth and World Affairs', clearly searched for partnerships at the bilateral level – thus being closer to the definition of bilateral 'competitive liberalisation'.

Although these minor discrepancies about 'when' the EU shifted towards a bilateral stance exist, it is still clear that since Lamy's 'pure multilateralism', Europe has transited to a more bilaterally oriented trade policy. This approach has evolved throughout time, only to be officially confirmed in the new 'Trade for All' strategy, under the administration of Cecilia Malmström (2014–). In this document, she openly advocates for the FTA as an effective method to open markets for EU goods and services.[5] She argues:

> To boost EU's capacity to benefit from trade and investment, [we] have developed a trade agenda that complements EU engagement in the WTO. . . . While FTAs in force covered less than a quarter of EU ten years ago, that is not the case for more than a third of EU trade. It could reach to two thirds if all ongoing negotiations are concluded. (European Commission 2015, 9)

Malmström's new bilateral trade policy is a response to a growing competitive world pressured by the emergence of China as a trade power. She continues with the de Gucht strategy to secure FTAs, especially in the ASEAN region which is considered 'crucial to European Commercial interests' (European Commission 2015, 31). In that sense, the EU currently considers as 'top priorities' the negotiations with MERCOSUR (ongoing since 1999 and relaunched in 2012), Japan (started in 2013 and signed in 2017), Canada (started in 2009 and signed in 2017) and Vietnam (started in 2009 and a first agreement concluded in 2018). Furthermore, the European Commission has

---

5 Which makes 40 per cent of total exports and 70 per cent of the GDP (European Commission 2015, 9).

authorised, in May 2018, the negotiation of future FTAs with Australia and New Zealand.

Also, the Malmström administration has changed EU previous commitment to multilateral organisations, namely the Doha Ministerial Conferences (officially in impasse since the 2009 Potsdam meeting). Clearly, the EU position has changed from Mandelson's 'Doha remains our priority' to the pragmatic Malmström's 'turning the page on it' approach (European Commission 2015, 9–10).

However, when it comes to China, the EU still simultaneously advocates for bilateral and multilateral forums. The 'Trade for All' claims to 'rebalance' the EU–China relationship in terms of market access, investment limitations and transparency. At the multilateral level, the EU seeks to bind China through WTO pacts in order to secure a better playing field for European firms. These pacts include: The Technology and Information Agreement (which aims to eliminates tariffs to IT products), the Trade in Services Agreement (which aims to liberalise transport, health care and banking) and the Government Procurement Agreement (which aims for transparency in the procurement market) (European Commission 2019c). At the bilateral level, the EU also pursues to finalise a bilateral investment agreement. It aims to reduce pending limitations to European investors in the Chinese market, improving transparency concerning licencing and authorisation procedures. This measure is deemed to start a balanced protection of European investors in China whose participation in joint ventures is restricted to the 49 per cent of company's ownership, whereas in Europe, Chinese investors went from controlling 5,000 firms in 2007 to 28,000 in 2017. The EU formally started negotiations in 2014 (European Commission 2013, 6).

Although the EU undertook initial steps to engage bilaterally with China, it is not yet considering an FTA. Europe still expects some Chinese domestic reforms concerning intellectual property and transparency (European Commission 2010, 2).

As part of the new 'rebalance' effort, on 12 March 2019, the EU released its 'EU-China—A Strategic Outlook' which complements the already existing '2020 Strategic Agenda for Cooperation with China' and the 'Trade for All' strategy, by analysing the challenges and opportunities China as a power trade presents for the EU (European Commission 2019b). In this document, the bloc considers that China no longer holds the 'developing country' status; instead, *it should be considered as a trade and technological power, and therefore be treated by the EU as a cooperation partner, an economic competitor as well as a systemic rival.* In Sbragia's (2010) terms, the EU has established a CI relationship with China. Moreover, the newly released EU strategy proposes that future negotiations should rely on three clear principles: (1) the deepening of commercial links, although following

EU multilateral principles (most notably in terms of climate change), (2) the pursuit of robust and reciprocal policies (to secure EU's interest in China), and (3) the internal adaptation of the EU to fast-changing economic realities (especially technological challenges).

However, the bloc still faces old coordination problems which limits its ability to speak with a unitary voice: on the one hand, Italy has signed a non-binding memorandum of understanding (MoU) opening its participation in the *Belt and Road* initiative (*The Guardian* 2019); on the other, Emmanuel Macron has reacted in a 'more multilateral way' by inviting the European Commission president, Jean-Claude Juncker, and the German chancellor, Angela Merkel, to his bilateral summit with the Chinese president Xi Jinping.

Furthermore, during the 2019 EU–China Summit, both actors agreed to three MoUs which set the basis for their future relationship. They have addressed topics concerning: (1) state aid-control and fair competition, (2) expert dialogues on antitrust law and enforcement, and (3) initial topics for negotiations in relation to energy policy and climate change (European Council 2019).

Undoubtedly, the EU has already been making consistent steps on its purpose of setting a 'balanced' playground with China. Under the Malmström administration, the bloc has changed its approach to China, recurring to a more selective bilateral negotiations, while trying to constrain it at the multilateral level.

UNITED STATES

The United States, different from the EU, has consistently led the race for market liberalisation since the creation of the WTO in 1994. Under President Bush, the United States drastically increased their FTAs. In turn, Obama's administration adopted a more pragmatic stance seeking to advance U.S. interests by reinvigorating the role of multilateralism, while also revising some of the FTAs deemed harmful to American interests (i.e. North American Free Trade Agreement [NAFTA] labour section). More recently, upon the election of President Donald Trump, the U.S. trade policy adopted a novel unilateral stance and a harsh line with China. We describe how the United States opted for different trade choices in the past decade.

Pragmatic Multilateralism

Upon the election of Obama as the U.S. president, the previous bilateral liberalisation doctrine championed by President Bush faced strong criticism. The presumed benefits of the FTAs to the American local industries were called into question.[6] Cooper (2014, 11), for instance, reports that some interest groups (i.e. United Auto Makers) considered that FTAs 'undermine the ability of governments in the region to regulate their economies in the interests of their citizens and intensify the downward pressure on workers' incomes through competition for jobs and investments'. Other actors did also manifest their concerns: the U.S. steel manufactures, for instance, argued that the South Korean FTA (KORUS) would potentially damage U.S. trade remedies through countervailing duty laws. A similar claim came from the American Federation of Labour and Congress of Industrial Organisation (Williams et al. 2014).

Moreover, criticism extended to existing trade agreements, such as to NAFTA and its absence of a clear labour section.

Obama responded to these concerns by proposing a 'new template' to establish future bilateral negotiations (Zepeda, Wise and Gallagher 2009, 2). In his inaugural trade policy agenda in 2009, President Obama announced a revision of the NAFTA's labour section, which was considered damaging to the U.S. industry as they did not include workers' rights, nor did they include income schemes sections (in relation to Mexico's flawed labour regulations).[7]

Eventually, Obama's reconsideration of FTAs gradually evolved into a full doctrine. In 2016, in his Trade Policy Agenda, President Obama coined a term for his approach: '*pragmatic multilateralism*' (USTR 2016, 26). As presented in Table 2.1, this concept elicits the pragmatic usage of multi-lateral institutions to advance a country's interests. In practice, while the United States considered bilateral relationships crucial, it also 'opted for a multi-faceted regional and economic relationship', which could project an international image of a 'competent and committed partner' (USTR 2016, 26). In other words, the United States opted to advance its interests through both bilateral and multilateral schemes.

Applied to China, U.S. pragmatism operated in two levels. On the multi-lateral level, the administration committed to finalise the Transpacific Part-nership (TPP) negotiations as a mechanism to counter China's expansion, by setting strict trade rules with analogous Asian partners (e.g. antipiracy

---

6 Although President Bush's bilateral trade policy received strong criticism from the upcoming Obama administration, the Democrat US Congress – after a period of reconsideration during the 110th and 111th legislatures – approved pending FTAs with Colombia, Panama and South Korean (USTR 2008; Arregui 2015) that the Bush administration had negotiated.

7 President Obama stated:

We will also work with Canada and Mexico to identify ways in which NAFTA could be improved without having an adverse effect on trade. We will do this in a collaborative spirit and emphasize ways in which this process can benefit the citizens of all three countries. And, we will consider proposals for new bilateral and regional agreements when they promise to deliver significant benefits consistent with our national economic policies. If new negotiating authority is required, we will seek that from Congress. (USTR 2009, 4)

laws and intellectual property regulations), while at the same time the United States repeatedly challenged China's trade practices in the WTO. In 2010, the United States formulated a dispute against China over the blockade that this country imposed to American electronic payment firms – a yearly market of US$1 trillion (USTR 2015, 13). Also, in 2011, the United States opened another dispute in the WTO against China, claiming that the country must align with the General Procurement Agreement Pact to guarantee U.S. access to China's large government 'procurement market' (USTR 2015, 13). In one of his administration's last actions against China, the 2016 U.S. President Trade Agenda reports that the United States has opened a dispute to China concerning the limitations imposed to the exports of 'rare earth materials' (tungsten and molybdenum). China produces 97 per cent of all rare materials that are important for 'advanced electronics' (Arregui 2015; USTR 2016).

On the bilateral level, in turn, President Obama established with China a Joint Commission on Commerce and Trade that sought to reach formally a coordinated solution to issues concerning China's internet piracy, its violation of intellectual property rights (IPR) and wind energies. Furthermore, in 2016, the United States also considered the possibility of a bilateral investment treaty (BIT) with China, which could have eased the prior requirement to American companies to partner with Chinese ones in order to penetrate its market (USCBC 2014).

Arguably, most U.S. trade policy changes were a response to China's emergence as a trade power. Yet Obama's pragmatic stance did also extend to the EU,[8] although with marked emphasis during his initial administration years. Between 2009 and 2013, the U.S. Trade Policy Agendas showed that President Obama actively searched for a mutual partnership based on the Transatlantic Trade and Investment Partnership (TTIP) (USTR 2013). However, since 2014, mentions to the TTIP gradually reduced until barely mentioned in the 2015 and 2016 U.S. Trade Policy Agendas. Most recently, in

---

8 In 1995, the United States and the EU agreed on the New Transatlantic Agenda which sought joint action for their participation in the Uruguayan round, while also opening talks for a multilateral Organisation for Economic Co-operation and Development trade agreement, named the Transatlantic Marketplace (Bown and Crowley 2016). Subsequently, in 2000, both actors set the Transatlantic Economic Partnership conveying on issues such as the elimination of regulatory barriers and preparation of the ground for future multilateral negotiations in the WTO (European Commission 2002). Following these efforts, in 2007, they also set the Transatlantic Economic Council (TEC), which was deemed conduce to high level negotiations. It was integrated by three advisory groups: legislator's dialogue, consumer dialogue and business dialogue. But it was not until 2013 that this entity – along with the US-UE High Level Working Group on Jobs and Growth – chaired by Ron Kirk, USTR, and Karel de Gucht, European Commissioner for Trade, started negotiations towards a comprehensive TTIP. The TTIP aimed to (1) reduce barriers to trade in goods (tariffs and tariff-rate quotas), (2) eliminate barriers in goods services and investment, (3) enhance compatibility of regulations and standards, (4) eliminate 'behind the border' non-tariff barriers to trade in all categories and (5) improve regulation (European Commission 2002, 5–10).

2015 the European Commission reported that after fifteen negotiation rounds, they have not been continued (European Commission 2015, 5).

Unilateralism

In 2016, following the election of President Donald Trump, the U.S. trade policy changed to a path characterised by strong unilateralism (Brinkley 2018). The inaugural president's 2017 U.S. Trade Policy Agenda establishes four clear objectives: (1) consider the U.S. trade policy a national security issue, meaning that any action to secure favourable trade deals would be taken (possible under WTO agreements); (2) a special focus on strengthening U.S. exports of goods and services, which means any possible means to encourage positive trade balances would also be taken; (3) the renegotiation of existing deals (in particular, NAFTA), while simultaneously searching for better deals worldwide; and (4) the reform of the multilateral trade system towards on a country-to-country (one-to-one) relationship basis (USTR 2017).

In practice, American new unilateralism promotes the withdrawal from various ongoing multilateral negotiations, including most prominently the TPP and TTIP. On the former, the administration advocates direct negotiation of FTAs following a bilateral basis, given that the TPP has 'no way to [be] fixed' (CNBC 2018). On the latter, the administration mentions that there has been a lack of interest from the European counterpart to conclude negotiations.[9]

Moreover, the Trump administration's preference for direct negotiations, different from the Bush's 'competitive bilateralism' or Obama's 'multilateral pragmatism', involves the rejection of existing multilateral organisations that he considers biased in favour of third countries (especially to China). Thus, the U.S. new unilateralism rejects WTO's dispute settlement panel arguing that 'it does not automatically translate in changes, [therefore] posing a threat to US trade sovereignty'. Henceforth, the adoption of a 'unilateral action [should] support the country's effort to enforce US laws' (USTR 2018, 1), not leaving everything to the agreements eventually reached in WTO Ministerial Conferences.

Applied to China, President Trump's unilateral framework translates into sanctions. He has imposed tariffs to China's imports worth US\$250 billion, which started in September 2018 at 10 per cent rate until reaching 25 per cent rate in January 2019 (CNBC 2018). These tariffs aim to bring China into the negotiation table – a scheme that could rely in the previous BIT pursued by

---

9 Moreover, he also mentioned that 'as a general matter we [Trump's administration] believe that goals . . . can be accomplished by focusing on bilateral negotiations rather than multilateral and revising trade agreements when our goals are not being met' (USTR 2017, 1).

President Obama. President Trump also commissioned an investigation to the USTR under section 301 of the 1974's Trade Act to determine whether China's policies related to technology transfer, intellectual property and innovation are discriminatory (USTR 2018, 16). A 'Section 301' investigation determines whether a country (1) violates or is inconsistent with U.S. trade agreements and (2) creates an unjustifiable burden to U.S. commerce. The results of the investigation should produce a dispute under WTO terms, and in cases when the disputed country violation relates to intellectual property or is bounded by an FTA, the USTR determines a retaliation measures in the form of increased tariffs. Finally, on 5 May 2019, he announced his intention to slap a 25 per cent tariff on another $200 billion worth of Chinese imports.

Since the early 1990s, China's trade policy (particularly its IPR policy) has been object of section 301 investigations in the United States. In 1992, the United States launched an investigation to China's IPR and threatened to apply tariffs for up to $3.9 billion. In 2010, the United States launched another investigation about presumed limitations to US firms' investments in the Chinese market and wind power subsidies. In 2012, the United States challenged China for its restriction to exports of rare earth materials. In every case, these cases 'resulted in bilateral agreements before tariff hikes were implemented' (U.S. Congress 2019). In March 2018, President Trump announced a series of measures to retaliate to China's 'economic aggression', based on tariffs on China's imports (which he implemented in September 2018), initiated a WTO dispute on China's discriminatory licencing (filed in March 2018) and set investment restrictions to China's acquisition of U.S. firms working on sensitive technologies (*The Economist Times* 2018).

President Trump's approach has provoked spirited debates among scholars. While some argue that President Trump unilateralism is novel and resembles early nineteenth-century protectionist policies (Irwin 2017; Noland 2018), others argue that the U.S. trade policy under Trump presents clear continuities, although by different means to those employed under Presidents Obama and Bush. His reliance on a 'one-to-one' scheme might respond to a long story of unresolved disputes with China's subsidies and lack of enforcement of IPR policies. What is undeniable, however, is that in the current U.S. trade policy, China plays a major role.

CONCLUSION

Has previous CI between the EU and the United States shifted towards China? The revision of both actors' trade policies after Sbragia's analysis (1995–2009) seems to confirm this path.

Previous EU-U.S. relationships, where each actor adjusted their policies relative to the other, are currently facing the challenge of China's rise. Recent figures show that China's export power expansion has had an impact on both EU and U.S. global market share.

This scenario has provoked a re-evaluation of the trade strategies followed by these two actors. Previously focused on constraining each other either multilaterally through the WTO and bilaterally through FTAs, both Europeans and Americans have redirected their efforts to contain China's impact. To do so, they have modified their trade choices accordingly.

In the period of analysis (2009–2018), EU trade policy has moved towards a more bilateral stance. Its aim is to secure FTA agreements globally.

When it comes to China, the EU has followed a dual path simultaneously using multilateral forums (the WTO) to constrain China while also advancing towards a bilateral agreement in terms of investment. The 'EU-China—A Strategic Outlook' document, released ahead of the two trade actors' summit in April 2019, reveals that EU has moved to consider China both a partner and a competitor. This new strategy also reveals that further negotiations with the Asian power must rely on multilateral forums, while pushing to reciprocal policies in terms of investment.

The United States has been an active player in opening markets and strengthening its influence globally. After the U.S. administration change in 2009 and the criticism to the benefits of FTAs to U.S. industries, President Obama searched for a 'new template' for his trade policy, labelled as 'pragmatic multilateralism' – a new approach that combines both the multilateral and the bilateral. This approach also changed in form under the administration of President Trump (2016) who has adopted a more 'unilateral' stance; although, in substance, the United States presents important continuities in its trade policy towards China.

Since the Obama era – and even before – the U.S. trade policy has repeatedly challenged China at both the multilateral and the bilateral levels. Moreover, the Asian power has been object of 'Section 301' investigations in multiple years (1992, 2010 and 2012) and avoided tariff impositions by recurring to bilateral agreements which have not been properly enforced. President Trump's actions could be read as the manifestation of a harsher line against China's fail to comply with intellectual property policies, and discriminatory practices concerning American company's participation in its market. So far, the U.S. approach has been tariff-based, looking to accelerate bilateral negotiations with the final objective to reach a deal that facilitates U.S. industries participation in China's digital market – a negotiation that started during the Obama era under the name of BIT.

In sum, more than dramatic discontinuities, the U.S. change to unilateralism still aims to ensure more general American trade policy goals, although this time through more controversial means, such as the use of tariffs.

Arguably, the growing role of China as a trade powerhouse has had important implications for both European and American trade policy choices. European and American multilateral and bilateral efforts to bring the Asian country accountable through WTO rules have seen frustrated results (e.g. through the Trade in Services Agreements, Government Procurement Agreement and other bilateral negotiations such as the Bilateral Trade Agreement).

Undoubtedly, China's overriding economic growth has changed the bilateral structure of EU-U.S. CI towards a trilateral one, where both actors worry about China's policy choices and thus design adequate responses through either multilateral (WTO) or bilateral means (agreements or a potential FTA).

BIBLIOGRAPHY

Arregui, Javier M. 2015. 'TTIP/EU-US Economic Relations: The TTIP Negotiations and Its Implications.' *Revista CIDOB d'Afers Internacionals*, no. 110: 43–66.

Baldwin, Richard E. 1997. 'The Causes of Regionalism.' *World Economy*, 20.7: 865–888.

Baldwin, Richard E. 2010. 'Unilateral Tariff Liberalisation.' *The International Economy*, 14: 10–43.

Baldwin, Richard E. 2016. 'The World Trade Organization and the Future of Multilateralism.' *Journal of Economic Perspectives*, 30.1: 95–116.

Baldwin, Richard E. and Rikard Forslid. 2016. 'Trade Liberalization with Heterogeneous Firms.' *Review of Development Economics*, 14.2: 161–176.

Bhagwati, Jagdish N. 1988. 'Export-Promoting Trade Strategy: Issues and Evidence.' *The World Bank Research Observer*, 3: 27–57.

Bown, Chad P. and Meredith A. Crowley. 2016. 'The Empirical Landscape of Trade Policy.' Policy Research Working Paper, no. WPS 7620: 1–98. Washington, DC: World Bank Group.

Brinkley, John. 2018. 'What Trump Calls Nationalism Looks More Like Isolationism.' *Forbes*, 16 October 2018. https://www.forbes.com/sites/johnbrinkley/2018/03/21/what-trump-calls-nationalism-looks-more-like-isolationism/#5870875928f1.

Campos Filho, Leonardo. 1998. 'Unilateral Liberalisation and Mercosur: Implications for Resource Allocation.' *Revista Brasileira de Economia*, 52.4. 601–636.

Cass, Deborah Z. 2005. *The Constitutionalization of the World Trade Organization: Legitimacy, Democracy, and Community in the International Trading System.* Oxford: Oxford University Press.

Chorev, Nitsan. 2009. 'International Trade Policy under George W. Bush.' In *Assessing the George W. Bush Presidency: A Tale of Two Terms*, edited by Andrew Wroe and Jon Herbert, 129–148. Edinburgh: Edinburgh University Press.

CNBC. 2018. 'Trump Dismisses TPP But Might Have Lost Opportunity in China Trade Skirmish.' *CNBC*, 16 October 2018. https://www.cnbc.com/2018/04/18/trump-dismisses-tpp-but-may-have-missed-opportunity-in-china-trade-skirmish.html.

Cooper, William H. 2014. 'Free Trade Agreements: Impact on US Trade and Implications for US Trade Policy.' Cornell University ILR School—Key Workplace

Documents: 1–15. https://digitalcommons.ilr.cornell.edu/cgi/viewcontent. cgi?article=2252&context=key_workplace.

Corbet, Hugh. 1970. *Trade Strategy and the Asian-Pacific Region.* London: George Allen & Unwin Ltd.

De Ville, Ferdi and Gabriel Siles☐Brügge. 2018. 'The Role of Ideas in Legitimating EU Trade Policy: From the Single Market Programme to the Transatlantic Trade and Investment Partnership.' In *Handbook on the EU and International Trade,* edited by Sangeeta Khorana and María García, 243–262. Gloucestershire, UK: Edward Elgar Publishing Limited.

The Economic Times. 2018. 'US Drags China to WTO on Discriminatory Technology Licensing Requirements.' *The Economist Times,* 23 March 2018. https://economic times.indiatimes.com/news/international/us-drags-china-to-0wto-on-discriminatory- technology-licensing-requirements/articleshow/63433503.cms?from=mdr.

Edwards, Sebastian, and Daniel Lederman. 1998. 'The Political Economy of Unilat- eral Trade Liberalization: The Case of Chile.' NBER Working Paper No. 6510: 1–74. Cambridge, MA: National Bureau of Economic Research.

European Commission. 2002. 'The Tras-Atlantic Economic Partnership. Over- view and Assessment.' Online: http://trade.ec.europa.eu/doclib/docs/2003/october/ tradoc_111712.pdf

European Commission. 2006a. 'Global Europe: Competing in the World. A Contri- bution to the EU's Jobs and Growth Strategy.' Brussels: European Commission. https://eur-lex.Europa.eu/legal-content/EN/TXT/?uri=celex:52006DC0567.

European Commission. 2006b. 'New strategy Puts EU Trade Policy at Service of European Competitiveness and Economic Reform.' Published on 4 October 2006. Brussels: European Commission—Press Release Database. http://Europa.eu/rapid/ press-release_IP-06-1303_en.htm.

European Commission. 2010. 'Trade, Growth and World Affairs. Trade Policy as a Core Component of the EU's 2020 Strategy.' Brussels: European Commission. https://library.euneighbours.eu/content/trade-growth-and-world-affairs-trade-pol- icy-core-component-eu%E2%80%99s-2020-strategy.

European Commission. 2013. 'Impact Assessment Report on the EU-China Invest- ment Relations.' Commission Staff Working Document: 1–127. Brussels: Euro- pean Commission. http://ec.Europa.eu/smart-regulation/impact/ia_carried_out/ docs/ia_2013/swd_2013_0185_en.pdf.

European Commission. 2014. 'Trade Policy in the Prodi Commission 1999–2004. An Assessment.' Brussels: EU Commission. https://pascallamyeu.files.wordpress. com/2016/11/1999_2004_pl_legacy_e.pdf.

European Commission. 2015. '"Trade for All": Towards Responsible Trade and Investment Policy.' Luxembourg: Publications Office of the European Union. http://trade.ec.Europa.eu/doclib/docs/2015/october/tradoc_153846.pdf.

European Commission. 2019a. 'Association of Southeast Asian Nations.' Accessed on 17 August 2019. https://ec.Europa.eu/trade/policy/countries-and-regions/regions/ asean/.

European Commission. 2019b. 'Countries and Regions: China.' Accessed on 5 May 2019. http://ec.Europa.eu/trade/policy/countries-and-regions/countries/china/.

European Commission. 2019c. 'EU-China Strategic Outlook: Commission and HR/VP contribution to the European Council (21–22 March 2019).' Accessed on 26 July 2019. https://ec.Europa.eu/commission/publications/eu-china-strategic-outlook-commission-contribution-European-council-21-22-march-2019_en.

European Council. 2019. 'EU-China Summit, 09/04/2019—Main Results.' Accessed on 26 July 2019. https://www.consilium.Europa.eu/en/meetings/international-summit/2019/04/09/.

European Parliament. 2011. 'EU-China, Trade Relations.' Brussels: European Parliament-Directorate-General for External Policies Policy Department. http://www.Europarl.Europa.eu/RegData/etudes/etudes/join/2011/433861/EXPO-INTA_ET(2011)433861_EN.pdf.

Eurostat. 2019. 'EU-China Trade in Goods: 185 Million Euros Deficit.' *Eurostat*, 4 April 2019. https://ec.Europa.eu/Eurostat/web/products-Eurostat-news/-/EDN-20190409-1.

Fergusson, Ian F., William H. Cooper, Remy Jurenas and Brock R. Williams. 2013. 'The Trans-Pacific Partnership: Negotiations and Issues for Congress.' Cornell University ILR School. https://digitalcommons.ilr.cornell.edu/cgi/viewcontent.cgi?referer=https://scholar.google.de/&httpsredir=1&article=2160&context=key_workplace.

The Guardian. 2019. 'Italy and China in Plan for New Silk Road-Style Trade Network.' *The Guardian*, 23 March 2019. https://www.theguardian.com/world/2019/mar/23/italy-china-new-silk-road-belt-and-road-g7.

Handley, Kyle and Nuno Limão. 2017. 'Policy Uncertainty, Trade, and Welfare: Theory and Evidence for China and the United States.' *American Economic Review*, 107.9: 2731–2783.

Heron, Tony and Gabriel Siles☐Brügge. 2012. 'Competitive Liberalization and the "Global Europe" Services and Investment Agenda: Locating the Commercial Drivers of the EU—ACP Economic Partnership Agreements.' *JCMS: Journal of Common Market Studies*, 50.2: 250–266.

Hudec, Robert E. 1975. *The GATT Legal System and World Trade Diplomacy.* New York: Praeger Publishers.

Irwin, Douglas A. 1994. 'The GATT's Contribution to Economic Recovery in Post-War Western Europe.' National Bureau of Economic Research Working Paper No. 4944: 1–38. https://www.dartmouth.edu/~dirwin/docs/GATT%20contribution.pdf.

Irwin, Douglas A. 2017. 'The False Promise of Protectionism: Why Trump's Trade Policy Could Backfire.' *Foreign Affairs*, 96.3 (May–June 2017): 45+. https://www.foreignaffairs.com/articles/united-states/2017-04-17/false-promise-protectionism.

Irwin, Douglas A. 2018. 'Trade Policy in American Economic History.' In *The Oxford Handbook of American Economic History, vol. 2*, edited by Louis P. Cain, Price V. Fishback and Paul W. Rhode, 306–324. Oxford: Oxford University Press.

Jacoby, W. and S. Meunier. 2010. 'Europe and the Management of Globalization.' *Journal of European Public Policy*, 17.3: 299–317.

Jaura, Ramesh. 2003. 'WTO-Cancun: Mixed Feelings about the Debacle.' *Inter Press Service*, 15 September 2003. http://www.ipsnews.net/2003/09/wto-cancun-mixed-feelings-about-the-debacle/.

Lardy, Nicholas. 2001. 'Issues in China's WTO Accession.' Brookings Institution, 9 May 2001. https://www.brookings.edu/testimonies/issues-in-chinas-wto-accession/.

Meunier, Sophie and Kalypso Nicolaïdis. 2006. 'The European Union as a Conflicted Trade Power.' *Journal of European Public Policy*, 13.6: 906–925.

Noland, M. 2018. 'US Trade Policy in the Trump Administration.' *Asian Economic Policy Review*, 13.2: 262–278.

Rodrik, Dani. 1995. 'Political Economy of Trade Policy.' In *Handbook of International Economics, vol. 3*, edited by Gene M. Grossman and Kenneth Rogoff, 1457–1494. Amsterdam: Elsevier B.V.

Sally, Razeen. 2007. 'The Political Economy of Trade Liberalisation: What Lessons for Reforms Today?' *Trade Policy Report* 18: 1–54. Johannesburg: South African Institute of International Affairs. http://www.lse.ac.uk/internationalrelations/centresandunits/itpu/docs/sallytradeliberalism.pdf.

Sally, Razeen. 2008. *Trade Policy, New Century: The WTO, FTAs and Asian Rising*. London: The Institute of Economic Affairs. http://www.iea.org.uk/sites/default/files/publications/files/upldbook432pdf.pdf.

Sbragia, Alberta M. 2010. 'The EU, the US, and Trade Policy: Competitive Interdependence in the Management of Globalization.' *Journal of European Public Policy*, 17.3: 368–382.

US Census Bureau. 2019. 'Trade in Goods with China.' Accessed on August 2018. https://www.census.gov/foreign-trade/balance/c5700.html.

US Congress. 2019, 'Enforcing US Trade Laws: Section 301 and China.' Washington, DC: Congressional Research Service. https://fas.org/sgp/crs/row/IF10708.pdf.

USCBC. 2014. 'US-China Bilateral Investment Treaty: What It Means for US Jobs.' *The US-China Business Council*. https://www.goldmansachs.com/insights/pages/us-china-bilateral-investment-dialogue/multimedia/papers/us-china-treaty-what-it-means-for-us-jobs.pdf.

USTR. 2002. *2002 Trade Policy Agenda and 2001 Annual Report*. Washington, DC: Office of the US Trade Representative.

USTR. 2003. *2003 Trade Policy Agenda and 2002 Annual Report*. Washington, DC: Office of the US Trade Representative.

USTR. 2004. *2004 Trade Policy Agenda and 2003 Annual Report*. Washington, DC: Office of the US Trade Representative.

USTR. 2007. *2007 Trade Policy Agenda and 2006 Annual Report*. Washington, DC: Office of the US Trade Representative.

USTR. 2008. *2008 Trade Policy Agenda and 2007 Annual Report*. Washington, DC: Office of the US Trade Representative.

USTR. 2009. *2009 Trade Policy Agenda and 2008 Annual Report*. Washington, DC: Office of the US Trade Representative.

USTR. 2010. *2010 Trade Policy Agenda and 2009 Annual Report*. Washington, DC: Office of the US Trade Representative.

USTR. 2011. *2011 Trade Policy Agenda and 2010 Annual Report*. Washington, DC: Office of the US Trade Representative.

USTR. 2012. *2012 Trade Policy Agenda and 2011 Annual Report*. Washington, DC: Office of the US Trade Representative.

USTR. 2013. *2013 Trade Policy Agenda and 2012 Annual Report.* Washington, DC: Office of the US Trade Representative.

USTR. 2014. *2014 Trade Policy Agenda and 2013 Annual Report.* Washington, DC: Office of the US Trade Representative.

USTR. 2015. *2015 Trade Policy Agenda and 2014 Annual Report.* Washington, DC: Office of the US Trade Representative.

USTR. 2016. *2016 Trade Policy Agenda and 2015 Annual Report.* Washington, DC: Office of the US Trade Representative.

USTR. 2017. 'The President's 2017 Trade Policy Agenda and 2016 Annual Report.' Washington, DC: Office of the US Trade Representative. https://ustr.gov/sites/default/files/files/reports/2017/AnnualReport/Chapter%20I%20-%20The%20President%27s%20Trade%20Policy%20Agenda.pdf.

USTR. 2018. 'Generalised System of Preferences?' Washington, DC: Office of the US Trade Representative. https://ustr.gov/issue-areas/trade-development/preference-programs/generalized-system-preference-gsp.

Williams, Brock, Mark Manyin, Remy Jurenas and Michaela Platzer. 2014. 'The US-South Korea Free Trade Agreement (KORUS-FTA0): Provisions and Implementation.' Congressional Research Service. https://fas.org/sgp/crs/row/RL34330.pdf.

WTO. 2019. 'Preferential Trade Agreements.' World Trade Organization. http://ptadb.wto.org/ptaList.aspx.

Zepeda, Eduardo, Timothy A. Wise and Kevin P. Gallagher. 2009. 'Rethinking Trade Policy for Development: Lessons from Mexico under NAFTA.' *Carnegie Endowment for International Peace*, 2009: 1–22.

Zhao, Suisheng, ed. 2016. *Chinese Foreign Policy: Pragmatism and Strategic Behavior.* London: Routledge.

Chapter 3

Of Magnets and Centrifuges

The U.S. and EU Federal Systems and Private International Law

Ronald A. Brand

Each of the federal systems in the United States and the European Union (EU) has come into being in a very different way. One combined the affiliation of nascent interconnected states breaking away from a common colonial power, while the other began as a treaty framework between mature nations with global stature. Some commentators are even hesitant to refer to the EU as a "federal" system (for an excellent discussion of Alberta Sbragia's comparative federalist approach to the study of the EU, see chapter 1 [this volume]). When viewed in the context of a single area of law—private international law—however, it becomes apparent that the EU system is both more centralized and more predictably developed than is its counterpart in the United States.

In the past, I have described the different approaches to private international law in the United States and the EU by referring to the EU magnet and the U.S. centrifuge (Brand 2009a, 2013). Through over twenty-five years of participation in negotiations with the EU at the Hague Conference on Private International Law, I have had the opportunity for firsthand observation of the evolution of EU competence in private international law and its effect on global developments. In this chapter, I begin by discussing my personal experience in observing this process. I then review the developments that have led to centralization of private international law within the EU. This then allows me to consider how the federal system in each of the United States and the EU has influenced this area of the law, and to draw some conclusions about how each has used its own federal approach in this area of the law to influence global development of the law. As Alberta Sbragia (2004a) contends in her keynote address at the European Community Studies Association-Canada (ECSA-C) 2004 Biennial Conference, "Federalism is one of the oldest lens through which to view the process of European integration."

A PERSONAL STORY

In 1989–1990, I was privileged to be the recipient of a Fulbright Fellowship
to teach and do research at the Vrije Universiteit Brussel (VUB). The experience allowed me, as a relatively young scholar and teacher, to be in the middle of developments in the European Community at that time. Those teaching
at the VUB Program on International Legal Cooperation consisted of both
a strong core group of teacher-scholars from that university and others in
Belgium, as well as some of the best civil servants from the European Commission and Council of Ministers. It was a time of change in Europe, with
the lead-up to 1992 and the constant development of core legal instruments
delineating community law. As is the case with many Fulbright scholars, the
experience changed the course of my career by deepening my understanding
of the world, my host country and institution, my scholarly discipline, the
developing EU, and myself.

   My scholarly focus while in Brussels was on dispute resolution under the
General Agreement on Tariffs and Trade. I was a trade law scholar, with a
focus on how private parties could use the developing trade law system (soon
to become the World Trade Organization) and how they were yet excluded
from benefitting from rules otherwise designed to implement economic theories that required private party participation. But I had also begun delving
into the world of private international law, thinking it to have clear relationships with the issues of private party protection of interests through dispute
resolution.

   These two areas of study, international trade law (for which the developing
European Community was becoming a major player as the premier example
of a customs union) and private international law (with its focus on rules of
jurisdiction, applicable law, and the recognition and enforcement of foreign
judgments in private party litigation), came together when I returned from
Brussels to the University of Pittsburgh and was asked to prepare a paper
for a conference on law and economics and trade law. At the same time, as
a result of my time in Brussels and some early publications on judgments
recognition, I was asked by lawyers from the Office of the Legal Adviser to
the U.S. Secretary of State to join the U.S. delegation at the Hague Conference on Private International Law for the consideration of a global treaty on
jurisdiction and the recognition and enforcement of judgments. Reflecting on
this latter experience, I prepared my paper for the law and economics conference by proposing that the free movement of judgments was a basic element
of the free movement of goods, services, and capital—three of the four pillars
of the European Community. I played with my nascent understanding of law
and economics theory to justify the recognition of judgments (a private international law pillar) as a trade law matter, thus bringing trade law and private

international law together and allowing me to explore the intersection of the two legal disciplines with which I had been working at the time.

When I had completed the law and economics paper in late 1994, I shared a copy with a colleague from the VUB who was then at the Belgian Foreign Ministry. He responded with the kind of nice note you receive from a colleague who is also a friend, stating that he had enjoyed reading the paper. But he added that he had shared it with some of the lawyers at the European Commission and that they had found it to be quite interesting as well.

I had continued to participate in the U.S. delegation's work in The Hague on the convention on jurisdiction and judgments, which in 1996 took on official project status. During the first half of the twentieth century, the Hague Conference on Private International Law was largely a Eurocentric organization, developing private international law conventions for its largely European set of member states. That was changing at the end of the twentieth century with the conference becoming a truly global player. In Europe, however, each of the member states of the European Community was also a member state of the Hague Conference, and each of them retained competence for the areas of law being discussed at The Hague. Thus, at the Special Commission meetings on our developing convention text, each of the European states had a voice, and many of them had strong delegations who were both active and effective. The European Community was represented by two or three persons from the Commission who sat in the back of the room as observers.

In June of 1997, I traveled with the U.S. delegation to The Hague for a two-week Special Commission meeting on the jurisdiction and judgments project. On the Sunday in the middle of that meeting, I traveled to Brussels to meet with my VUB colleague and friend, who had then moved from the Belgian Foreign Ministry to the European Commission. As we sipped coffee in the Grand Place, he handed me a portion of the draft of the coming Treaty of Amsterdam and asked, "Doesn't this have something to do with what you are involved with at The Hague?" That portion of the Treaty of Amsterdam set out rules providing for competence on matters of private international law —and in particular the rules on jurisdiction and the recognition of judgments within the European Community—to be transferred from the member states to the institutions of the Community.

On the next morning, as I entered The Hague Academy lecture hall in which we were engaged in negotiations, I found the representative from the Commission and asked her what the language in the draft Amsterdam treaty meant. She suggested that I should not be concerned about it. I then approached the UK delegation, where one representative responded by saying, "Why, it can't mean what it says." The private international law experts from the Community member states were all in The Hague, developing new global rules on jurisdiction and judgments recognition, while it appeared that the trade law lawyers at the European Commission had inserted language in the Treaty of Amsterdam that would take away the ability to have the member states' direct participation in the very institution that was developing those rules. And the private international law experts, including those in member state governments, seemed wholly unaware of the changes being prepared in Brussels.

This change in the law in Brussels, while member state experts on private international law were focused on other matters in The Hague, has had a dramatic effect on EU law, which demonstrates a very centralized federal system that leaves little for the constituent member state units in the allocation of competence. At the same time, as described later, the U.S. system of private international law, with more than 200 years of history, has remained diffused, decentralized, and determined by case law rather than the more predictable language of statutes. This dichotomy of approach has also had an impact on the development of the law on a global basis, with the United States and the EU being major players in that development.

PRIVATE INTERNATIONAL LAW AND THE PATH OF FEDERALISM IN THE EU AND THE UNITED STATES[1]

The development of private international law in the EU demonstrates a very centralized and focused, centrally controlled federal system in the EU. In the United States, this development demonstrates a very fractured and diffused system, in which law is developed in the states, with very limited law at the federal level. Unlike the work of Alberta Sbragia, which focuses on the political context for shared levels of governance (see Sbragia 2002; Damro and Sbragia 2003; Sbragia 2004b; Sbragia and Stolfi 2008; Sbragia 2011); my view of the development of the EU focuses on a small area, private international law, which is "below the radar" not only for most citizens but also for political science scholars. I believe, however, that it is an area that holds lessons worth considering for the broader context.

The European Union

Upon the creation of the European Economic Community (EEC) in 1957, the original six member states demonstrated a realization that private international law plays an important role in, and thus overlaps with, trade law. Originally, article 220 of the Treaty of Rome (later changed to article 293 of the Treaty

---

1 This section relies on the author's earlier work; see Brand (2013).

establishing the European Community (TEC) and now repealed as unneces-
sary) declared that the member states of the Community should "enter into
[further] negotiations with each other with a view to securing for the benefit
of their nationals . . . the simplification of formalities governing the reciprocal
recognition and enforcement of judgments of courts or tribunals and of arbitration awards" (TEC [Nice consolidated version] article 293, December 24,
2002[2]). Consistent with the idea that the EEC was a new and very different
kind of experiment in international law, a decade later its member states
concluded the 1968 Brussels Convention on jurisdiction and the recognition
and enforcement of judgments in civil and commercial matters (September 9,
1968; hereinafter Brussels Convention).[3] Just as article 220 had recognized
the importance of the free movement of judgments to a functioning common
market (for a discussion on the rationale for including private international
law rules under the rubric of a trade law regime, see Brand 1998), the Brussels Convention carried out the mandate of the Treaty of Rome to conclude a
further treaty to put that realization into effect in the law of the EEC.

When the Treaty of Amsterdam was concluded in 1997 (Treaty of Amsterdam amending the Treaty on EU, the Treaties Establishing the European
Communities and Certain Related Acts, October 2, 1997), it included article
61, providing that "the Council shall adopt . . . measures in the field of judicial cooperation in civil matters as provided for in Article 65" (TEC, article
61c, December 24, 2002). Article 65, in turn, itemized such authority for the
purposes of service of process, taking of evidence, the recognition of judgments, rules of conflict of laws and jurisdiction, and rules of civil procedure
(TEC, article 65, December 24, 2002). Thus, while the Treaty of Rome had
addressed one element of private international law (the recognition of foreign judgments) by prodding the member states to take an international law
(treaty) approach to the matter, the Treaty of Amsterdam addressed the full
package of private international law, transferring competence for these issues
from the member states to the EU institutions.

The Treaty of Amsterdam unleashed an internal process that has rapidly
moved the sources of private international law from the member states—
largely found in codes of private international law—to the EU institutions,
using regulations and directives to make the matter clearly governed by centralized EU law.

---

2 For original article 220, see "Treaty Establishing the European Economic Community." Open
for Signature on March 27, 1957. *Europa.eu*. https://Europa.eu/European-union/sites/Europaeu/files/
docs/body/treaties_establishing_the_European_communities_single_European_act_en.pdf.

3 The consolidated and updated version of the 1968 Convention and the Protocol of 1971, fol-
lowing the 1996 accession of the Republic of Austria, the Republic of Finland, and the Kingdom of
Sweden, is available at *Eur-Lex* Document 41997A0115(01). https://eur-lex.Europa.eu/legal-content/
EN/TXT/?uri=CELEX:41997A0115(01).

The centralization of European private international law after the Treaty of Amsterdam has been dramatic, regarding both the internal law of the EU and external legal developments (for further discussion of the nature and impact of the Treaty of Amsterdam on the Hague Convention negotiations, see Brand 2009b). Regulations have been adopted establishing rules on insolvency (Council Regulation [EC] No. 1346/2000 [2000]);[4] recognition and enforcement of judgments in civil and commercial matters (Council Regulation [EC] No. 44/2001 [2001]); taking of evidence (Council Regulation [EC] No. 1206/2001 [2001]); judicial cooperation (Council Regulation [EC] No. 743/2002 [2002]); recognition and enforcement of family law judgments (Council Regulation [EC] No. 2201/2003 [2003]); uncontested claims (Regulation [EC] of the European Parliament and of the Council No. 805/2004 [2004]); common payment procedures (Regulation [EC] of the European Parliament and of the Council No. 1896/2006 [2006]); small claims procedure (Regulation [EC] of the European Parliament and of the Council No. 861/2007 [2007]); applicable law for noncontractual obligations (Regulation [EC] of the European Parliament and of the Council No. 864/2007 [2007]); service of documents (Regulation [EC] of the European Parliament and of the Council No. 1393/2007 [2007]); applicable law for contractual obligations (Regulation [EC] of the European Parliament and of the Council No. 593/2008 [2008]); jurisdiction, applicable law, and recognition of judgments in maintenance obligation matters (Council Regulation [EC] No. 4/2009 [2009]); applicable law for divorce and separation (Council Regulation [EU] No. 1259/2010 [2010]); and matters of succession (Regulation [EU] of the European Parliament and of the Council No. 650/2012 [2012]). In each case, the regulation moved a matter from member states law to EU law, unifying and centralizing the source of the rules.

These regulations have made clear the exclusive nature of EU institutional competence for the development of private international law under the authority granted in the Treaty of Amsterdam. What was not so clear at the outset was the allocation of competence between the member states and the EU institutions for private international law in external matters.

The debate about competence for developing external rules of private international law was largely settled in 2006 with the *Lugano Convention* opinion of the European Court of Justice (Opinion 1/03, Opinion pursuant to article 300(6) EC [2006]), which answered any outstanding questions about the extent and effect of the transfer of authority to Brussels.

---

4 See also the Proposal for a Regulation of the European Parliament and of the Council Amending Council Regulation (EC) No 1346/2000 on Insolvency Proceedings, COM(2012) 744 final of December 12, 2012.

The opinion procedure under article 300(6) is used only occasionally and is separate from the normal "case" procedure by which most matters reach the European Court of Justice. The Lugano Convention originally was developed to extend the rules of the Brussels Convention beyond the confines of the European Community to the member states of the European Free Trade Association (EFTA). Completed in 1988, its provisions generally track those of the Brussels Convention, setting up a parallel regime for jurisdiction and judgments recognition. As most of the EFTA member states have now joined the EU, the importance of the Lugano Convention has diminished but has not been extinguished. It remains in effect for relationships between EU member states and Iceland, Norway, and Switzerland. With the changes to internal rules brought about by the Brussels I Regulation, parallel changes were proposed to the Lugano Convention. Because competence for those rules internally had shifted in the interim from the EU member states to the Community institutions, there was lack of clarity on whether the member states or the Community held the external competence to become a party to the Lugano Convention. This question was submitted to the European Court of Justice for clarification (see Borrás 2004).

The Lugano Convention case involved a challenge to the competence of the Community to enter into a treaty with EFTA member states that would parallel the rules the then-recent Brussels I Regulation had established for jurisdiction and the recognition of foreign judgments when a case involved a defendant from another member state. In the *Lugano Convention* opinion, the Court followed the 1999 Opinion of the European Council Legal Service, which had stated that "once the Community has exercised its internal competences adopting positions by which common rules are fixed [pursuant to article 65 of the ECT], the Community competence becomes exclusive, in the sense that the Member States lose the right to contract, individually and even collectively, obligations with third countries which affect the said rules" (Borrás 2004, 100). Based on the 1971 *ERTA/AETR* decision (Case 22/70, Judgment of 31 Mar. 1971, *Commission v Council* [1971] E.C.R. 263 (European Rail Transport Agreement (ERTA/AETR) Case), as further developed in the *Open Skies* judgments of 2002 (*Commission v Denmark* [2002], *Commission v Sweden* [2002], *Commission v Finland* [2002], *Commission v Belgium* [2002], *Commission v Luxembourg* [2002], *Commission v Austria* [2002], and *Commission v Germany* [2002]), the Court stated that "whenever the Community has included in its internal legislative acts provisions relating to the treatment of nationals of non-member countries or expressly conferred on its institutions powers to negotiate with non-member countries, it acquires an exclusive external competence in the spheres covered by those acts" (*Commission v Denmark* [2002], I-9522) and "the same applies, even in the absence of any express provision authorizing its institutions to negotiate with non-member countries, where the Community has achieved complete harmonization in a given area" (I-9523). Thus, "the conclusion of the new

Lugano Convention on jurisdiction and the recognition and enforcement of judgments in civil and commercial matters . . . falls entirely within the sphere of exclusive competence of the European Community" (ibid., Conclusion).

The *Lugano Convention* opinion laid to rest any claim of remaining competence with the member states for external relations on matters of jurisdiction and the recognition and enforcement of judgments—as well as, effectively, for any other area of private international law and judicial cooperation covered by TEC article 65.

The United States

Unlike the situation in the EU, in the United States, the law has not developed through codes. Only two U.S. states have codes of private international law, and those have come only very recently. While the original six member states of the EEC were all civil law states, with a focus on development of the law through legislative codes, the United States is a common law legal system, with the law developing primarily through case law. This has been true in the realm of private international law as well. The result is that the sources of the law are not centrally located in clear texts.

U.S. rules of applicable law and the recognition of foreign country judgments have developed largely as state law and not as federal law. While developments in the law of jurisdiction have focused largely on the Due Process Clauses of the federal Constitution (see Brand 1999), even there, the analysis in each case normally begins with the state "long-arm" jurisdiction statute (ibid., 669–671), giving states an important role in the process.

In the United States, the development of private international law has also been heavily influenced by the legal profession in a process that occurs in neither the legislature nor the courts. This has happened in the American Law Institute (ALI). The ALI describes itself as

> the leading independent organization in the United States producing scholarly work to clarify, modernize, and otherwise improve the law. ALI drafts, discusses, revises, and publishes Restatements of the Law, Model Codes, and Principles of Law that are enormously influential in the courts and legislatures, as well as in legal scholarship and education. (American Law Institute 2019)

In the realm of applicable law, in particular, the ALI has been especially influential, with both the First and Second Restatements of Conflict of Laws playing significant roles in the law applied in the courts (Hay, Borchers, and Symeonides 2010, 27–78, describing the "dissatisfaction with the fixed and thus mechanical rules of the First Restatement" and the resulting "'revolution' in American conflicts law" leading to the Second Restatement).

The law on choice of law in the United States is thus more diverse, and often less clear, than is the case in Europe. EU law has a distinctly civil law, code-based, texture developed in a centralized fashion, while U.S. law is primarily found in cases at the state level such that "the Restatement continues, by hypothesis, the litigation-oriented pattern of American conflicts approaches. In other words, it is self-defining through litigation. By providing an approach for the elaboration of rules often yet unknown rather than suggesting rules for judicial acceptance, it shares with most other approaches a lack of certainty and predictability for conflicts situations in which there has been no prior litigation. . . . The precise direction of the case law—in terms of the 'coexistence' of the various approaches and their value-goals—continues to remain unclear" (Hay, Borchers and Symeonides 2010, 71).

Some unification has occurred in the United States through the National Conference of Commissioners on Uniform State Laws (the National Conference of Commissioners on Uniform State Laws has recently begun using the name "Uniform Law Commission" [ULC]. Its website states that "the Uniform Law Commission . . . provides states with non-partisan, well-conceived, and well drafted legislation that brings clarity and stability to critical areas of state statutory law" [Uniform Law Commission 2019]), such as with the 1962 Uniform Foreign-Money Judgments Recognition Act[5] and 2005 Uniform Foreign-Country Money Judgments Recognition Act.[6] But these Acts become law only when enacted by each of the states, and some states have enacted neither of the Acts (thirty-one states, plus the District of Columbia and the Virgin Islands, currently have either the 1962 Act or the 2005 Act as law, leaving nineteen states without either of the two Acts, even though the first of the two Acts has been available for over fifty years).

Comparisons–of Magnets and Centrifuges

The intersection of these two legal systems has occurred in negotiations at the Hague Conference on Private International Law. In the Hague Conference, the EU has become the single spokesperson for all of its member states. This occurred in 2005, following the *Lugano Convention* opinion, when the Statute of the Hague Conference on Private International Law was amended[7] to

---

5 For the 1962 Uniform Foreign-Money Judgments Recognition Act, see https://www.uniform-laws.org/committees/community-home?CommunityKey=9c11b007-83b2-4bf2-a08e-74f642c840bc.

6 For the 2005 Uniform Foreign-Country Money Judgments Recognition Act, see https://www.uniformlaws.org/viewdocument/enactment-kit-24.

7 See Statute of the Hague Conference on Private International Law, Final Act, C, amended on June 30, 2005, approved by members on September 30, 2006, and entered into force on January 1, 2007.

allow membership by Regional Economic Integration Organizations, that is, by the EU. It amended article 3(1) of the Statute to provide that

> the Member States of the Conference may, at a meeting concerning general affairs and policy where the majority of Member States is present, by a majority of the votes cast, decide to admit also as a Member any Regional Economic Integration Organisation which has submitted an application for membership to the Secretary General. References to Members under this Statute shall include such Member Organizations, except as otherwise expressly provided. The admission shall become effective upon the acceptance of the Statute by the Regional Economic Integration Organisation concerned. (Hague Conference on Private International Law, Statute of the Hague Conference on Private International Law, article 3, section 1, June 30, 2005)

EU Membership in the Hague Conference became effective on March 4, 2007.[8] This external competence of the EU has been explicitly claimed as well through EU Regulations dealing with procedures for external negotiation regarding applicable law according to Council Regulation (EC) No. 662/2009 (2009) and procedures for external negotiation regarding jurisdiction and the recognition of judgments in family law matters according to Council Regulation (EC) No. 664/2009 of 7 July 2009 (2009).

The 2005 Hague Convention on Choice of Court Agreements entered into effect for the EU on October 1, 2015 (Hague Conference on Private International Law 2015), after completion of the Brussels I Recast Regulation. That Regulation was approved by the Council on December 6, 2012, and went into effect in early 2015 (Council of the European Union 2015). This reflected an internal and external coordination of development of the law.

In the United States, progress on the external front has been markedly less successful. While negotiations have been led by the U.S. State Department, the states, through the Uniform Law Commissioners, have sought state-by-state implementation of the 2005 Hague Convention. This method for implementation has not been found acceptable at the federal level. So, while the United States signed the Hague Convention in January of 2009, it has not moved forward toward ratification. The signing followed two internal developments, which demonstrate the federalism problems that have slowed the U.S. participation in the global development of private international law. In 2005, the ALI promulgated its *Proposed Federal Statute* that would not only serve as the implementing legislation for the 2005 Hague Convention but would also federalize a significant part of an area of law that has been

---

8 See Hague Conference on Private International Law Membership Status table, available at http:// www.hcch.net/index_en.php?act=conventions.status&cid=29.

mostly found in state law in recent times (American Law Institute 2006). The same year, the National Conference of Commissioners on Uniform State Laws ("ULC") completed the Uniform Foreign-Country Money Judgments Recognition Act, which was a substantial revision of its 1962 Uniform Foreign-Money Judgments Recognition Act. Some commentators saw this as driven not so much by changes in the law subsequent to the 1962 Act as by the ULC's desire, in response to the Hague Convention, to claim state law dominance in the area of recognition and enforcement of foreign judgments (Burbank 2012, 639–640).

At about the same time, the ULC also began preparation for a uniform act designed to implement the Hague Convention through state law that would be combined with a federal statute (Uniform Choice of Court Agreements Implementation Act 2012). This Act was initiated as the result of a Study Committee recommendation in 2007 and approved as final by the ULC in July 2012. According to article 2 of the Act, it "implements in [the state of enactment] the Convention on Choice of Court Agreements, done at The Hague on June 30, 2005" (Uniform Choice of Court Agreements Implementation Act, section 2 [2012]).

The U.S. Department of State attempted to work closely with the ULC to design implementation of the Convention in a manner that has been referred to as "cooperative federalism," using a combination of federal and state legislation to implement a treaty that deals with matters that previously have been governed by both federal and state laws (for a discussion of cooperative federalism from the viewpoint of one Uniform Law Commissioner, see Henning [2011]. For a somewhat contrary perspective, see Trooboff [2009], who argues that "whatever else can be said from a theoretical perspective about this debate, some points are clear—'cooperative federalism' will never be as easy to understand for non-U.S. parties as federal legislation alone. . . . [T]he greater complexity of 'cooperative federalism' puts a burden on the advocates of 'cooperative federalism' to make a compelling case and to show this approach can be accomplished without needless ambiguity and increased cost to litigants" [Trooboof 2009, 246–247]). That process led to disagreements on the extent to which state law would govern matters that, if the treaty were implemented solely through federal law, would be a matter of federal law under article VI of the Supremacy Clause of the U.S. Constitution that states that this "Constitution, and the Laws of the United States which shall be made in Pursuance thereof; and all Treaties made . . . shall be the supreme Law of the Land" (U.S. Constitution, article VI, clause 2). Harold Koh, then legal advisor to the U.S. secretary of state, led discussions held at the American Society of International Law in an effort to reconcile the states' rights positions of the ULC and the preference for normal federal treaty law implementation advocated by others (for a more detailed discussion of the negotiations to reach a "cooperative federalism" approach, see Burbank [2013]). This effort failed when, in 2012, the ULC rejected a final compromise effort proposed by Koh.

The State Department followed the ULC rejection of a compromise approach with a new proposed implementing statute based largely on the model of chapter 2 of the Federal Arbitration Act[9] (which implements the United Nations Convention on the Recognition and Enforcement of Foreign Arbitral Awards [New York Convention]). This approach draws logic from the fact that the Hague Convention, if widely ratified, would serve to place choice of court on a parallel footing with arbitration agreements under the very successful New York Convention. It would implement the Hague Convention through federal law, consistent with standard treaty practice in the United States. At the same time, it would allow state law to remain important in matters fundamental to many Hague Convention cases (e.g., whether a choice of court agreement is "null and void" for purposes of decisions made under articles 5, 6, and 9 of the Convention). The results of this effort have not reached the U.S. Senate for advice and consent, however, largely because of concerns that those wanting a larger state role in this area of law could easily find senators who would block the process.

CONCLUDING THOUGHTS: FEDERALISM AND THE INTERNAL AND EXTERNAL DEVELOPMENT OF PRIVATE INTERNATIONAL LAW IN THE EU AND THE UNITED STATES

Internally, the development of private international law in each of the EU and the United States reflects the legal system in which it has occurred. In the EU, the process and result are characteristics of Europe's majority civil law systems in which law is promulgated by the legislature and exists in reasonably predictable codes. In the United States, the development is consistent with American common law roots and the historic process that has kept much of law creation in the hands of the states rather than the federal government. This means that the rules are neither uniform nor clearly organized. While the Treaty of Amsterdam moved competence for private international law development from the member states to the institutions of the EU, there has been no equivalent transfer to the central government in the United States.

The centralization of the process of development of private international law within the EU has also had an impact on the external development of private international law. At the Hague Conference on Private International

---

9 See US Code chapter 2—Convention on the Recognition and Enforcement of Foreign Arbitral Awards, 9 U.S.C. § 201. Available at https://uscode.house.gov/view.xhtml?path=/prelim@title9/chapter2&edition=prelim.

Law, the EU delegation speaks for all member states as well as for the Union. At the same time, however, the EU and the member states account for twenty-nine seats at the table. This provides considerable influence both visually and as a matter of substance. The *Lugano Convention* opinion of the Court of Justice has not only brought external competence in line with internal competence but has allowed the EU to present an effective negotiating front in the development of new global conventions on private international law. This effectiveness is enhanced by the fact that most Hague member states have civil law systems that are derived from the continental European model, which is at the core of EU law. The result is a clear magnet effect, which draws others to the EU model.

The United States faces a more difficult task on the external front. Its common law system is followed by a minority of countries of the world. Moreover, the diffuse nature of the resulting law, combined with the failure to move competence for this area of the law to the federal level at any time in our history, means that other Hague Conference member states are not inclined to easily understand the U.S. approach and thus are not as inclined to accept that approach in a global convention. The internal U.S. centrifuge does make the process of negotiation both more difficult and less effective.

BIBLIOGRAPHY

American Law Institute. 2006. "Recognition and Enforcement of Foreign Judgements: Analysis and Proposal Federal Statute." Philadelphia: American Law Institute. Accessed July 21, 2019. https://www.ali.org/publications/show/recognition-and-enforcement-foreign-judgments-analysis-and-proposed-federal-statute/.

American Law Institute. 2019. "About ALI." About ALI. Accessed July 21, 2019. http://www.ali.org/index.cfm?fuseaction=about.overview.

Borrás, Alegría. 2004. "The Effect of the Adoption of Brussels I and Rome I on the External Competences of the EC and the Member States." In *Enforcement of International Contracts in the European Union: Convergence and Divergence between Brussels I and Rome I*, edited by Johan Meeusen, Marta Pertegás, and Gert Straetmans, 99–125. Antwerp: Intersentia.

Brand, Ronald A. 1998. "Recognition of Foreign Judgments as a Trade Law Issue: The Economics of Private International Law." In *Economic Dimensions in International Law: Comparative and Empirical Perspectives*, edited by Jagdeep S. Bhandari and Alan O. Sykes, 592–641. Cambridge: Cambridge University Press.

Brand, Ronald A. 1999. "Due Process, Jurisdiction and a Hague Judgments Convention." *University of Pittsburgh Law Review*, 60.3: 661–706.

Brand, Ronald A. 2009a. "The European Magnet and the U.S. Centrifuge: Ten Selected Private International Law Developments of 2008." *ILSA Journal of International & Comparative Law*, 15.2: 367–393.

Brand, Ronald A. 2009b. "External Effects of Internal Developments: A US Perspective on Changing Competence for Private International Law in Europe." In *Liber Fausto Pocar: New Instruments of Private International Law, Volume 2*, edited by Gabriella Venturini and Stefania Bariatti, 163–179. Milan: Giuffrè Editore.

Brand, Ronald A. 2013. "Implementing the 2005 Hague Convention: The EU Magnet and the US Centrifuge." In *Entre Bruselas Y La Haya, Estudios Sobre La Unificatión Internacional Y Regional Del Derecho International Privado: Liber Amicorum Alegría Borrás*, edited by Joaquim Forner Delaygua, Cristina Gonzalez Beilfuss, and Ramon Vinas Farre, 267–276. Madrid: Marcial Pons Ediciones Jurídicas y Sociales, S.A.

Burbank, Stephen B. 2012. "Our Courts and the World: Transnational Litigation and Civil Procedure: Judgement Enforcement: A Tea Party at the Hague?" *Southwestern Journal of International Law*, 18.2: 629–645.

Burbank, Stephen B. 2013. "Symposium: Eighteenth Annual Herbert Rubin and Justice Rose Luttan Rubin International Law Symposium: Tug of War: The Tension between Regulation and Internal Cooperation: Whose Regulatory Interests? Outsourcing the Treaty Function." *New York University Journal of International Laws and Politics*, 45.4: 1037–1062.

Commission of the European Communities v Belgium (2002). Case C-471/98, Judgement of November 5, 2002. *European Court Reports*, I-9690–I-9739.

Commission of the European Communities v Council (1971). Case 22/70, Judgment of March 31, 1971. *European Court Reports*, 263–284.

Commission of the European Communities v Denmark (2002). Case C-467–98, Judgment of November 5, 2002. *European Court Reports*, I-9519–I-9526, I-9807–I-9854.

Commission of the European Communities v Finland (2002). Case C-469/98, Judgment of November 5, 2002. *European Court Reports*, I-9635–I-9680.

Commission of the European Communities v Germany (2002). Case C-476/98, Judgment of November 5, 2002. *European Court Reports*, I-9865–I-9917.

Commission of the European Communities v Luxembourg (2002). Case 472/98, Judgment of November 5, 2002. *European Court Reports*, I-9750–I-9796.

Commission of the European Communities v Sweden (2002). Case C-468/98, Judgment of November 5, 2002. *European Court Reports*, I-9583–I-9626.

"Council Regulation (EC) No. 4/2009 of 18 December 2008 on Jurisdiction, Applicable Law, Recognition and Enforcement of Decisions and Cooperation in Matters Relating to Maintenance Obligations." January 10, 2009. *Official Journal of the European Communities*, L 7/1–L 7/79.

"Council Regulation (EC) No. 44/2001 of 22 December 2000 on Jurisdiction and the Recognition and Enforcement of Judgments in Civil and Commercial Matters (Brussels I)." January 16, 2001. *Official Journal of the European Communities*, L 12/1–L 12/23.

"Council Regulation (EC) No. 664/2009 of 7 July 2009 Establishing a Procedure for the Negotiation and Conclusion of Agreements between Member States and Third Countries Concerning Jurisdiction, Recognition and Enforcement of Judgments and Decisions in Matrimonial Matters, Matters of Parental Responsibility and Matters Relating to Maintenance Obligations, and the Law Applicable to Matters

Relating to Maintenance Obligations." July 31, 2009. *Official Journal of the European Communities*, L 200/46–L 200/51.

"Council Regulation (EC) No. 743/2002 of 25 April 2002, Establishing a General Community Framework of Activities to Facilitate the Implementation of Judicial Cooperation in Civil Matters." May 1, 2002. *Official Journal of the European Communities*, L 115/1–L 115/5.

"Council Regulation (EC) No. 1206/2001 of 28 May 2001 on Cooperation between the Courts of the Member States in the Taking of Evidence in Civil or Commercial Matters." June 27, 2001. *Official Journal of the European Communities*, L 174/1–L 174/24.

"Council Regulation (EU) No. 1259/2010 of 20 December 2010 Implementing Enhanced Cooperation in the Area of the Law Applicable to Divorce and Legal Separation." December 29, 2010. *Official Journal of the European Communities*, L 343/10–L 343/16.

"Council Regulation (EC) No. 1346/2000 of 29 May 2000 on Insolvency Proceedings." June 30, 2000. *Official Journal of the European Communities*, L 160/1–L 160/18.

"Council Regulation (EC) No. 2201/2003 of 27 November 2003, Concerning Jurisdiction and the Recognition and Enforcement of Judgments in Matrimonial Matters and the Matters of Parental Responsibility (Repealing Council Regulation 1347/2000) (Brussels II *bis*)." December 12, 2003. *Official Journal of the European Communities*, L 338/1–L 338/29.

Damro, Chad and Alberta M. Sbragia. 2003. "The New Framework in Transatlantic Economic Governance: Strategic Trade Management and Regulatory Conflict in a Multilateral Global Economy." In *EU Economic Governance and Globalization*, edited by Miriam Campanella and Sylvester Eijffinger, 105–141. Gloucestershire, UK: Edward Elgar Publishing Limited.

Hague Conference on Private International Law. 2005. "Statute of the Hague Conference on Private International Law." Amendments adopted on June 30, 2005, approved by Members on September 30, 2006, and entered into force on January 1, 2007. *HCCH*. Accessed July 21, 2019. https://assets.hcch.net/docs/d7d051ae-6dd1-4881-a3b5-f7dbcaad02ea.pdf.

Hague Conference on Private International Law. 2015. "2005 Choice of Court Convention to Enter into Force on 1 October 2015 Following the Approval by the European Union." *HCCH*, released June 25, 2015. Accessed July 21, 2019. https://www.hcch.net/en/news-archive/details/?varevent=412.

Hay, Peter, Patrick J. Borchers, and Symeon Symeonides. 2010. *Conflict of Laws*. St. Paul, MN: West, 5th edition.

Henning, William H. 2011. "The Uniform Law Commission and Cooperative Federalism: Implementing Private International Law Conventions through Uniform State Laws." *Elon Law Review*, 2.1: 39–55.

"1968 Brussels Convention on Jurisdiction and the Enforcement of Judgments in Civil and Commercial Matters." Opened for Signature on September 27, 1968. *Eur-Lex* Document 41968A0927(01). Accessed July 21, 2019. https://eur-lex.Europa.eu/legal-content/EN/ALL/?uri=CELEX%3A41968A0927%2801%29.

"Opinion 1/03, Opinion Pursuant to Article 300(6) EC." Opinion of the Court (Full Court) of February 7, 2006. *European Court Reports* 2006 I-01145. Accessed July 21, 2019. https://eur-lex.Europa.eu/legal-content/EN/TXT/?qid=1563801093 699&uri=CELEX:62003CV0001.

"Regulation (EC) No. 593/2008 of the European Parliament and of the Council of 17 June 2008 on the Law Applicable to Contractual Obligations (Rome I)." July 4, 2008. *Official Journal of the European Communities*, L 177/6–L 177/16.

"Regulation (EU) No. 650/2012 of the European Parliament and of the Council of 4 July 2012 on Jurisdiction, Applicable Law, Recognition and Enforcement of Decisions and Acceptance and Enforcement of Authentic Instruments in Matters of Succession and on the Creation of a European Certificate of Succession." July 27, 2012. *Official Journal of the European Communities*, L 201/107–L 201/134.

"Regulation (EC) No. 662/2009 of the European Parliament and of the Council of 13 July 2009 Establishing a Procedure for the Negotiation and Conclusion of Agreements between Member States and Third Countries on Particular Matters Concerning the Law Applicable to Contractual and Non-Contractual Obligations." July 31, 2009. *Official Journal of the European Communities*, L 200/25–L 200/30.

"Regulation (EC) No. 805/2004 of the European Parliament and of the Council of 21 April 2004 Creating a European Enforcement Order for Uncontested Claims." April 30, 2004. *Official Journal of the European Communities*, L 143/15–L 143/39.

"Regulation (EC) No. 861/2007 of the European Parliament and of the Council of 11 July 2007 Establishing a European Small Claims Procedure." July 31, 2007. *Official Journal of the European Communities*, O.J. Eur. Comm. L 199/1–L 199/22.

"Regulation (EC) No. 864/2007 of the European Parliament and of the Council of 11 July 2007 on the Law Applicable to Non-Contractual Obligations (Rome II)." July 31, 2007. *Official Journal of the European Communities*, L 199/40–L 199/49.

"Regulation (EU) No. 1215/2012 of the European Parliament and of the Council of 12 December 2012 on Jurisdiction and the Recognition and Enforcement of Judgments in Civil and Commercial Matters (Recast)." February 26, 2015. *Official Journal of the European Communities*, L 351/1–351/32.

"Regulation (EC) No. 1393/2007 of the European Parliament and of the Council of 13 November 2007 on the Service in the Member States of Judicial and Extrajudicial Documents in Civil or Commercial Matters (Service of Documents), and Repealing Council Regulation (EC) No. 1348/2000." December 10, 2007. *Official Journal of the European Communities*, L 324/79–L 324/120.

"Regulation (EC) No. 1896/2006 of the European Parliament and of the Council of 12 December 2006 Creating a European Order for Payment Procedure." December 30, 2006. *Official Journal of the European Communities*, L 399/1–L 399/32.

Sbragia, Alberta M. 2002. "The Dilemma of Governance with Government." The Jean Monnet Program—European Union Jean Monnet Chair, Paper 3/02. New York: New York University School of Law. Accessed July 21, 2019. *https://jean-monnetprogram.org/archive/papers/02/020301.rtf.*

Sbragia, Alberta M. 2004a. "The Future of Federalism in the European Union." Keynote Address Delivered at the European Community Studies Association-Canada (ECSA-C) 2004 Biennial Conference "A Constitution for Europe? Governance and

Policy Making in the European Union," May 27–29, 2004. Accessed July 21, 2019. aei.pitt.edu/1877/2/Sbragia_ECSA-Canada_keynote_address_May_2004.rtf.

Sbragia, Alberta M. 2004b. "Shaping a Polity in an Economic and Monetary Union: The EU in Comparative Perspective." In *Euros and Europeans*, edited by Andrew Martin and George Ross, 51–75. Cambridge: Cambridge University Press.

Sbragia, Alberta M. 2011. "The European Union: A New Form of Governance." In *The Ashgate Research Companion to Regionalisms*, edited by Timothy Shaw, J. Andrew Grant, and Scarlett Cornelissen, 91–111. London: Ashgate Publishing Limited.

Sbragia, Alberta M. and Francesco Stolfi. 2008. "Key Policies." In *The European Union: How Does It Work?* edited by Elizabeth Bomberg, John Peterson, and Alexander Stubb, 115–137. Oxford: Oxford University Press, 2nd edition.

"Treaty of Amsterdam Amending the Treaty on European Union, the Treaties Establishing the European Communities and Certain Related Acts." Open for Signature on October 2, 1997. *Eur-Lex* Document 11997D/TXT. Accessed July 21, 2019. https://eur-lex.Europa.eu/legal-content/EN/TXT/?uri=CELEX:11997D/TXT.

"Treaty Establishing the European Community (Nice Consolidated Version)." Entered into force December 24, 2002. *Eur-Lex* Document 12002E/TXT. Accessed July 21, 2019. https://eur-lex.Europa.eu/legal-content/EN/TXT/?uri=CELEX%3A 12002E%2FTXT.

Trooboff, Peter D. 2009. "Proposed Principles for United States Implementation of the New Hague Convention on Choice of Court Agreements." *New York University Journal of International Law and Politics*, 42.1: 237–251.

Uniform Law Commission. 2012. "Uniform Choice of Court Agreements Implementation Act." Adopted on July 18, 2012. *National Conference of Commissioners on Uniform State Laws*. Accessed July 21, 2019. https://www.uniformlaws.org/HigherLogic/System/DownloadDocumentFile.ashx?DocumentFileKey=5e7a9920-15af-c2c1-7f9d-53ef0185a4a5&forceDialog=0.

Uniform Law Commission. 2019. "About Us." Overview. Accessed July 21, 2019. https://www.uniformlaws.org/aboutulc/overview.

US Constitution, article VI, clause 2.

Chapter 4

Citizenship and Free Movement in Comparative Federalism

Willem Maas

In a keynote address to the European Community Studies Association-Canada 2004 Biennial Conference, Alberta Sbragia (2004) examined the balance between "shared rule and self-rule" identified by federalism scholars and argued that the process of writing a constitutional treaty was prompting a significant movement on the part of the European Union's (EU) member states toward a greater degree of "shared rule" outside both the predominant supranational and intergovernmental models.[1] She suggested that scholars should reexamine confederal kinds of "shared rule" arrangements rather than simply federalism conceived narrowly as the traditional form of division of powers within a federal government: "Discussions of federalism in the European Union need to incorporate serious analyses of the confederal form of governance" (Sbragia 2004).

Sbragia's argument for the relevance of reexamining different kinds of shared rule arrangements, most notably confederal models, was based on an analysis and evaluation of the draft constitutional treaty. She argued that the treaty did not represent a step toward a federation as traditionally defined but was a step toward a deeper and more sophisticated form of shared rule—not a step toward a *government* as traditionally defined in a federal state but instead a step toward more *governance* understood as expanded, deeper, and more intrusive shared rule (Sbragia 2004). Subsequent developments have proven Sbragia's analysis largely correct: the balance between self-rule and shared rule within the EU has continued to tilt in the direction of the latter, sometimes dramatically so—and the form of that shared rule is more confederal than federal, more "governance" than "government" as traditionally defined

---

1 One major author in the federalism literatures examined by Sbragia is Elazar, whose arguments can be found succinctly in Elazar (1995).

in a federal state. In this contribution, I examine the difficult rise of shared rule over questions of citizenship and the free movement of people within a shared political space.[2]

Both in Europe and in North America, the regulation of the movement of people, and issues of citizenship more broadly, have always interacted with federalism. In the United States, the Great Depression epitomized barriers on the movement of unwanted Americans from other states. But incentives and disincentives to crossing jurisdictional borders continue to exist even today. Similarly, in Canada, interprovincial movement of people has been hampered historically as well as in the present day by the existence of "semi-sovereign" provinces responsible for their own labor markets and welfare provisions such as health care and education. In Europe, the movement of people between states was for the first half of the twentieth century purely an issue for inter-national migration and international relations between sovereign states. But starting from the free movement rights granted to coal and steel workers (most significantly Italian workers) in the early 1950s (Maas 2005), through all the ups and downs of the slow rise of EU citizenship (Maas 2007, 2017a), the movement of Europeans within Europe has become more akin to internal migration such as that which occurs between provinces within Canada or states within the United States. Yet, as demonstrated by populist and nativist responses, or even simply the innocent operation of governments working at different levels, this slow and ongoing transition toward a shared European citizenship with shared rights raises fundamental questions about the status of the nation-state and the role of national governments. As noted also in this volume by Fabbrini (see chapter 11), the question raised by Sbragia in 1992 is still unanswered, namely, "Is it possible to 'federalize' the Community significantly while retaining a key policy-making role for national govern-ments?" (Sbragia 1992, 258). Along these lines, the question should be asked to what extent it is possible or desirable to "Europeanize" citizenship and free movement while retaining a key role for national governments.

WANTED VERSUS UNWANTED MIGRANTS AND THE QUESTION OF GOVERNANCE

Questions of citizenship and free movement have marked the EU throughout its evolution and are also key issues for federal states and scholarship in

---

2 Thus, this contribution does not analyze the movement of people *into* the EU, which is covered in this volume by Jacoby and Jevtic-Somlai (this volume, chapter 8), who identify a trade-off between the desire to respond humanely to massive refugee flows into Europe and the capacity to integrate large numbers of refugees into national life.

comparative federalism, the lens that Alberta Sbragia has examined throughout her career. "We must break free of the EU and take back control of our borders" declares a poster unveiled by UK Independence Party leader Nigel Farage during the Brexit referendum campaign—and the continued free movement rights of British citizens in the EU and EU citizens in the United Kingdom remain a political hot potato in the Brexit negotiations (Maas forthcoming). "If You Ain't Got the Do Re Mi," sang Woody Guthrie in Dust Bowl Ballads, "The police at the port of entry say. . . . Better get back to beautiful Texas, Oklahoma, Kansas, Georgia, Tennessee"—and the *Los Angeles Times* lauded the police presence at California's borders as providing much-needed "protection against such swarms of two-legged locusts," meaning jobless fellow Americans. "Nearly one in seven new welfare recipients in B.C. last year were from out-of-province," affirmed *The Province* newspaper in 2016, arguing that, as "more homeless and unemployed people continue to arrive here, British Columbia should make it clear to other provinces that offloading their poor on B.C. is not acceptable." These are manifestations of nativism or protectionism against fellow citizens, but the Brexit referendum has resulted in a resurgence of Europhilia in the United Kingdom, California's "bum blockade" resulted in the U.S. Supreme Court affirming the primacy of federal over state citizenship, and the British Columbia statistics prompted the province's Housing Minister to affirm that "we don't have border security here that says you can't come into British Columbia. If you arrive at a shelter here, we don't judge you by where you come from. We try to help you." In all three cases, then, the nativist or protectionist backlash against in-migration by fellow citizens sparked a counternarrative of fellow citizenship. Adapting the comparative federalism lens developed by Sbragia demonstrates that questions of free movement and citizenship are fundamental not only in federations such as the United States and Canada but also in Europe.

Looking comparatively at internal migration policies reveals that governments generally favor rich people and want to attract them or retain them, while governments also generally discourage poor people to in-migrate and may encourage out-migration. It does not matter whether the government in question is municipal, regional, state, or otherwise: all governments engage in such calculations about the utility or desirability of residents and migrants. To the extent that this is true, attempts by some EU member states to attract wealthy Europeans and to discourage poor Europeans from in-migrating (or encourage them to out-migrate) are not at all unexpected but can be analyzed through the lens of comparative federalism.

As an example from the United States, Puerto Rico has special tax incentives to attract millionaires and billionaires from the rest of the United States: zero tax on dividends, interest, and capital gains. Florida, too, actively works to attract wealthy Americans from other states—often with success. In 2016, the relocation of a single taxpayer (hedge-fund billionaire David Tepper) from New Jersey to Florida caused New Jersey's income to fall by hundreds of millions of dollars: in "New York, California, Connecticut, Maryland and New Jersey, the top 1 percent pay a third or more of total income taxes. Now a handful of billionaires or even a single individual like Mr. Tepper can have a noticeable impact on state revenues and budgets" (Frank 2016). Meanwhile, Connecticut holds discussions with top earners in hopes of keeping them from moving out of state.

The key point is that this type of competition among jurisdictions is nothing new: governments have long competed for "desirable" immigrants. For example, during the sixteenth-century Dutch revolt, northern Dutch cities actively recruited refugees from the south (present-day Belgium, Luxembourg, and parts of northern France) with incentives and inducements, including reimbursing moving costs, extending capital to (re)start businesses, making available manufacturing space, and providing tax incentives (Maas 2013b). The existing population sometimes envied these incentives, with complaints that the immigrants were "favored, advanced, and less taxed than residents" (ibid., 394). Dutch cities nevertheless competed with each other to attract the best immigrants. For example, Leiden in 1577 sent an agent to Gloucester, England, to attract southern Dutch linen and woolworkers, and the leaders of Haarlem in 1578 exhorted the Walloon community of London to relocate, promising to pay the salary of a French-speaking church minister and lauding their city's stability and prosperity. These efforts to recruit refugees from the south paid off; by 1622, there were approximately 150,000 southerners residing in the Dutch Republic, approximately 10 percent of the total population. Because most southerners settled in the cities, the concentration of immigrants in urban areas was much higher: an estimated one-third of Amsterdam residents, two-thirds of Leiden and Middelburg residents, and similarly significant groups in the smaller cities (ibid.). What distinguishes contemporary efforts by governments to attract and retain desirable migrants from this historical example is today's relative ease of information, transportation, and communications technology—and of course the rise of the nation-states which generally guarantee the right to internal migration (Maas 2017c).

As an example of governments encouraging the out-migration of unwanted people, San Francisco has been expanding a program that buses over 1,000 homeless people out of the city annually (Sabatini 2016).[3] Similarly, New York City also pays for destitute residents to "return," usually to other parts

---

3 Since February 2005, the city has provided nearly 10,000 homeless residents Greyhound bus tickets—also a $10 per travel day allowance for food—to cities across the United States under Homeward Bound, the bus ticket home program (Sabatini 2016).

of the United States, most notably Puerto Rico (Bosman 2009). In a system in which state and local governments are responsible for welfare provision, encouraging the out-migration of people who are "burdens" and encouraging the in-migration of people who are "contributors" makes financial sense. It may also make political sense. But seen from the perspective of the political system as a whole, such movements are zero-sum: one jurisdiction's loss is another's gain and vice versa. This raises fundamental questions about the relationship between citizenship and federalism, questions which can be examined comparatively.

CITIZENSHIP AND COMPARATIVE FEDERALISM

Federalism exists in uneasy tension with citizenship. Indeed, the question of what "federalism" means when it comes to the delineation of different peoples in a space or territory that is both shared and distinct can never be resolved completely. In "American Federalism and Intergovernmental Relations," Sbragia argues that federalism in the United States should be understood as a conflict between territorial and functional politics. National institutions such as Congress are organized by functional areas, while the representation of the interests of subnational governments "involves the insertion of territorial criteria into that functionally dominated process. Given the structural dominance of functional politics in the American national arena, and the weaknesses in the system by which states and local governments represent their own interests, it is not surprising that federalism as a value has become of secondary importance in Washington" (Sbragia 2008, 240).

   In the EU, by contrast, territorial politics is much more enshrined because of the dominant role of the European Council and of the member states continuing to act directly rather than through centralized policymaking. One way of capturing this is to view governance in the EU as a process that has evolved from a simple model based on hierarchical policymaking to a much more complex system of governance that employs both hierarchical and nonhierarchical governance modes (Tömmel 2016). Beyond both territorial and functional politics, the EU "engages in processes of meta-governance in order to transform fundamentally the economic and social organisation of the member states" (ibid., 410). Indeed, a longer-term analysis of the evolution of European governance over many decades demonstrates that the key achievement of European integration in the realm of policymaking is a radical transformation in governance which transcends simple notions of hierarchy and may take the form of direct intervention or the establishment of guidelines or norms, in which governance is shared by multiple institutional actors across multiple levels (Caviedes and Maas 2016).

According to Sbragia, the key to understanding the politics of federalism within the United States is the conflict between territorial and functional interests: the "'institutional self-interest' of subnational elected officials has to do with maintaining as much authority and control as they possibly can over their own geographic area. By contrast, the interest of Congress lies in exercising national control in functionally defined policy areas" (Sbragia 2008, 244). This conflict between the territorial and functional interests shapes federalism not only in the United States but also in the EU, where common institutions such as the Commission and the Court—one might add the European Central Bank, the European External Action Service, or even the European Court of Auditors—work to harmonize policies across the Union (Chang 2016; Cini 2016; Dominguez 2016; Guth 2016; Stephenson 2016).

Furthermore, in Europe just as in federal states, there is competition between levels of government. In the United States, as Sbragia argues, levels of government compete with one another: "Mayors want a direct relationship with Washington, whereas governors argue that states are best equipped to allocate resources to lower levels of government. Counties for their part argue that they are the critical local units" (Sbragia 2008, 255). And since in many areas the federal government does not itself deliver services, "the competition among other governments to be the key service provider in any policy area can be fierce," and partisan divisions can also be important (ibid.).

This mirrors in many ways the situation within the EU, where central authorities similarly do not themselves deliver services. As described below, however, governments both in Europe and in federal states also often engage in "offloading" responsibilities that are expensive or not rewarding, for example by denying responsibility for providing services to certain people or groups of people.

Another of Sbragia's intellectual concern, mirroring developments in the real world, has been the relationship between political identity (which is still largely presumed to be national) and supranational institutions. As she notes, many scholars "have focused on the problem posed by the lack of a European identity, the lack of a European public sphere in which citizens of different nationalities could debate with one another, and the lack of feelings of solidarity across national boundaries" (Sbragia 2005, 168).

While acknowledging the lack of feelings of solidarity across national boundaries—which today, fifteen years later, looks less like a lack than a relative paucity, given the growing feelings of supranational solidarity raised by the Brexit process (Maas forthcoming)—as a problem, Sbragia affirms that even a lack of demos would not stop the debate about democracy: those "arguing for greater democracy at the EU level have been listened to since 1979 when the European Parliament was directly elected for the first time.

Since then, the power of the European Parliament has been consistently expanded" (Sbragia 2005, 168).

This observation remains true, even in sensitive areas such as citizenship and free movement, though this underscores the necessity of developing robust new types of institutional arrangements to enable democratic control over policymaking in what Sbragia terms a postnational democracy. Whereas national democracy was closely linked to a nationally defined demos, "post-national democracy may in fact distinguish itself from its national predecessor by incorporating within itself the lack of such "we-feeling." New types of institutional arrangements will need to be developed in order that post-national democracy might be able to coexist with the lack of a political community" (ibid., 169).

As shown below, territorial identities and sovereignty are not nearly as fixed or immutable as often assumed by scholars of international relations and international relations-inspired analyses of European integration. Instead, a comparative politics approach—particularly a comparative federalism approach such as that championed by Sbragia, which analyzes governance rather than government and recalls confederal models rather than being fixated on particular federal models—demonstrates the complexity and the fluidity of policymaking in multi-level settings. And of course economic integration, though core, was never the only purpose of European integration; as I have argued elsewhere, European integration involves not only economic cooperation but also a political project of transcending borders and building a European community of people (Maas 2007).

FREE MOVEMENT AND FEDERALISM

Classic research in political science established that full-scale mobility of persons "followed every successful amalgamated security-community in modern times immediately upon its establishment" and that "the importance of the mobility of persons suggests that in this field of politics persons may be more important than either goods or money" (Deutsch 1957, 53–54). As the examples of the United States and Canada show, mobility even in these democratic states is not entirely full-scale, but Deutsch and his coauthors are certainly correct to insist on the primary importance of the free movement of persons. In Europe today, there is opposition to migration generally and specifically to perceived welfare tourism. But member states have been remarkably successful at limiting access to benefits for migrant Europeans, using welfare policies to limit mobility of poor or otherwise undesirable EU migrants (Geddes and Hadj-Abdou 2016; Lafleur and Mescoli 2018; Schenk and Schmidt 2018). One group which epitomizes the quandary facing member state governments and EU institutions are the Roma: the European Commission has taken significant steps to ensure that member states no longer engage in illegal expulsions of Roma, yet at the same time governments at all levels continue to limit the European rights of free movement and residence for Roma, leading to the conclusion that a weak Commission will likely continue to allow member states to engage in ethnically discriminatory policies against people who provide an easy scapegoat (Gehring 2013; Parker and López Catalán 2014). In many member states, support for free movement and EU citizenship remains the prevailing political message, but governments at some levels stoke fears about "poverty migration" or "welfare tourism" requiring limits on EU free movement (Mantu 2017). As noted earlier, Sbragia reminds us that different levels of governments compete with each other—and this is true also for citizenship.

Except for the middle of the twentieth century, when alternative levels had largely been subsumed or were not considered relevant, the reigning form of citizenship was multi-level.[4] Though the origins of unitary state citizenship can be traced back to Westphalia, local citizenships dominated in most countries until relatively recently. Common citizenship supplanted earlier forms of plural rather than singular citizenship in the United States only after the Civil War and the Fourteenth Amendment (1868) and state-level entitlements remain important today; German and Italian citizenship simply did not exist before the unifications of Germany and Italy in 1871. In Latin America, independence and state-building processes occupied most of the nineteenth century and it would be anachronistic to speak of homogeneous citizenships. The Austro-Hungarian, Ottoman, and Russian empires all featured forms of local status and rights that differed depending on territorial location or social membership. European colonial empires were characterized by forms of subjecthood in the colonies that were generally inferior to those in the metropole. Only since the end of World War I have unitary nation-states spread around the world; most of the world's states are less than one hundred years old and many are considerably newer.

These relatively recent mutations of sovereignty affect citizenship deeply. As Sbragia has argued, when a territorially based political identity is recognized as sovereign in the international arena, "the problems of constructing democratic governance with its overtones of some kind of majoritarian impulse are exacerbated" (Sbragia 2005, 171). Within the EU, giving greater autonomy to the territorially defined groups becomes particularly problematic because economic "integration requires a 'level playing field' for all

---

4 This paragraph draws on Maas (2017b).

economic actors regardless of their nationality or claims to uniqueness"—which is why subsidiarity concerning competition policy, the single market, and trade and monetary policy are explicitly precluded (ibid.). In the area of citizenship and free movement, too, the search for closer coordination and common guidelines flows from functional needs inevitably generated by superimposing a new supranational political community over existing territorially based national communities (Maas 2016) in ways analogous to the construction of federal states such as the United States and Canada.

The United States

The European Commission has suggested that interstate mobility in the United States is a model to be emulated when fostering intra-EU mobility, but actual interstate mobility has been declining steadily in the United States: the annual mobility rate between states (the proportion of U.S. citizens who change their residence from one state to another each year) dropped from 3.5 percent in the 1950s and 3.4 percent in the 1970s to only 1.6 percent more recently.[5] It is unclear what caused the change, but one hypothesis is housing: as the cost of housing has risen, people are more "tied" to where they live. This is true in the market sector (housing that costs 1.7 times annual income is easier to trade than housing that costs three or more times annual income).[6] It is even more true for the nonmarket sector: someone living in rent-controlled or subsidized social housing may be even less likely to move for employment or family reasons (the main reasons people move) than those who have market-rate housing.

As noted above, during the Great Depression, when many unemployed and poor U.S. citizens attempted to move from Dust Bowl states to California and other states in search of opportunity, the police chief of Los Angeles, James Davis, marched 136 police officers to the borders of California in a so-called bum blockade, wherever roads and railways entered California from Arizona, Nevada, and Oregon.[7] The *Los Angeles Times* lauded the police presence at California's borders for providing the much-needed "protection against such swarms of two-legged locusts." Characterizing jobless fellow U.S. citizens as "two-legged locusts" was a particularly stark image, but other newspapers

---

5 See Brookings analysis of annual mobility rates.

6 In 1950, the median U.S. home cost 2.2 times the annual median household income; by 1990, it was still 2.2 times, but households were more likely to be dual-earner rather than single-earner (which inhibits mobility, because it is harder to relocate two jobs instead of only one). By 2010—even after a severe drop in housing prices—the median U.S. home cost 3.3 times the annual median household income.

7 See http://thislandpress.com/2016/11/10/the-anti-okie-panic/.

referred to jobseekers as "criminals," "troublemakers," "parasites," "enemies of society," and deplored the "influx of undesirables" from other U.S. states.[8]

The "bum blockade" was not the first example of a conflict between federal and state protection of rights in the United States. For example, the U.S. Supreme Court in *The Slaughter-House Cases*, ruled that "there is a citizenship of the United States, and a citizenship of a State, which are distinct from each other, and which depend upon different characteristics or circumstances in the individual."[9] The existence of these two levels of citizenship could result in competition between the two levels, as predicted for other policy realms by Sbragia.

In contrast with most other federations, freedom of movement between states in the United States is not guaranteed by the Constitution. Many scholars consider the fact that freedom of movement within the United States is not mentioned in the Constitution a sign that it was so clearly intended as a freedom that the drafters of the Constitution did not think it needed to be stated,[10] with free movement intrinsic to the very nature of federalism.[11] Others contend that it was omitted deliberately, since article IV of the Articles of Confederation (1781), the Constitution's precursor, did include freedom of movement: "To secure and perpetuate mutual friendship and intercourse among the people of the different states in this Union, the free inhabitants of each of these states . . . shall have free ingress and egress to and from any other state."[12]

The most-cited constitutional source for freedom of movement was the Privileges and Immunities Clause (article IV), which protects federal rights from state infringement, but a minority of justices placed it within the Commerce Clause (article I), which enables federal oversight over interstate commerce (Longo 2013). This ambiguity was extended in the landmark *Edwards v California* case, decided in 1941, which struck down a California statute attempting to prosecute anyone who knowingly brought poor nonresidents across state lines. As Justice Robert H. Jackson (later the chief

---

8 See http://thislandpress.com/2016/11/10/the-anti-okie-panic/.

9 83 U.S. 36 (1873).

10 A. P. van der Mei, "Freedom of Movement for Indigents: A Comparative Analysis of American Constitutional Law and European Community Law," *Arizona Journal of International and Comparative Law* 19:3 (2002): 810, writes: "The omission of a reference to the right to travel, which encompasses both the right to cross inter-state borders and the right to migrate, has never been seen as a denial of the right. On the contrary, the framers of the Constitution probably took the right to travel so much for granted that they considered any reference to the right superfluous. . . . The right simply exists and the absence of an explicit reference to it may, if anything, symbolize how deeply the notion of freedom of movement is rooted in American thinking" (Longo 2013; Maas 2013a).

11 S. F. Kreimer, "The Law of Choice and Choice of Law: Abortion, the Right to Travel and Extraterritorial Regulation in American Federalism," *New York University Law Review* 67:3 (1992): 451–519 cited in (Longo 2013).

12 Articles of Confederation (1781) (article IV, §1).

U.S. prosecutor at the Nuremberg Trials) wrote in the judgment, to deny freedom of movement to the poor would "introduce a caste system utterly incompatible with the spirit of our system of government. It would permit those who were stigmatized by a State as indigents, paupers, or vagabonds to be relegated to an inferior class of citizenship."[13] Longo (2013) argues that *Edwards* was groundbreaking but did not resolve disagreement over the legal basis of freedom of movement, which continues today.

Canada

Just as in Europe and the United States, internal freedom of movement within Canada has a contentious history. Compared with U.S. states, Canadian provinces face fewer restraints from the federal government in terms of financial resources or scope for policy differences. Importantly, Canadian provinces are responsible for labor market regulation, leaving the federal government's role restricted to fostering general rights of citizenship. The 1999 Social Union Framework Agreement (SUFA) declared: "All governments believe that the freedom of movement of Canadians to pursue opportunities anywhere in Canada is an essential element of Canadian citizenship. Governments will ensure that no new barriers to mobility are created." But this was lukewarm language, since repeated at regular summits of the provincial premiers.

For example, the conclusions of the July 2019 summit meeting of Canada's premiers affirmed that provinces and territories would prioritize action to "identify and address outstanding impediments to labour mobility"—but with no specific details or timeline (Council of the Federation 2019).

Meanwhile, the Canadian Free Trade Agreement (CFTA), an intergovernmental trade agreement that entered into force in July 2017, promises to reduce measures that restrict or impair the free movement of workers within Canada but does not apply to "social policy measures including labour standards and codes, minimum wages, employment insurance qualification periods, and social assistance"[14]—leaving significant room for policy deviation by the provinces and territories.

---

13 *Edwards v California* 314 U.S. 160 (1941, 181–183). Jackson continued that restricting free movement "would prevent a citizen, because he was poor, from seeking new horizons in other states. It might thus withhold from large segments of our people that mobility which is basic to any guarantee of freedom of opportunity. The result would be a substantial dilution of the right of national citizenship, a serious impairment of the principles of equality . . . [it] is a privilege of citizenship of the United States protected from State abridgement, to enter any State of the Union either for temporary sojourn or for the establishment of permanent residence therein and for gaining resultant citizenship thereof. If national citizenship means less than this it means nothing."

14 CFTA (2017), article 701(2), available at https://www.cfta-alec.ca/wp-content/uploads/2017/06/CFTA-Consolidated-Text-Final-Print-Text-English.pdf.

Under the heading "Mobility Rights," section 6 of the Canadian Charter of Rights and Freedoms, part of the Constitution Act of 1982, provides that, "Every citizen of Canada and every person who has the status of a permanent resident of Canada has the right to move to and take up residence in any province; and to pursue the gaining of a livelihood in any province." But the Charter specifies that these rights are subject to "any laws providing for reasonable residency requirements as a qualification for the receipt of publicly provided social services." This means that the free movement rights in the Canadian constitution are not unlimited; indeed, the restrictions inserted into the text make free movement rights in Canada similar in many ways to free movement rights within the EU. The political dynamics are comparable.

An example illustrates these political dynamics.[15] Only days after the 1995 Quebec referendum, the government of Canada's westernmost province of British Columbia imposed a ninety-day residency requirement on persons entering the province before they would be eligible to receive social assistance.[16] Successive British Columbia governments had long complained of social dumping; in a poor fiscal climate exacerbated by funding cuts from the federal government, other provinces, notably Ontario (Canada's largest province by population) and Alberta (bordering on British Columbia and hence relatively easy to move from) were reducing their social benefits, resulting in an influx of Canadians moving from other provinces and claiming social assistance in British Columbia. The direct challenge to free movement in Canada posed by British Columbia's ninety-day residency requirement was ultimately resolved in 1997 by an agreement between the federal and British Columbia governments in which the federal government agreed to compensate British Columbia for "the special pressures faced by B.C. as a result of internal migration."[17] The agreement also set the stage for the SUFA by promising a review of internal mobility within Canada.

As a second example: preferential hiring practices are a long-standing issue between Ontario and Quebec, with Quebec often restricting Ontario construction workers from working in Quebec on the basis that they do not meet Quebec's training standards. In the late 1990s, there were six times as many Quebec construction workers in Ontario than Ontario workers in Quebec (Gomez and Gunderson 2007), and tension peaked when the government of Quebec excluded Ontario contractors from bidding on the construction of a new casino in Hull, immediately across the river from Ottawa (located in

---

15 This paragraph and the next two draw on Maas (2013a).

16 Order in Council No. 1348 of November 2, 1995.

17 British Columbia Government Communications Office: "PM, Premier Settle B.C. Residency Dispute, Agree to New Co-operation on Mobility, Immigration and Asia-Pacific," available at http://www2.news.gov.bc.ca/archive/pre2001/1997/0475.asp.

Ontario). The Ontario government promptly passed the 1999 *Fairness is a Two-Way Street Act*, resulting in hundreds of Quebec construction workers being dismissed from Ontario projects. Ontario also hired more inspectors to ensure Quebec workers were meeting health, tax, and labor regulations. The law was ultimately repealed as a result of negotiations between the two provinces, and similar interprovincial negotiations continue to mark Canadian federalism. For example, the Joint Labour Mobility Committee monitors progress in achieving full worker mobility under the Ontario-Quebec Trade and Cooperation Agreement, signed in 2009 and revised in 2015, and now subject to the CFTA.

In a key difference with free movement in Europe, federal involvement in free movement of Canadian workers is quite limited due to the constitutional division of powers, which gives provinces (rather than the federal government) the authority to regulate employment and services, including professions. The Supreme Court of Canada generally upholds the constitutionality of provincial statutes in core areas of provincial responsibility, including labor policy, education policy, social policy, election acts, and public safety (Kelly 2005, 195 and the section titled "Reconciling Rights and Federalism"). Because of this, there is a tension in Canada between the overarching Canadian citizenship and policies and laws which assert provincial difference. This means that "Canada will continue to combine features of both a territorial and a plurinational federation into the indefinite future" (Resnick 2012, 182), a conclusion which very much resonates with the tension between governance and government identified by Sbragia.

Europe

The rise of EU citizenship over decades of European integration means that the EU now increasingly resembles a federal state in terms of internal free movement. Just as in the United States and Canada, central authorities work to safeguard the rights of citizens to move unhindered, while decentralized jurisdictions often attempt to attract desirable individuals and repel undesirable ones. This development has been far from easy or linear, and in fact generated and continues to generate political opposition as well as support (Maas 2007, forthcoming). Yet facilitating free movement of persons within Europe has been central to European integration since its origins and developed alongside a supranational European citizenship, meaning that the political dynamics surrounding intra-European migration are now comparable to similar dynamics operating in other multi-level political systems (Maas 2017a).

Wong and Irrera (this volume, chapter 10) may be correct that a large part of the explanation for postwar European integration lies in the efforts of west European states to counteract the loss of national sovereignty by building common European institutions to reinforce national institutions which had lost capacity or legitimacy (compare Milward 1992, 2006). But a complementary impetus for European integration has also always been a political project to create, in the words of the European Coal and Steel Community treaty, a "broader and deeper community among peoples with a destiny henceforward shared." In place of previous bilateral and *ad hoc* arrangements to manage migration between their states, successive generations of political leaders in Europe created a new constitutional category: the European citizen, with rights that EU member states cannot infringe except under limited circumstances (Maas 2017a).

Wong and Irrera's observation that political leaders at member state and EU levels have different views on the uncertainty and urgency of the immigration pressures facing Europe and hence also have different views about appropriate responses fits within the general phenomenon of the inevitable conflicts that occur between different levels of government in multi-level polities, as Sbragia investigates in the United States as well as Europe from the perspective of comparative federalism.

The key point to take away from comparative federalism research is that free movement of people cannot be completely separated from the free movement of goods, services, and capital that defines a common market. Of course no large political community of the size or scope of the United States, Canada, or the EU has uniform free movement for all of these "four freedoms"; indeed, individual states and EU institutions themselves have either created or permitted the creation of direct and indirect barriers to mobility that undermine the promise of free movement (Carens 2013). But working to dismantle barriers to the free movement not only of goods, services, and capital but also of people defines a common political community in contrast to a simple free trade arrangement (Cameron 1992; Garrett 1998; Egan 2001; Schütze 2017). While a free trade arrangement can be modified or terminated with relative ease, the process of creating or dismantling a political community is much more difficult.

The final comparative point relevant to this chapter is that political ties across territorial boundaries are strengthening in Europe, in ways analogous to the manner in which such political ties strengthened when separate British colonies united to form the federal United States and, later, a federal Canada. A November 2018 flash Eurobarometer survey found that 59 percent of Europeans trust the EU, while only 42 percent trust their national government, continuing a trend toward more trust in the EU. In terms of social rights, a strong majority of Europeans favor harmonizing European social welfare systems: the 2017 Eurobarometer survey found 64 percent in favor, 26 percent opposed, and 10 percent don't know, continuing a trend of increasing support for Europeanization—and younger respondents (those aged between fifteen and thirty-nine) favored harmonization more than older respondents (those aged fifty-five plus), 67 to 61 percent.[18] The Schuman Declaration's determination to lay the "common foundations for economic development as a first step in the federation of Europe" foresaw that a common market would create "a wider and deeper community" and "lead to the realization of the first concrete foundation of a European federation." Since then, Europe has been transformed profoundly and the coexistence of "shared rule" and "self-rule" analyzed by Sbragia (1992, 2004) is undeniable, even in the area of citizenship and free movement.

CONCLUSION

One of Alberta Sbragia's seminal contributions to the comparative study of Europe argued that it is "nearly impossible to overestimate the importance of national boundaries as key organizers of political power and economic wealth" in the EU, largely because the "ties across territory are relatively weak in critical areas" (Sbragia 1992, 274). This chapter demonstrates that political tensions that are represented by borders and boundaries character-ize not only Europe but also federal systems such as the United States and Canada, and that the ties across territory may be strengthening in Europe, in ways analogous to the way in which they developed earlier elsewhere. Europeans have been attempting to manage free movement within a common European political space—which raises issues such as rights of residence, access to employment, rights of political participation, mutual recognition of credentials (see Van Riemsdijk 2013), and social security and welfare ben-efits—since the establishment of the European Coal and Steel Community. During that time, the economic logic originally used to justify freedom of movement—that economic integration requires free movement of labor—has been replaced by a political logic: a common EU citizenship requires free movement rights not only for workers but for ever increasing categories of people. EU citizenship grants rights throughout EU territory not only to lim-ited categories of workers but also to all member state citizens and members of their families. In this light, the question inspired by Alberta Sbragia's work on comparative federalism concerns the extent to which it is possible to "Europeanize" citizenship and free movement while retaining a key role for national governments.

---

18 The question was: "Today, each European Union Member State is responsible for its own social welfare system. To what extent would you be in favour or opposed to the harmonisation of social welfare systems within the European Union?"

Sbragia is correct in her exhortation to scholars to reexamine older con-federal models of "shared rule" rather than fixating on the extent to which the EU approaches the model of any contemporary federal state, such as the United States (or Germany, or Brazil, or India, or Canada, etc.). Reexamining confederal models of citizenship reminds us that decisions about member-ship need not be exercised solely by the central authority but can in fact be decentralized and left to local authorities—indeed this remains the practice in Switzerland today, although even in Switzerland the federal government has been playing more of a role than in the past.

Democracy assumes a political community, and citizenship is a means of delineating who does and who does not belong to the political "people"—but the introduction of EU citizenship over already-established national citizen-ships transforms citizenship in Europe into a multi-level phenomenon (Maas 2013c, 2017c). Scholars of European integration have generally accepted as an unexplored assumption that national identities are relatively fixed. But as eminent social scientists such as Max Weber long ago pointed out, dif-ferences in national sentiment are both significant and fluid: the "idea of the nation" is empirically "entirely ambiguous" and the intensity of feelings of solidarity is variable (Weber 1946, 175). As of this writing, we see the veracity of this claim in places such as Scotland (in light of the 2016 Brexit referendum), Northern Ireland (in light of that same referendum), Catalonia (in light of several officially unrecognized referendums), across Central and Eastern Europe (whose post-Soviet political identities remain mutable), and elsewhere. Furthermore, successive EU-wide opinion surveys show increas-ing numbers of Europeans identifying with Europe—certainly far more than was imagined even a few years ago.

A comparative federalism lens such as that developed by Alberta Sbragia demonstrates that questions of citizenship and free movement are funda-mental not only in federal states such as the United States and Canada but also in the EU. Cases such as the role of borders and migration in the Brexit debates, the popularity of the "bum blockade" during the Great Depression in the United States, and interprovincial migration in Canada demonstrate the enduring tension between "shared rule" and "self-rule" over the movement of people and the question of who is entitled to participate in politics as a citizen.

BIBLIOGRAPHY

Bosman, Julie 2009. "City Aids Homeless with One-Way Tickets Home." *New York Times*. July 29, page A1.

Cameron, David R. 1992. "The 1992 Initiative: Causes and Consequences." In *Euro-Politics: Institutions and Policymaking in the New European Community*, edited by Alberta M. Sbragia, 23–74. Washington, DC: Brookings Institution.

Carens, Joseph H. 2013. "Foreword." In *Democratic Citizenship and the Free Movement of People*, edited by Willem Maas, 5–8. Leiden: Martinus Nijhoff.

Caviedes, Alexander and Willem Maas. 2016. "Sixty-Five Years of European Governance." *Journal of Contemporary European Research*, 12 (1): 395–405.

Chang, Michele. 2016. "The (Ever) Incomplete Story of Economic and Monetary Union." *Journal of Contemporary European Research*, 12 (1). http://www.jcer.net/index.php/jcer.

Cini, Michelle. 2016. "Good Governance and Institutional Change: Administrative Ethics Reform in the European Commission." *Journal of Contemporary European Research*, 12 (1). http://www.jcer.net/index.php/jcer/article/view/705.

Council of the Federation. 2019. "Premiers Committed to Strengthening the Economy through Reducing Barriers to Internal Trade." http://www.canadaspremiers.ca/wp-content/uploads/2019/07/Internal_Trade_July10_FINAL-1.pdf.

Deutsch, Karl Wolfgang. 1957. *Political Community and the North Atlantic Area: International Organization in the Light of Historical Experience*. Princeton, NJ: Princeton University Press.

Dominguez, Roberto. 2016. "The EU Governance System of External Relations." *Journal of Contemporary European Research*, 12 (1). http://www.jcer.net/index.php/jcer/article/view/700.

Egan, Michelle P. 2001. *Constructing a European Market: Standards, Regulations, and Governance*. Oxford: Oxford University Press.

Elazar, Daniel J. 1995. "Federalism and the European Idea." In *Federal-Type Solutions and European Integration*, edited by C. Lloyd Brown-John, 19–28. Lanham MD: University Press of America.

Frank, Robert. 2016. "One Top Taxpayer Moved, and New Jersey Shuddered." *New York Times*, May 1, Section BU, Page 1.

Garrett, Geoffrey. 1998. "Global Markets and National Politics: Collision Course or Virtuous Circle?" *International Organization*, 52 (4): 787–824.

Geddes, Andrew and Leila Hadj-Abdou. 2016. "An Unstable Equilibrium? Freedom of Movement and the Welfare State in the European Union." In *Handbook on Migration and Social Policy*, edited by Gary P. Freeman and Nikola Mirilovic, 222–239. Cheltenham UK: Edward Elgar Publishing.

Gehring, Jacqueline. 2013. "Free Movement for Some: The Treatment of the Roma after the European Union's Eastern Expansion." In *Democratic Citizenship and the Free Movement of People*, edited by Willem Maas, 143–174. Leiden: Martinus Nijhoff.

Gomez, Rafael and Morley Gunderson. 2007. "Barriers to the Inter-Provincial Mobility of Labour." Working Paper Series—Economic Analysis and Statistics, Industry Canada, WP 2007–2009. http://www.ic.gc.ca/eic/site/eas-aes.nsf/eng/ra02043.html.

Guth, Jessica. 2016. "Transforming the European Legal Order: The European Court of Justice at 60+." *Journal of Contemporary European Research*, 12 (1). http://www.jcer.net/index.php/jcer/article/view/699.

Kelly, James B. 2005. *Governing with the Charter: Legislative and Judicial Activism and Framers' Intent*. Law and Society Series. Vancouver: UBC Press.

Lafleur, Jean-Michel and Elsa Mescoli. 2018. "Creating Undocumented EU Migrants through Welfare: A Conceptualization of Undeserving and Precarious Citizenship." *Sociology*, 52 (3): 480–496.

Longo, Matthew. 2013. "Right of Way? Defining the Scope of Freedom of Movement within Democratic Societies." In *Democratic Citizenship and the Free Movement of People*, edited by Willem Maas, 31–56. Leiden: Martinus Nijhoff.

Maas, Willem. 2005. "The Genesis of European Rights." *Journal of Common Market Studies*, 43 (5): 1009–1025.

Maas, Willem. 2007. *Creating European Citizens*. Lanham, MD: Rowman & Littlefield.

Maas, Willem. 2013a. "Free Movement and Discrimination: Evidence from Europe, the United States, and Canada." *European Journal of Migration and Law*, 15 (1): 91–110.

Maas, Willem. 2013b. "Immigrant Integration, Gender, and Citizenship in the Dutch Republic." *Politics, Groups, and Identities*, 1 (3): 390–401.

Maas, Willem. 2013c. "Varieties of Multilevel Citizenship." In *Multilevel Citizenship*, edited by Willem Maas, 1–21. Philadelphia: University of Pennsylvania Press.

Maas, Willem. 2016. "European Governance of Citizenship and Nationality." *Journal of Contemporary European Research*, 12 (1): 532–551.

Maas, Willem. 2017a. "Free Movement and the Difference That Citizenship Makes." *Journal of European Integration History*, 23 (1): 85–101.

Maas, Willem. 2017b. "Multilevel Citizenship." In *The Oxford Handbook of Citizenship*, edited by Ayelet Shachar, Rainer Bauböck, Irene Bloemraad, and Maarten Vink, 644–668. Oxford: Oxford University Press.

Maas, Willem. 2017c. "Boundaries of Political Community in Europe, the US, and Canada." *Journal of European Integration*, 39 (5): 575–590. https://doi.org/10.10 80/07036337.2017.1327526.

Maas, Willem. Forthcoming. "European Citizenship and Free Movement after Brexit." In *Europe after Brexit*, edited by Scott Greer and Janet Laible. Manchester: Manchester University Press.

Mantu, Sandra. 2017. "Alternative Views on EU Citizenship." In *Migration on the Move: Essays on the Dynamics of Migration*, edited by Carolus Grütters, Sandra Mantu, and Paul Minderhoud, 225–246. Leiden: Brill Nijhoff.

Milward, Alan S. 1992. *The European Rescue of the Nation-State*. London: Routledge.

Milward, Alan S. 2006. *The Reconstruction of Western Europe, 1945–51*. London: Routledge.

Parker, Owen and Óscar López Catalán. 2014. "Free Movement for Whom, Where, When? Roma EU Citizens in France and Spain." *International Political Sociology*, 8 (4): 379–395.

Resnick, Philip. 2012. "Canada: A Territorial or a Multinational Federation?" In *Federalism, Plurinationality and Democratic Constitutionalism: Theory and Cases*, edited by Ferran Requejo Coll and Miquel Caminal i Badia, 171–184. New York: Routledge.

Sabatini, Joshua. 2016. "SF Expanding Program that has Bused 10K Homeless Residents Out of Town in Past Decade." *San Francisco Examiner*. June 29, available at https://www.sfexaminer.com/news/sf-expanding-program-that-has-bused-10k-homeless-residents-out-of-town-in-past-decade/.

Sbragia, Alberta M. 1992. "Thinking about the European Future: The Uses of Comparison." In *Euro-Politics: Institutions and Policymaking in the New European*

Community, edited by Alberta M. Sbragia, 257–291. Washington, DC: Brookings Institution.

Sbragia, Alberta M. 2004. "The Future of Federalism in the European Union." Keynote Address delivered at the European Community Studies Association-Canada (ECSA-C) 2004 Biennial Conference. http://aei.pitt.edu/1877/.

Sbragia, Alberta M. 2005. "Post-National Democracy as Post-National Democratization." In *Democracy and Federalism in the European Union and the United States*, edited by Sergio Fabbrini, 167–182. London: Routledge.

Sbragia, Alberta M. 2006. "American Federalism and Intergovernmental Relations." *The Oxford Handbook of Political Institutions*, 239–260. Oxford: Oxford University Press.

Schenk, Angelika and Susanne K. Schmidt. 2018. "Failing on the Social Dimension: Judicial Law-Making and Student Mobility in the EU." *Journal of European Public Policy*, 25 (10): 1522–1540.

Schütze, Robert. 2017. *From International to Federal Market: The Changing Structure of European Law*. Oxford: Oxford University Press.

Stephenson, Paul J. 2016. "Sixty-Five Years of Auditing Europe." *Journal of Contemporary European Research*, 12 (1). http://www.jcer.net/index.php/jcer/article/view/691.

Tömmel, Ingeborg. 2016. "EU Governance of Governance: Political Steering in a Non-Hierarchical Multilevel System." *Journal of Contemporary European Research*, 12 (1). http://www.jcer.net/index.php/jcer/article/view/695.

Van Riemsdijk, Micheline. 2013. "Politics of Free Movement in the European Union: Recognition and Transfer of Professional Qualifications." In *Democratic Citizenship and the Free Movement of People*, edited by Willem Maas, 115–141. Leiden: Martinus Nijhoff.

Weber, Max. 1946. "The Nation." In *From Max Weber: Essays in Sociology*, edited by H. H. Gerth and C. Wright Mills, 171–179. New York: Oxford University Press.

Chapter 5

Multi-level Politics from within a Single European Legislature

Analyzing Early Exits from the Eighth European Parliament

William T. Daniel

In the introduction to her edited volume *Euro-Politics: Institutions and Policymaking in the "New" European Community*, Alberta Sbragia comments on the complex overlapping institutional arrangements present in what is now known as the European Union (EU). "It is precisely . . . the meshing between national institutions and leaders, on the one hand, and Community institutions and leaders, on the other, which makes it difficult for those with only a cursory knowledge of the Community to understand how it functions" (Sbragia 1992, 2). Nearly thirty years on, the EU institutions are arguably better understood—or at least studied—than they once were; however, the interplay between national- and EU-level institutions and leaders continues to present social scientists with new fora for theory-testing and -building.

Among the European institutional ecosystem, the European Parliament (EP) offers perhaps the most unique space for inquiry. Having moved from an unelected and mostly deliberative body of national members of parliament (MPs) to a committee-driven congress that is the only directly elected body of EU, the nature of its composition has also changed. Once considered by Sbragia (1993, 33) as the "clear the 'junior partner' within the Community's institutional scheme," members of the European Parliament (MEPs) were typically viewed as a colorful cache of political amateurs, faded retirees, or pseudocelebrity dilettantes. This view has also changed: the EP and its members are now the focus of a well-developed literature on political decision-making in Europe, whose scholarly breadth and depth is arguably only rivaled among the world's legislature by the literature on the U.S. Congress (e.g., Kreppel 2002; Hix, Noury, and Roland 2007; Yordanova 2013; Servent 2017).

MEP career paths have also garnered increased scholarly attention, both as indicators of the EP's increased institutionalization as a legislative body (Daniel 2015) and as a lens for viewing how national political movements incubate talents suited to the growing array of political offices that populate an integrated Europe (Whitaker 2014; Geffen 2016). According to this literature, tracing the professional pathways that MEPs have taken, to and from power, can reveal important information about both the status of the EP among the broader constellation of European political offices and the multiple levels of governance at play on the continent.

However, the EP also continues to present a set of logistical quandaries for the national political parties who select would-be candidates to stand for election. EP elections remain *the* prime example of the "second-order election" (SOE) model (e.g., Reif and Schmitt 1980) and routinely attract both lower voter turnout rates and weaker levels of public knowledge about candidates than do national elections. At the same time, a set of EU-level electoral rules that can be more "permissive" than their national analogues in some cases (to use the language of Prosser [2016b]) compounds the ease with which smaller parties can more easily gain access to the EP than to their national legislative bodies. In the divisive political landscape currently observed across the EU, this can oftentimes entail big gains and top billing for fringe and extremist movements in EP elections. Taking the sum of these dynamics into consideration, this chapter benefits from the complexity alluded to by Sbragia (1992) to demonstrate how the configuration of the EP in a multi-level political European space has impacted on the development of political party careers that would have traditionally been contained by the nation state.

In order to do so, I take stock of the career trajectories for those MEPs who resigned early from the eighth and current session of the EP (2014–2019). As of the formal close of session for the Eighth European Parliament in April 2019, 106 of the originally elected 751 MEPs (14.11 percent) had resigned their position in the EP. While this set of early departures is somewhat lower in the current EP than in previous sessions (see comparative rates across all EP electoral periods in Daniel and Metzger [2018]), it is still much higher than the generalized, average turnover rate of 9.56 percent observed by Matland and Studlar (2004, 93) for 25 national parliamentarians from industrial democracies. Indeed, the most recent figures for within-session turnover are actually higher in the EP—however low they may now be, as compared with earlier sessions—than for any of the yearly national averages calculated by Matland and Studlar, apart from Portugal.

While intrasession turnover in the EP is quite high, MEP "dropouts" from the most recent session contained a highly important set of politicians: cabinet members and chief executives (35), current national MPs (23), key regional and local politicians (seven), European Commissioners (seven), and even members of the EU Court of Auditors (two). In short, the EP may have become an increasingly important legislative body in its own right, but it is also responsible for cultivating a growing class of top-flight political talent from across the EU.

I use the remaining sections to contextualize a snapshot of these outgoing MEPs within the broader contours of the literature on EP elections and national party system developments. I first link this to new work on the SOE model, before examining mechanisms by which EP elections may provide political parties—particularly those at the ideological or structural fringes—with the sorts of fertilizer needed to help them grow into ostensibly national movements. In doing so, I point out that the present state of the literature mostly omits a focus on the microlevel of these developments—the individual politicians, themselves. I make use of the current session of the EP to illustrate these mechanisms at work, paying specific attention to the career progression of those outgoing MEPs who failed to complete their current term.

Using originally collected descriptive and biographical data on this set of politicians, the ensuing discussion demonstrates the extent to which the EP's development has impacted the career paths of its politicians across multiple levels and for reasons that remain unique among the legislative offices of Europe. I find that, while the EP may have become an important legislative player and career destination in its own right—it remains an important "training ground" or "holding pattern" for national political parties to grow politicians of prominence, prior to future political work at the national and/ or European levels.

NATIONAL USES OF THE SUPRANATIONAL LEGISLATURE

As mentioned in the introduction of the chapter, voting in European elections and thus the electoral fortunes of the MEPs remains highly conditioned by the SOE model. The SOE model, in turn, has unique ramifications for the growth of smaller, newer, and/or ideological fringe parties—first in the EP and later in national political office. In this section, I review recent developments from the literature on SOEs. I then move on to link up this discussion with the analytical aim of the chapter: the ambition of individual MEPs who resign their seats, prior to the end of their current legislative term.

SECOND-ORDER ELECTIONS AND THE EP

Reif and Schmitt's (1980) seminal argument on SOEs identified a set of electoral contests of lesser (hence, "second-order") importance than those in national office. Using the first, direct EP elections of 1979 as a basis for their analysis, the SOE model has evolved to posit three, central expectations: (1) voter turnout in SOEs will be lower than in national contests, (2) voters will use SOEs as a referendum on national governing parties and larger/governing parties will tend to fare worse than in national contests, and (3) due to their perceived secondary importance, voters will be more likely to reward fringe and/or protest parties in SOEs (see, for instance, Schmitt and Teperoglu 2017). While the SOE model has generally performed consistently within the EP context (Schmitt 2005; Träger et al. 2015), it has also been used as the basis for a set of more nuanced predictions.

For instance, Schakel's (2015) evaluation of regional elections in Central and East European (CEE) countries shows that the SOE model hangs upon more than just in or out of government status but rather functions as a combination of party size and economic indicators, such as national unemployment and inflation rates. The mechanism at play in this refined version of the familiar SOE story is that, because CEE party systems continue to be less static and voters less bound to specific parties, exogenous factors like the economy may be more relevant for analyzing party vote choices—even if they still correspond roughly with the original dynamics of the SOE model. However, in terms of work on the EP, this also suggests that European elections may continue to function differently between CEE enlargement countries and those in the mostly West European EU-15 bloc. This result is comparable to the earlier findings of Koepke and Ringe (2006), which indicated that EP voters from CEE countries may be prone to vote more sincerely and without the typical protest behavior characteristic of the pre-2004 member states.

More broadly, Golder et al.'s (2017) work uses the SOE model as a basis for examining the variations in the decisions of elites to seek election, the strategy of campaigns, and the eventual vote choice made across multiple levels of elections (subnational, national, and European) in France, Germany, and Spain. Their aim is to call attention to the intrinsically multi-level nature of elections in the European space: when politicians and parties seek office at multiple levels, the decisions that they make are endogenous to the variation present at each level of representation—a frame that certainly resonates with the spirit of Sbragia's (1992) volume. In terms of the EP, the authors find that smaller parties in their case countries focus their attention predominantly on EP elections, where barriers to entry are oftentimes lower—as EP elections must use proportional representation, whereas national elections do not always do so.

In a similar vein, Prosser (2016b) examines how the SOE model can be used as a way for parties to first grow at the European level, prior to making electoral advances into national office. As his theory goes, the more "permissive" nature of EP elections[1] permits new parties to get an initial foothold in European office, before increasing their following in national elections. A range of other studies corroborate the general finding of Prosser's investigation, either between the EP and national levels or between local and national contests (e.g., Bytzek 2015; Giebler and Wagner 2015; Marien, Dassonneville, and Hooghe 2015; Prosser 2016a).

At this point, it is important to note how EP elections have been viewed as breeding grounds for the development of ideologically "fringe" parties, due to the aspects of structural permissiveness noted above. However, it is also worth mentioning here that the mechanism described above does not require that parties benefitting from the EP's permissiveness be either extremist or even fringe movements. The important point to underline is that, at least for many of the major member states, a seat in the EP is easier to win than a seat in the national parliament; this comparative ease relies upon SOE voting behavior, more permissive electoral rules, lower/absent electoral thresholds, or some combination of the three. However, as with most things in the EP, the combination of relevant factors varies along national and partisan lines and may be impossible to fully disentangle. Nonetheless, as we shall see in the next section, it is oftentimes those parties with outlying ideological positions who do empirically benefit the most from the SOE model in the EP.

THE EP AND NEW POLITICAL MOVEMENTS

In van der Brug and de Vreese's (2016) discussion of the "unintended" consequences of European elections, Markowski's piece focuses on how EP elections lead to the development of new parties at the national level. Exploiting the permissiveness of EP electoral rules, he examines the ability of these new parties to succeed in national contests in the long run. However, he finds that only 11 of the 42 "new" parties that first emerged from the EP level between the 1999 and 2009 EP elections were able to retain seats in their corresponding national legislatures, after a second wave of national elections. This suggests that new parties are able to first gain traction at the EP level—where the factors discussed above make it easier for "party start-ups" to succeed—but that this success is rarely replicated back at the national level.

For those parties that are successful in maintaining a new position within the national political space, however, he suggests that such parties must represent a coherent ideological position that is demanded by the national

---

1 This is particularly true in Great Britain and France, where plurality elections in national contest promote higher barriers to entry than in the fully proportional representation-based EP—although it is also true of the largest member state of Germany, where electoral thresholds are present in the *Bundestag* and not for the EP.

electorates. Related to an earlier point, he also finds that the majority of these successful "new" parties are found in Western European countries. Nonetheless, the results of the chapter suggest that the EP may offer political entrepreneurs with a new basis for growing their parties. To put it more bluntly, in the language of Nielsen and Franklin (2016), the EP serves as a "midwife" for new parties. Specific to Franklin's chapter in the volume (Nielsen and Franklin 2016: 223–238), the EP "pumps" new parties into European contests that can then attract and socialize new sets of voters that will then support them in the national political space. However, what makes these newly born parties among the most extreme or fringe in the European political space?

Schulte-Cloos (2018) examines how EP elections create a structural incentive for "challenger" parties to flourish. Beyond the electoral system effects discussed earlier, she notes that these parties are oftentimes from the ideological fringe, in part because the nature of EP elections makes it easier for voters to lodge a protest vote that will not lead to the danger of creating an actual government (unlike in national, parliamentary elections, where legislative majorities are the building blocks for the executive branch). However, once elected to the EP, institutional supports mean that such parties will also benefit from a variety of new supports and material resources that they would not otherwise have.

Reungoat (2015) pays specific attention to how the SOE model has allowed for the far-right French *Rassemblement National* (RN) party[2] to grow a national support base through the "back door" of the EP. Although the party's platform is inherently Eurosceptic and thus against the values advanced by the EP, European elections retain a "first-order" significance for the RN, as France's majoritarian election system has historically made it difficult for third parties to win seats in the National Assembly, as compared with the lengthy national party lists that have traditionally been used in French EP votes. In examining the RN predecessors' participation in the EP since the 1980s, she finds that the EP has ironically promoted the RN's respectability and legitimacy, while providing it with valuable material resources.

For instance, RN MEPs have long benefited from a livable salary and travel resources that allow them to augment their focus on French politics (they are also among the most absent from the EP) in ways that they wouldn't be able to—were they having to work jobs in the private sector while using EP-paid assistantships to cultivate a bevy of professional party staffers. This material advantage also provides RN leadership with a mechanism for instilling party discipline: wayward members can be quickly annihilated from public life via electoral lists and new office hires, as was the case with long-serving

2 As of July 2018, the National Front (FN) party changed its name to the *Rassemblement National* party—or "National Rally." I use the current nomenclature here, when referring to the present version of the party.

FN MEP Bruno Gollnisch. Under the newly created Europe of Nations and Freedom (ENF) political group—following the 2014 EP vote—the RN has benefited even further from resources not previously afforded to them as an independent (*non-inscrit*) party.

In the 2017 national elections, this situation of institutional support helped to translate into yet another presidential election face-off between the then-FN leader and outgoing MEP Marine Le Pen and now-French president Emanuel Macron, as had similarly been the case in 2002 between Le Pen's father (FN founder and former MEP Jean-Marie Le Pen) and the then-French president Jacques Chirac. While both Macron and Chirac cruised to an easy victory, the FN was able to effectively move French political discourse further to the right and even netted a reasonably large handful of seats in the National Assembly in 2017—its best-ever electoral result at the national level. Cultivated and professionalized by a legislature that it is theoretically opposed to, the RN will continue to be a dominating force in French politics for the foreseeable future, as seen once again in the strong result in the 2019 EP elections.

Of course, success at the EP level does not always translate into national victory. The UK Independence Party (UKIP) provides an interesting cautionary tale of how EP success may not yield seats in the national parliament. Cutts, Goodwin, and Milazzo (2017) examine how the party was unable to translate a first-place finish in 2014 EP elections into a net gain of any seats in the 2015 UK general elections, even when a referendum on EU membership was at the height of the national conscience. Through a lack of professionalism and expertise in its local ground game and a miscalculation that led the party to target broadly, instead of strategically focusing on districts that it could likely win, UKIP finished the election with only one seat out of the more than 500 present in the House of Commons.

Naturally here, once again, the EP served as a key source of support for the would-be UKIP MPs. It is also clear, however, that the party was unable to "pump" its protest votes from 2014 into a 2015 result. If we take the then-leader Nigel Farage's statement about UKIP as a party that advances "cooperation among sovereign European states and rejects the bureaucratization of Europe and . . . a single, centralized . . . super-state" to heart (Filimon 2015), we clearly see an example of how voters may favor nongoverning parties in SOEs, while being less clear on what they are meant to do with them in the more traditional national contests. On a smaller scale, this mismatch between EP and national victories was recently replicated. In the May 2019 EP elections, UK voters accorded a massive win to the upstart Brexit Party, just prior to losing out to a Labour candidate in the June 2019 Peterborough by-elections—a loss that has been attributed to a weak knowledge of the ground game required for generating voter turnout by the new party.

CONNECTING THE SOE LITERATURE TO
INDIVIDUAL MEP CAREER MOVES

Thus far, my discussion of the SOE literature has suggested that EP contests may be used to grow national parties—particularly when such organizations are disadvantaged for national-institutional reasons or disfavored from the ideological fringes. We've also seen how the EP connects to a broader, multi-level system of representation, across the ideological spectrum. Notably omitted from this literature, however, is a focus on career movements made by the politicians, themselves. Indeed the view of the literature remains mostly at the party level and neglects to trace the footsteps of those MEPs who might use their time in Brussels and Strasbourg to set the groundwork for a future career change for themselves. In the remainder of this section, I bring in literature from the study of MEP careers to account for how and when these individual shifts may take place.

The study of political ambition traditionally focuses on those politicians with a "discrete" or "static" interest in remaining elected to a particular office—or conversely with a "progressive" ambition toward a (generally higher) level. Although this literature is developed within the context of American presidential elections (Schlesinger 1966), it has also been exported to a variety of other national systems (Samuels 2003) and the EP (Daniel 2015). It is also keenly suited to the study of comparative federalist literatures advocated by Sbragia (2005). Of key interest to this particular chapter, however, is how connections between the party level and the SOE model may manifest themselves among the political ambitions of individual MEPs who anticipate further professional lives elsewhere.

Earlier work in Daniel (2015) traced the displayed career ambitions of MEPs across the full elected history of the EP, 1979–2014, and thereby provided evidence of the legislature's institutionalization and professionalization (*à la* Polsby 1968). However, the focus of the analysis in this particular chapter is on those MEPs who failed to complete their terms. I choose this approach to provide a current snapshot of MEP behavior at the individual level and because the decision to leave an elected mandate early demonstrates the rawest type of individual ambition. In my view, the decision to quit one's job early for another professional post would almost require something viewed as "better" for the individual in question. In the context of the EP, this is oftentimes a national political office—all of which relates back to the previous discussion on SOE dynamics and the interconnectedness of multi-level politics in the EU.

In the following, I summarize a set of four key expectations that we might anticipate from the "progressive" ambitions of such politicians.

Expectation 1: Federal and Unitary Systems

Previous work indicates that MEPs from federal and functionally decentralized systems are more likely than those from unitary and centralized ones to build lengthy careers at the EP level (Daniel 2015) and are generally less likely to leave the EP prior to the end of a term (Daniel and Metzger 2018). In both cases, the logic goes that MEPs from federal/decentralized systems are more accustomed to functional distinctions between the various levels of government and therefore display a "static" ambition for service at the level that best aligns with their policy interests. Federal systems are also more likely to have more devolved party systems, where individual politicians are more able to control the trajectory of their own careers. As relates to our discussion of SOEs, we also see a similar story advanced by Golder et al. (2017).

Conversely, unitary/centralized MEPs are more likely to operate at the mercy of national political parties, who typically treat national legislative office as the predominant goal for party vote-, office-, and policy-seeking. Accordingly, MEPs from these systems are less likely to stay in the EP, when a space at the national legislature becomes available (as will oftentimes occur during national elections that are out of sync with European ones). It is worth noting here that the typical dynamics of European governance—among them, strong parties, multiparty competition, a generally weaker version functional federalism, smaller geographies, and the heightened presence of proportional representation—all serve to reinforce this mechanism in ways that are not present in other, major federal systems like the United States.

Thus, at a systemic or structural level, we might expect that when MEPs from federal or decentralized systems do fail to complete their elected term at the EP, it will likely be associated with personal or nonpolitical reasons (such as retirement or private sector ventures) and have less to do with political "level hopping." I view the decision to drop out early as a nonpolitical baseline, against which other career destinations can be compared. Empirically, the expectation is that MEPs from federal/decentralized countries who do drop out will do so for disproportionally nonpolitical reasons.

Expectation 2: Second-Order and Fringe Parties

As mentioned in the earlier sections of this chapter, the SOE theory has been used to explain why smaller and more ideological fringe movements are rational to focus their attentions on SOEs, in which they stand to benefit disproportionally. Related to the movement of individual MEPs, previous work has also addressed why these "fringe parties" are more likely to protect incumbent MEPs for renomination and reelection, as a means of growing their party organizations for further national contests (Daniel 2016). However, MEPs from fringe and smaller parties do occasionally choose to leave the EP. I would expect that when this occurs prior to the end of their mandate, such MEPs are destined to disproportionally focus on national legislatures or key local and regional offices, relative to mainstream parties that are more accustomed to occupying these offices, and where they can begin to build out an electoral base for future contests.

Expectation 3: Mainstream Parties

Although the theory anticipates that major parties and those in government will suffer the biggest losses from SOEs, it's also the case that second-order bodies like the EP can serve as repositories of talent for mainstream parties—particularly in those policy areas in which the EU is the most competent. Accordingly, we might expect MEPs from mainstream or national governing parties who leave the EP to be headed toward national jobs of some importance. Unlike fringe and smaller parties, these mainstream groups are also more likely to be competitive for leadership roles in national races and should be more likely to receive national cabinet portfolios. Such a logic would lead us to anticipate that MEPs from mainstream and larger parties are more likely to quit the EP for national cabinets or executive campaigns. Of course, this expectation is also somewhat automatic to the extent that fringe and smaller parties are (typically—though not always!) less likely to enter into national governments.

Expectation 4: Parties from Central and Eastern Europe

The post-2004 CEE enlargement states represent a newer set of European democracies; they are also notable for the high degree of churn experienced by their party systems, with parties based less along ideological lines and more in relation to individual personalities, networks, or other historical-cultural distinctions. On the other hand, previous work (Daniel 2015) has shown that from 2004 to 2014, a number of MEPs from these systems have also come from among the ranks of their countries' first-order politicians.

Whether this is due to the perceived political prestige of an EU institution, to the restrictive lustration laws at home pertaining to former political service under state socialism, or to the more practical material benefits of European office, a number of the region's most prominent politicians have made a tour of duty in the EP. This is likely also an artifact of the more recently democratized countries of CEE, where top-line national politicians were likely to have worked on EU accession and have a higher esteem for the EP (or, more cynically, value EP salaries that can more than double those of national MPs).[3]

However, the uses of EP service by CEE politicians have not always matched with the actual functions of the legislature, as noted by Daniel's (2015) chapter on Polish MEPs, who sought out committee assignments on powerful-sounding, yet functionally underutilized committees like Foreign Affairs (AFET). Therefore, as both the former national political heavy hitters and key sources of political institutional knowledge, we might view MEPs from CEE countries as among the most likely to quit their positions for a return to mainline national offices—and likely for a key executive position. On the other hand, the EP also proposes a space within which such politicians can become socialized to the broader EU norms that may serve newcomers to the Union in a way that may lead them to its other institutions, particularly when a shallow bench of international experience exists back at home. Therefore, we might also see MEPs from the CEE countries to be more likely to move from the EP to other EU institutions such as the European Commission or the Court of Justice of the EU.

TAKING STOCK OF THE MEP DROPOUTS FROM EP 8

The remainder of the chapter examines the previous expectations within the context of those MEPs who have resigned early, prior to the conclusion of the current EP. The choice of the current EP is a deliberate one. The eighth EP was elected in May 2014 and adjourned for the 2019 electoral campaign in late April 2019. The 2014 elections provided some of the most dramatic pieces of support for the SOE model since the 1970s, with radical right-wing, populist, and other Eurosceptic parties amassing an unusually large number of seats. In some cases—such as in France and the United Kingdom—such parties even won a plurality of the available seats. Even in the most Euro-enthusiast countries, these parties came to power via a combination of challenges to home governments and a questioning of the mainstream consensus that has traditionally characterized the EP's political discourse. As such, it is worth considering how this legislature's members have since evolved.

The data collected for this chapter only examine those MEPs who were originally seated to the EP in 2014 and then chose to leave early—or "drop

---

3 It is important to note here that this effect is likely also enhanced by a number of the CEE countries to also be among the smaller EU member states and accordingly have fewer MEPs. MEPs from smaller states are disproportionately more likely to be top-line politicians anyway, with fewer seats available for election in their delegation. This may bias the CEE effect upward, with more important CEE politicians being more likely to have occupied EP seats to begin with, and therefore more likely to move on to the national executive and/or other EU positions.

out" of the legislature. This is also a deliberate choice. The EP is among the most volatile legislatures in the democratic world, in terms of both "between" and "within session" turnover (see Daniel and Metzger 2018). As a test of progressive ambition, however, an examination of dropout MEPs displays those politicians with the rawest ambitions to serve elsewhere. Not only did such politicians not wish to continue in the EP for further mandates, but they also deliberately chose to renounce their mandate early and seek work elsewhere.

I begin by assembling a baseline dataset of all 110 outgoing MEPs mentioned by the EP's official website, as of the close of the session in April 2019. Further investigation reveals that three of the listed MEPs did not actually leave the legislature; this is likely due to data entry errors from the EP site. One additional MEP was seated late (assuming the role of another dropout) and then left early to take up a seat in the Estonian national parliament. The remaining total yields a total population of 106 dropout MEPs from the current session who were initially elected.

From there, I examine online biographies from a variety of webpages (personal and campaign sites, Wikipedia pages, LinkedIn accounts, other social media spaces, etc.) to discern the reason for each MEP's departure. I group these reasons into broad and exclusive categories (viz., national executive, national legislative, regional and local office, EU institutions, or nonpolitical/personal reasons) that are roughly derived from the *outcome* variable in Daniel (2015) and then overlay these reasons with additional background information gathered on each MEP from Daniel and Thierse (2018). Table 5.1 displays summary descriptive statistics for the 106 dropout MEPs.

In order to assess the explanatory power of the expectations posited above, the data can also be examined at a finer grain. The first expectation was that, when MEPs left their mandate early from federal and decentralized countries, it would be primarily for personal or nonpolitical reasons. After excluding 6 of the 106 dropout MEPs due to death in office, 16 MEPs were identified as having left for personal reasons not related to further political goals. Their distribution across Norris's (2008) measure for formal federalism is shown in Table 5.2.

Table 5.1. MEP Dropouts, July 2014–April 2019

Reason for leaving	Number	Dropouts (%)
National legislature	27	25.47
National executive	35	33.02
Regional of local office	13	12.26
EU office	9	8.49
Personal reason	22	20.76
Total	106	100.00

Table 5.2. **Federalism and Early EP Departures**

	Personal reasons	*Other reasons*
Federal MEPs	13	49
Formally unitary MEPs	3	41
Total	16	90

Table 5.3. **National Legislative Early EP Departures**

Party group	*National legislature*	*Other reason*	*Total*
EPP	6	17	23
S&D	3	18	21
ALDE	5	12	17
ECR	5	9	14
Greens/EFA	0	8	8
GUE/NGL	3	8	11
EFDD	1	1	2
ENF	4	3	7
NI	0	3	3
Total	27	79	106

Although certainly not meant to be a causal test, it is interesting to note that a visibly larger proportion of MEPs from federal countries who left early did so for personal or nonpolitical reasons. For the most part, these 16 MEPs simply retired for reasons of age (one was actually the EP's oldest member at the time, well into his nineties), although five others of the set went out to future careers in nonpolitical sectors (two into banking, one to focus on family life and consulting, another into a global nongovernmental organization focused on digital openness, and the other returned to a previous position in academia). A further examination of the data suggests that the retiring MEPs oftentimes had lengthy EP careers, which itself is endogenous to predictions made about MEPs from federal systems.

Moving on to the second expectation, which anticipated that MEPs from fringe and other smaller parties would be disproportionately more likely to leave the EP early for a national legislature, Table 5.3 disaggregates dropout MEPs by their European party group (EPG). While the coding scheme allows for the reader to make their own judgments about those EPGs that are "fringe," I follow the convention developed in Daniel (2016) to consider the far-left GUE/NGL, Eurosceptic EFDD, far-right ENF, and independent NI MEPs as all being ideologically fringe. Greens/EFA and liberal ALDE MEPs are oftentimes from structurally smaller (if not ideologically extreme) national parties, so the mechanism at play here should be predominantly the same.

Here, a few quick observations can be made, namely, the total, raw number of dropouts from the largest EPP (Christian Democrats) group is not far off from those of the liberals (ALDE) and the national conservatives (ECR), even though the latter represent much smaller portions of the total number of MEPs. Even more striking is the incidence of the MEP dropouts from ideological fringe elements. Among them, dropouts from the far-left (GUE/NGL) and far-right (ENF) party groups were much more likely to be headed for national legislatures than those dropouts from the more ideologically mainstream Greens.

A closer examination of the data reveals that dropout MEPs from parties on the ideological periphery—such as Germany's *Die Linke* and *Alternative für Deutschland*, Italy's *Lega Nord*, the Netherlands' *Partij voor de Vrijheid*, and France's *Front National*—each contained a number of the MEPs headed for national legislative positions. This is in line with the theories discussed earlier. These extremist MEPs are disproportionately likely to leave the EP for national seats—as they become available—and as compared with the much larger, mainstream blocs.

On the other hand, it is further worth noting that about a fifth of MEPs leaving early for a national legislature—and the bulk of those coming from mainstream parties—were UK politicians. Historically, this is an interesting anomaly, as both Daniel (2015) and (Scarrow 1997) have noted the relatively unusual tendency for British MEPs to later find themselves in Westminster. However, in this case, UK dropout MEPs were able to take advantage of by-elections and the 2017 snap election to exit the EP for a legislative position that would not be subject to fulfillment of Brexit's article 50.[4]

The third expectation was that MEP dropouts from the mainstream and larger party groups would be disproportionately more likely to head to national executive branch positions, such as cabinet ministers, than would be MEPs from the ideologically fringe parties. Table 5.4 reveals that this is clearly the case. Beyond the general findings, 20 of the 35 MEPs featured in Table 5.4 became cabinet ministers, nine others resigned their position to run for a top national executive posting (such as president, vice president, or prime minister), and the remaining handful of MEPs moved into key bureaucratic positions—such as chairperson of their country's central bank or director of national intelligence services.

Among the many mainstream politicians, a closer reading of the national parties involved presents a laundry list of the national electoral victors from

---

4 Here, it is also interesting to note that the UK government reportedly set aside public funds as early as mid-2018 to run a 2019 EP campaign, in the event that the United Kingdom did not complete Brexit negotiations by May 2019 and was still present in the EU (and thus the EP), following the 2019 European elections.

Table 5.4.   National Executive Early EP Departures

Party group	National executive	Other reasons	Total
EPP	8	15	23
S&D	7	14	21
ALDE	7	10	17
ECR	7	7	14
Greens/EFA	4	4	8
GUE/NGL	1	10	11
EFDD	0	2	2
ENF	1	6	7
NI	0	3	3
Total	35	71	106

Table 5.5.   CEE Countries and Early EP Departures

	National executive	Other reasons
CEE country	14	11
Non-CEE country	21	60
Total	35	71

the past five years. In France, Macron's government recruited a handful of former liberal MEPs to serve in his cabinet, while the incoming Polish president, Andrzej Duda, was himself an MEP who brought a number of his national conservative (*PiS*) colleagues into national office with him, when his (now former) party also took hold of the Polish *Sejm*. Latvia's Krišjānis Kariņš now serves as his country's prime minister.

Only two of these nearly three dozen MEPs come from national parties that would regularly be considered to be on the ideological fringe: Italian deputy prime minister Matteo Salvini (formerly an MEP for the ENF group) and Greek cabinet minister Georgios Katrougalos (formerly an MEP for the GUE/ NGL group). While it was heretofore unprecedented for their national parties (*Lega Nord* in the case of Salvini and *SYRIZA* in the case of Katrougalos) to enter into national government, electoral victories have led to the main-streaming of their parties—producing exactly the sort of symbiotic feedback loop predicted by recent work on SOEs. This suggests that when a party does enter into government—however ideologically extreme—it may look to its MEPs for support and expertise.

Finally, the fourth expectation was that for those MEPs who dropped out for national executive positions, a number would come from CEE countries. This tendency is also borne out by the data in Table 5.5, with a majority of the CEE dropouts headed to the sorts of national executive positions described earlier. Beyond three from the Polish case that were already mentioned, another four of the 14 went on to cabinet-level positions in Romania; others from the CEE countries made runs for head of state or government in Estonia, Latvia, and Croatia. In each case, the EP functioned as a legitimizing force—not for an extremist viewpoint but for the sort of personal prestige or professional development needed to attract the recognition and attention of the region's consolidating party systems.

Relatedly, it is interesting that six of the nine MEPs who departed the EP for another EU post were also from CEE and post-2004 enlargement states. Of these nine, seven are now European Commissioners (Belgium, Bulgaria, Cyprus, Estonia, Latvia, Romania, and Spain) and two went on to become members of the EU Court of Auditors (Finland and Romania).

MULTIPLE DETERMINANTS FOR MEP CAREER OUTCOMES

Having taken stock of dropout MEPs from a descriptive perspective, I now move on to analyze patterns of behavior across the dropout MEPs in a way that allows for me to take multiple factors into account simultaneously, including the individual roles of MEPs, themselves. To do, I estimate a series of logistic regression models, where the dependent variable is manipulated across the various career outcomes from the dropout MEPs that were considered in Table 5.1. Independent variables in each model align with the central expectations discussed in the previous section and are collected from the earlier data sources, along with control variables used by Daniel and Thierse (2018). Here, the goal is not to confirm causality but rather to take multiple driving forces into account for career outcomes. Table 5.6 displays the results of these regressions.

Table 5.6. Multiple Logistic Regression for the Determinants of MEP Dropout Career Outcomes, 2014–2019

Dependent variable	1. Personal reason	2. National MP	3. Regional or local	4. National executive	5. EU institution
Previous national MP	−0.437 (1.02)	−1.342* (0.74)	−0.144 (0.90)	1.233* (0.63)	1.691 (1.65)
Previous national party officer	−2.103* (1.22)	0.815 (0.71)	0.201 (1.06)	−0.789 (0.70)	1.890 (1.59)
EP committee leader	3.248*** (1.16)	0.472 (0.79)	0.470 (1.26)		1.930 (2.13)
Female	1.911** (0.90)	−0.081 (0.56)	0.595 (0.76)	−0.484 (0.56)	−0.571 (1.47)

Dependent variable	1. Personal reason	2. National MP	3. Regional or local	4. National executive	5. EU institution
Age	1.126***	−0.043	0.026	−0.035	−0.086
	(0.05)	(0.03)	(0.03)	(0.03)	(0.09)
Days spent	0.000	−0.000	−0.001*	0.000	0.002**
in EP (as of	(0.00)	(0.00)	(0.00)	(0.00)	(0.00)
July 2014)					
Formally	−2.452**	0.620	−2.455**	0.943	6.960*
unitary	(1.20)	(0.67)	(1.22)	(0.64)	(3.59)
system					
National	5.328	−2.036	3.461	−3.444	11.926*
delegation	(3.34)	(2.00)	(2.50)	(2.11)	(6.33)
turnover					
(EP7)					
Party group	0.002	0.000	0.006	−0.001	0.008
size (seats)	(0.01)	(0.00)	(0.01)	(0.00)	(0.01)
Post-2004		−1.623*	1.099	0.676	1.913
enlargement		(0.96)	(1.31)	(0.79)	(2.10)
country					
Constant	−12.157***	2.639	−4.986**	2.214	−17.683***
	(3.83)	(1.61)	(2.16)	(1.50)	(7.98)
Pseudo	0.357	0.162	0.180	0.161	0.547
R-squared					
N	74	99	99	88	99

Note: Standard error in parenthesis; $*p<0.1$, $**p<0.05$, $***p<0.01$.

Starting with those MEPs who left for nonpolitical reasons, we see that not a single MEP from the 13 post-2004 enlargement countries left their position for a nonpolitical goal. This suggests support for the fourth expectation that CEE MEPs are more likely to use the EP as a step up from national legislative office, perhaps toward an even higher goal. In support of the first expectation, MEPs from unitary systems were much less likely (13.1 percent, using calculated marginal effects) to leave the EP for nonpolitical reasons. Demographically, older (1 percent per year) and female (19.22 percent) MEPs were more likely to retire or shift jobs, as were committee leaders—suggesting something of an "elder statesperson" and perhaps even a gendered effect for retirements. "Party animal" MEPs who had previously served as national party officers were also less likely to retire (9.7 percent).

Moving on to those MEPs who left early for positions in national legislatures, we see only two significant trends, with former MPs being much less likely (19.1 percent) to return to their previous jobs and post-2004 enlargement MEPs also not likely (22.15 percent) to return to national legislatures. This suggests the lack of a stepping-stone effect for CEE MEPs back into national office (similar to the fourth expectation), as well as the continued

presence of a contingent of previous national MPs among the MEPs. Returning to the first expectation in the third model, we see that MEPs from unitary
countries are highly unlikely (15.9 percent) to leave the EP for a regional or
local job, as are veteran MEPs (2 percent less likely, per term served), which
suggests a rough hierarchy of prestige among the differing levels of office.

Finally, moving on to the "top jobs" categories, we see relatively little in the
way of a discernable pattern for those MEPs headed to the national executive
branch. While MEPs with former national parliamentary experience are naturally
more likely (29.26 percent) to become a minister or chief executive, the only
other variable that comes close to a reasonable level of statistical significance
is for those MEPs from national delegations with very high degrees of interses-
sion turnover to be less predisposed to heading to national executive office.
This effect becomes highly significant, if the committee leadership variable is
excluded from the model (no committee leaders became chief executives).

Among the EU positions in the Commission, Courts, and elsewhere, we
see a mixed bag of effects. MEPs with some degree of seniority, but who
come from volatile national delegations and unitary states were among the
most likely to leave early for a top EU post. A word of caution is warranted
here, however, as there were relatively few MEPs who left early to take on
another EU post, so it would be foolish to generalize too much from the
regression results, which are driven by only a few examples (and thus, countries). While not meant to demonstrate an exhaustive and causal discussion
by any means, the regressions do allow for increased support of the bivariate
comparisons from the previous section.

DISCUSSION AND CONCLUSION

This chapter has aimed to assess the career behavior of dropout MEPs from
the current session of the EP, while contextualizing these results in light
of expectations derived from the SOE model and related theories on the
multi-level nature of European politics. By examining only those MEPs from
EP 8 who have left their seats early, it is able to bring new data to light, while
also filling a void in the SOE literature on the individual-level movements
inherent among politicians. Using original data, I am able to show that individual MEPs do indeed demonstrate a variety of the career behaviors that the
broader literature on their parties might expect from them.

Namely, when MEPs from federal systems depart early, it is oftentimes in
conjunction with personal or nonpolitical reasons—such as a career change
or a retirement. MEPs from fringe and extremist parties are more likely to
resign early for national legislative seats, as they use the EP for the resources

necessary to win national contests. MEPs from larger, mainstream parties are naturally predisposed to leaving the EP when key executive positions become available—particularly as cabinet ministers. Both of these effects suggest, however, that some MEPs are still predominantly interested in national politics—the mainstream ones are just more likely to get there (for now, anyway). Ironically, in this case, the EP may be undercutting itself: offering a home for the would-be "assassins" of the European project from within their own gates and sponsoring them handsomely for the privilege. Finally, MEPs from post-enlargement CEE countries who leave are disproportionally headed for top-line executive careers at home or even to powerful individual postings within the EU.

Naturally, the data and methodology employed for this chapter are very tentative and mostly inductive. I have deliberatively shied away from conclusive causal language and have mostly eschewed a more traditional analysis in favor of a review of the descriptive data. However, at the same time, the present contribution is meant to be both "theory building" and illuminating for a number of the mechanisms that the literature might expect for dropout MEPs to display. As we head into the new 2019–2024 session of the EP, it will be interesting to see how these sources of early departure align with the career behaviors of MEPs at the end of their 2019 mandates.

BIBLIOGRAPHY

van der Brug, Wouter and Claes H. de Vreese. 2016. *(Un)intended Consequences of EU Parliamentary Elections*. Oxford: Oxford University Press.

Bytzek, Evelyn. 2015. "The Nexus between National Party Preferences and State Elections—a Long-Term Perspective." *German Politics*, 24 (1): 85–98.

Cutts, David, Matthew Goodwin, and Caitlin Milazzo. 2017. "Defeat of the People's Army? The 2015 British General Election and the UK Independence Party (UKIP)." *Electoral Studies*, 48 (August): 70–83.

Daniel, William T. 2015. *Career Behaviour and the European Parliament: All Roads Lead through Brussels?* Oxford: Oxford University Press.

Daniel, William T. 2016. "First-Order Contests for Second-Order Parties? Differentiated Candidate Nomination Strategies in European Parliament Elections." *Journal of European Integration*, 38 (7): 807–822.

Daniel, William T. and Shawna K. Metzger. 2018. "Within or between Jobs? Determinants of Membership Volatility in the European Parliament, 1979–2014." *The Journal of Legislative Studies*, 24 (1): 90–108.

Daniel, William T. and Stefan Thierse. 2018. "Individual Determinants for the Selection of Group Coordinators in the European Parliament." *JCMS: Journal of Common Market Studies*, 56 (4): 939–954.

Filimon, Luiza Maria. 2015. "Beneficiaries of the Second Order Election Model: Radical Right Parties in the European Parliament." *Europolity—Continuity and Change in European Governance*, 9 (2): 193–223.

Geffen, Robert van. 2016. "Impact of Career Paths on MEPs' Activities." *JCMS: Journal of Common Market Studies*, 54 (4): 1017–32.

Giebler, Heiko, and Aiko Wagner. 2015. "Contrasting First- and Second-Order Electoral Behaviour: Determinants of Individual Party Choice in European and German Federal Elections." *German Politics*, 24 (1): 46–66.

Golder, Sona Nadenichek, Ignacio Lago, André Blais, Elisabeth Gidengil, and Thomas Gschwend. 2017. *Multi-Level Electoral Politics: Beyond the Second-Order Election Model*. http://public.eblib.com/choice/publicfullrecord.aspx?p=5061702.

Hix, Simon, Abdul Noury, and Gérard Roland. 2007. *Democratic Politics in the European Parliament*. Cambridge: Cambridge University Press.

Koepke, Jason R., and Nils Ringe. 2006. "The Second-Order Election Model in an Enlarged Europe." *European Union Politics*, 7 (3): 321–346.

Kreppel, Amie. 2002. *The European Parliament and Supranational Party System: A Study in Institutional Development*. Cambridge: Cambridge University Press.

Marien, Sofie, Ruth Dassonneville, and Marc Hooghe. 2015. "How Second Order Are Local Elections? Voting Motives and Party Preferences in Belgian Municipal Elections." *Local Government Studies*, 41 (6): 898–916.

Matland, Richard and Donley Studlar. 2004. "Determinants of Legislative Turnover: A Cross-National Analysis." *British Journal of Political Science*, 34: 87–108.

Nielsen, Julie Hassing and Mark N. Franklin. 2016. *The Eurosceptic 2014 European Parliament Elections: Second Order or Second Rate?* London: Palgrave Macmillan.

Norris, Pippa. 2008. *Driving Democracy: Do Power-Sharing Institutions Work?* Cambridge: Cambridge University Press.

Polsby, Nelson. 1968. "The Institutionalization of the U.S. House of Representatives." *The American Political Science Review*, 62 (1): 144–168.

Prosser, Christopher. 2016a. "Do Local Elections Predict the Outcome of the Next General Election? Forecasting British General Elections from Local Election National Vote Share Estimates." *Electoral Studies*, 41 (March): 274–278.

Prosser, Christopher. 2016b. "Second Order Electoral Rules and National Party Systems: The Duvergerian Effects of European Parliament Elections." *European Union Politics*, 17 (3): 366–386.

Reif, Karlheinz and Hermann Schmitt. 1980. "Nine Second☐order National Elections—a Conceptual Framework for the Analysis of European Election Results." *European Journal of Political Research*, 8 (1): 3–44.

Reungoat, Emmanuelle. 2015. "Mobilizing Europe in National Competition: The Case of the French Front National." *International Political Science Review*, 36 (3): 296–310.

Ripoll Servent, Ariadna. 2017. *The European Parliament*. London: Macmillan International Higher Education.

Samuels, David. 2003. *Ambition, Federalism, and Legislative Politics in Brazil*. Cambridge: Cambridge University Press.

Sbragia, Alberta M. 1992. Ed. Euro-Politics: Institutions and Policymaking in the "New" *European Community*. Brookings Institution Press.

Sbragia, Alberta M. 1993. "The European Community: A Balancing Act." *Publius: The Journal of Federalism*, 23 (3): 23–38.

Sbragia, Alberta M. 2005. "Territory, Electorates and Markets in the US: The Construction of Democratic Federalism and Its Implications for the EU." In *Democracy and Federalism in the European Union and the United States: Exploring Post-National Governance*, edited by Sergio Fabbrini, 93–103. London: Routledge.

Scarrow, Susan E. 1997. "Political Career Paths and the European Parliament." *Legislative Studies Quarterly*, 22 (2): 253–263.

Schakel, Arjan H. 2015. "How to Analyze Second-Order Election Effects? A Refined Second-Order Election Model." *Comparative European Politics*, 13 (6): 636–655.

Schlesinger, Joseph A. 1966. *Ambition and Politics: Political Careers in the United States*. Chicago: Rand McNally.

Schmitt, Hermann. 2005. The European Parliament Elections of June 2004: Still Second-Order? *West European Politics*, 28 (3): 650–679.

Schmitt, Hermann and Eftichia Teperoglu. 2017. "The Study of Less Important Elections." In *The SAGE Handbook of Electoral Behaviour*, edited by Kai Arzheimer, Jocelyn Evans, and Michael S. Lewis-Beck, 56–79. Los Angeles: SAGE.

Schulte-Cloos, Julia. 2018. "Do European Parliament Elections Foster Challenger Parties' Success on the National Level?" *European Union Politics*, 19 (3): 408–426.

Träger, Hendrik, Michael Kaeding, and Niko Switek. 2015. Die Europawahl 2014 als second-order election. In Michael Kaeding (ed.) Die Europawahl 2014: Spitzenkandidaten, Protestparteien, Nichtwähler (pp. 33–44). Wiesbaden: Springer Fachmedien Wiesbaden.

Whitaker, Richard. 2014. "Tenure, Turnover and Careers in the European Parliament: MEPs as Policy-Seekers." *Journal of European Public Policy*: 21 (10): 1509–1527.

Yordanova, Nikoleta. 2013. *Organising the European Parliament: The Role of the Committees and Their Legislative Influence*. Colchester: London: ECPR Press.

Chapter 6

Building a Bridge to Europe?

National Legislators' Views on Their Role in the European Union

Lauren K. Perez

The European Union (EU) has continually evolved, meaning that our efforts to understand it, especially in comparative perspective, must continue to evolve with it. As Alberta Sbragia wrote, "The evolution of institutions, the allocation of power among institutions, and the questions of legitimacy linked to such allocation are critical to the governance of the Community and its policy capacity" (Sbragia 1992b, 257), so it is important to understand these changes and where they may go in the future. One such change, especially in the past decade, is the increased involvement of the national parliaments in the legislative process.

This change has occurred, at least in part, as an effort to increase the legitimacy of EU policy-making. The formal role that the Lisbon Treaty gives to the national parliaments (more later) is one of the changes made to the EU's institutions in an effort to reduce the EU's democratic deficit or the sense of disconnection between Europe's citizens and its institutions. "Not only do [practical politicians] acknowledge [the democratic deficit] rhetorically, but they acknowledge it by consistently changing the institutional arrangements which govern the making of legislation" (Sbragia 2005, 169). Since the national parliaments are closer to citizens, they are one potential bridge between citizens and the EU. This chapter builds on a series of interviews with national legislators to get a better sense of how they understand their role in the EU and what potential role they see in the future.

NATIONAL PARLIAMENTS IN THE EUROPEAN UNION: A COMPARATIVE PERSPECTIVE

Combining the perspectives of democratic accountability and comparative federalism, Europe's national parliaments have a greater potential role in the EU than we might imagine subfederal parliaments having in most federal systems. In many federal systems, such as the United States, subnational politicians do not simultaneously serve at the federal level. Without a formal role and direct chains of accountability, most subnational influence on the national level comes through informal and party relationships. However, in the EU, national ministers serve on the Council of Ministers, making this institution more like the German *Bundesrat*, where government ministers from the subfederal level (the German *Länder* or the EU's member states) serve in a federal legislative body. Referring to the European Community, the former name of the EU, Sbragia (1992a, 2) highlighted this difference: "The governments of the twelve members of the Community exert immeasurably more influence on Community policies than American state governments exert on federal policies within the United States." This greater role for national governments creates a potential role for the legislatures to which they are accountable. The standard chains of scrutiny and accountability that make national ministers responsible to the national parliament on domestic or foreign affairs should also hold at the European level.

Despite these structural differences, Europe's national parliaments have not always played much of a role in the EU's legislative process. That role has generally increased over time as concerns about the democratic deficit have become more prominent and EU legislation has touched more policy areas. Norton (1996) outlines three historical phases for the national parliaments, showing progress toward greater involvement. From the EU's founding to the mid-1980s, there was essentially a period of noninvolvement and little interest in involvement.[1] During this period, the national parliaments' role was relatively comparable to that of most subfederal legislatures, since it was essentially nonexistent or based on individual relationships with ministers or members of the European Parliament (MEPs).

During Norton's (1996) second phase, in the second half of the 1980s and into the 1990s, national parliaments began to fight for more information about EU policy-making, to establish EU affairs committees and procedures to process information, and to influence the Council by monitoring their governments. In the final phase, they have become a potential solution to the democratic deficit and gained additional powers. For example, the Lisbon Treaty offered the first formal recognition of the national parliaments. The Commission now sends proposed legislation and other information directly

---

1 The clear exception to early noninvolvement is that some national legislators served in the European Parliament (EP) prior to direct elections in 1979. These individual members were clearly involved with the EU, but the parliamentary chambers as a whole were not.

to the parliaments and must respond to opinions it receives from them (the "political dialogue"). The parliaments also have a formal role in preserving the EU's principle of subsidiarity, or the idea that legislative decisions should be taken at the closest possible level to citizens. Parliaments now have eight weeks after legislation is proposed to provide a "reasoned opinion" arguing that the legislation violates subsidiarity, and if enough of them do so, they may be able to delay or help block legislation (the "Early Warning System").[2] These changes allow the national parliaments to serve as a direct link between the citizens and the EU institutions (Cooper 2012), and as such, they are the only actors that "combine a close attachment to the citizens" with formal powers at the EU level (Neyer 2012, 38). During these two phases, the differences between the role of Europe's national parliaments and that of most subfederal parliaments became more distinct. Another important difference is that most European citizens still view the national parliaments as the primary legislature that represents them, giving them more legitimacy than most subfederal legislatures.

However, it is worth noting, as Fabbrini (this volume, chapter 11) does, that the ability of a single national parliament to block or drastically alter EU legislation is limited, since each parliament can only influence one minister and Council decisions are made collegially. Additionally, these efforts toward further involvement have been met with a variety of challenges, including political, procedural, institutional, and ideological ones (discussed later). Opinion is not necessarily united on whether the national parliaments should be involved, and it is certainly not unanimous on how they should do so. These differences of opinion exist within parliaments and member states as well as between them.

Given these challenges and differences of opinion, what role is there for the national parliaments in the EU? In particular, how do national legislators view their role and what potential future role do they envision? While the remainder of this chapter does not directly compare the EU's national parliaments to subfederal parliaments elsewhere, it aims to understand how these legislators view their role. Having a better understanding of these views could inform future attempts at more direct comparison, while also highlighting some important differences. The role of national parliaments speaks to governance questions facing the EU, both those raised by the democratic deficit and those raised by potential reforms to reduce it, such as those discussed by Fabbrini (this volume, chapter 11).

---

2 It should be noted, however, that the requirements for coordination are quite high and the parliaments have not had much formal success yet.

COMPARING PARLIAMENTARY CHAMBERS

Much of the existing work on parliamentary involvement in the EU has been done at the parliamentary chamber level. There is important variation at this level, with different chambers showing different patterns of involvement. Auel and Hönig (2014) divide the chambers into four main types. The first are "policy shapers," who focus primarily on issuing resolutions and mandates to affect their governments' positions on EU legislation. The second are "debating arenas," who focus on public debates. Third, "Commission watchdogs" focus on sending opinions on proposed legislation to the Commission as part of the political dialogue and the Early Warning System. Finally, there are the "scrutiny laggards," who could technically be put into the aforementioned groups, but whose overall activity is so low that they are better grouped together.

Parliamentary chambers also have different powers to get involved in EU affairs. The *Observatory of Parliaments after the Lisbon Treaty* project scored each parliament on its institutional strength in EU affairs. These scores are based on three dimensions: how much access each parliament has to information about EU legislation and proceedings, and their government's position on those; the level of parliamentary infrastructure, based on the European affairs committee, the role of other committees, and so forth; and the strength of the parliament's oversight and influence rights over its government's position on EU affairs (Auel, Rozenberg, and Tacea 2015a). Looking at average scores from 2010 to 2012, these range from a score above 0.8 for Finland to a score around 0.2 for Belgium (Auel, Rozenberg, and Tacea 2015b).

Most of the explanations for different patterns of involvement have focused on two main factors: the strength of parliamentary institutions, both generally and for EU affairs, and the level of public Euroscepticism. In general, stronger parliaments vis-à-vis their executive and those with stronger institutions have been more involved (Bergman 1997; Pahre 1997; Bergman 2000; Martin 2000; Maurer and Wessels 2001; Rozenberg 2002; Raunio 2005; Saalfeld 2005; Kietz 2006; Hamerly 2007; Raunio 2009; Karlas 2012). More specifically, strengths and weaknesses of government/policy scrutiny for domestic policy seem to be mirrored for EU policy (Dimitrakopoulos 2001; Damgaard and Jensen 2005). However, in more recent periods, especially during the Euro crisis, institutional strength on crisis policy areas and on EU matters was important, while general institutional strength was not (Auel and Höing 2015; Auel, Rozenberg, and Tacea 2015b; Auel, Eisele, and Kinski 2016). Higher levels of public Euroscepticism have also strongly predicted greater involvement (Bergman 1997; Pahre 1997; Bergman 2000; Raunio and Wiberg 2000; Rozenberg 2002; Kietz 2006; Hamerly 2007; Winzen 2013;

Auel, Rozenberg, and Tacea 2015b; Auel, Eisele, and Kinski 2016), although some work suggests this effect was less important during the Euro crisis (Auel and Höing 2015).

CASE SELECTION

I chose cases for my interviews that were spread across these various dimensions. The interview data used in the remainder of this chapter[3] come from five member states: Belgium, Denmark, Germany, Poland, and the United Kingdom. Using the four types described earlier, Germany and the United Kingdom are both policy shapers and debating arenas, Denmark is a policy shaper, Poland is a (partial) Commission watchdog and a scrutiny laggard, and Belgium is a scrutiny laggard (Auel and Höing 2014). In terms of institutional strength on EU affairs, Germany ranks second among twenty-seven countries with a score of about 0.8, Denmark is fifth (0.7), the United Kingdom ranks twelfth (0.5), Poland ranks eighteenth (0.4), and Belgium is last (0.2) (Auel, Rozenberg, and Tacea 2015b). In terms of Euroscepticism, Poland had the most positive vision of the EU of all twenty-seven countries in 2014, with 61 percent of respondents reporting a positive image of the EU and only 6 percent reporting a negative image. Ranked according to percentage positive, Belgium (42 percent positive, 22 percent negative) is tenth and above the EU average (39 percent positive, 22 percent negative), while Denmark (39 percent positive, 18 percent negative) and Germany (38 percent positive, 20 percent negative) are fifteenth and sixteenth, respectively, just below the average. The United Kingdom is third from the bottom (30 percent positive, 32 percent negative; above Cyprus and Greece).[4] These countries are also relatively spread out across the waves of EU accession. They include small and large states, federal and unitary states, bicameral and unicameral legislatures, and more majoritarian and more consensual systems. Together, these legislatures should be fairly representative of the larger group.

---

3 The interviews referenced in this chapter are drawn from a larger sample of 170 interviews I conducted in five capitals (Berlin, Brussels, Copenhagen, London, and Warsaw) with legislators and their staff. The interviewees come from almost all political parties represented in these legislatures and served on a wide array of committees. There was an extra effort to speak with those legislators on the European Affairs committees, as well as with those who had also been ministers and could discuss both sides of parliamentary oversight. The broader sample also included some MEPs, subnational legislators, and many of the national parliamentary representatives to the EU. The interviews were conducted over three periods: May–June 2013, September–December 2014, and June–July 2015.

4 Based on the fall 2014 Eurobarometer survey, in order to coincide with the interview data. The question asked, "In general, does the EU conjure up for you a very positive, fairly positive, neutral, fairly negative, or very negative image?" I combined both "very positive" and "fairly positive" into a total positive category, and did the same for the negative categories.

COMPARING INDIVIDUAL LEGISLATORS: TWO DIMENSIONS OF OPINION

Why Individual Legislators?

There is clearly variation between parliamentary chambers, but this chapter focuses on the variation between individual legislators and members of parliament (MPs). Institutions are important, but institutions do not exist in a vacuum; they have to be created, utilized, and strengthened. Institutions can create opportunities for involvement, but legislators still need to want to be involved, especially to create or strengthen future institutions. Therefore, it is important to understand the opinions and motivations of individuals that function within and help shape these institutions. Auel, Rozenberg, and Tacea (2015b) make a similar argument: "Our general assumption is that European activities depend on both the institutional capacities of the parliaments and MPs' motivation to act."

For example, all of the parliaments have European affairs committees. However, are their members active? Do they put in the work required to meaningfully contribute to EU legislation? The Irish *Dail* was one of the first parliaments to create such a committee in the 1970s, but most parliamentarians at the time saw it as "a complete backwater" and "its impact was very limited and its work was generally far in arrears" (O'Halpin 1996, 128–129). Similarly, a member of the Belgian *Sénat*'s committee remarked that it was a "stepchild" and an "extra committee," which was not always attended by other members (interview 9).

Other tools, like questions or debates, exist in all parliaments. But the question remains whether legislators are motivated to use them for EU issues. When they have the opportunity to question ministers, do they ask about the EU or only about national issues? Do they choose to speak in and attend EU-focused debates? Therefore, this chapter tries to understand how national legislators view their role within the EU and its future potential.

A Typology of Involvement

Based on my interviews, I identify two main dimensions along which legislators' opinions differ: how interested a legislator is in being involved in European affairs and how optimistic or pessimistic they are about the practicality of involvement. These are separate from the ideological dimensions of what they should try to achieve with their influence, which likely varies with party and ideology. Using these two dimensions, I create a typology that separates legislators into four main groups (see Table 6.1). Those who show little interest and are pessimistic about involvement's practicality are "disinterested

Table 6.1. Four Types of National Legislators' Opinions on EU Involvement

	Low interest	*High interest*
Pessimistic	Disinterested pessimist	Interested pessimist
Optimistic	Disinterested optimist	Interested optimist

pessimists," while those who are low on interest but more optimistic are "disinterested optimists." Similarly, among those legislators with a higher interest in involvement, there are both "interested pessimists" and "interested optimists." I discuss the two dimensions in more detail later, explaining many of the reasons legislators gave for their levels of interest and practicality. Toward the end of the chapter, I discuss an example of a legislator in each group and discuss which legislators are more likely to fall into each category.

Interest in Involvement

Legislators varied substantially in their interest in EU involvement. Some legislators recognized that they were national legislators and thought they should focus on national issues. Others recognized how much policy comes from the EU level and thought it was essential for them to influence that policy, especially as close representatives of their constituents. These differences of opinion were not as influenced by Euroscepticism as one might imagine; both Europhiles and Eurosceptics wanted to be involved, although they obviously differed in what they would do with that involvement. However, having a particularly strong opinion on Europe, whichever opinion it was, seemed to drive interest in EU involvement. The other main factor driving interest in involvement seemed to be the sectoral policy areas that legislators specialized in. Those members who worked on areas with a lot of EU legislation, such as the environment or agriculture, were more likely to show an interest in European policy-making. Similarly, those on the European affairs committees also tended to be more interested. There was a fair amount of within-parliament variation, but in general, interest was more consistent among the German and Danish legislators than in other countries.

Those legislators who were disinterested in EU involvement provided a few reasons why they did not think such involvement was relevant or worthwhile. These reasons mostly centered on the idea that they had enough national work to do; their role was a national one and dealing with European issues was the role of the EP. If they felt particularly strongly about a topic, they could make a recommendation to the EP, but otherwise they do "not really play a role" (interview 8).

Others also expressed disinterest because they sensed legislation had already been decided at the EU level. As one legislator said, they have "almost no role" because they were "faced with things that have already happened" and the main discussions within the parliament or party were to discuss how they could not actually do anything (interview 5). Legislators also raised this as a concern about the practicality of additional involvement, so it will be discussed more later.

A philosophical or normative concern was that Europe is already too dependent on national interests. As one senator said, "It is not a Europe of the citizens, but one of governments and sometimes of parliaments" (interview 13). Another MP argued that ministers on the Council have to report to national parliaments and electorates, which makes it difficult for them to make more "European" decisions. They become "national egoists." He thought this made the EU more unproductive and inefficient, such as through national rebates. Therefore, he was against any changes that would bring more national egoism into the equation, including more parliamentary involvement (interview 10).

Other legislators expressed interest in their current role but not in an increased future role. A *Land* staff member, who assisted with preparations for *Bundesrat* meetings on Europe, described the current role as "constructive" and "fitting for their role in the whole system" (interview 23). Similarly, a member of the House of Lords thought the chamber "fulfills its role well. It has always been good at committee work, especially on the EU, and performs careful scrutiny of both major and minor matters" (interview 36). Additionally, many legislators thought there had been recent improvement, especially via dialogue with the Commission and the Early Warning System. This was a "good role for the national parliaments," allowing them to "turn on the yellow light" (interview 10). Other legislators discussed this subsidiarity monitoring as their "most important role" (interview 14).

Legislators who were interested in more involvement provided many reasons for why it was important. They most often cited the democratic deficit. Some legislators, especially the more Eurosceptic ones, had particularly strong opinions on the EU's lack of democracy. One British MP went so far as to say the EU has "robbed men on the street of the right to govern" (interview 34), while a Belgian MP called the EU "a civilized dictator" (interview 3). While these views were certainly on the stronger end, many legislators recognized a problem and saw their own institutions as a potential solution.

One MP explained that "national parliaments have an important role, because their job or task is to bring the discussion from Brussels to the member state and its citizens." She thought it was disgraceful that MPs do not take responsibility for EU legislation and argued that blaming the EU was no longer acceptable, as legislators now "have the opportunities for influence, even if they don't win every time." She then cited a recent example of EU legislation that banned a certain type of lamp, for which German politicians blamed Brussels. However, in truth, German politicians had asked for that legislation. Despite this, she saw signs of change, such as public *Bundestag* debates about the EU's proposed free trade agreements with Canada and the United States (interview 22).

A related argument for more involvement was that the EP was not a sufficient democratic representative. Some legislators argued that there is no real European *demos*, so the EP did not really have a group to represent (interview 33). A parliamentary staff member raised the issue that EP constituencies are much larger than national constituencies, so MEPs have a more distant link to the people (interview 18). Another argument combined democratic concerns with the powers of the EP itself. A Polish senator argued that the EP is not "like a real parliament" because its elections are not the same as national elections and because it cannot adopt any laws it would like but rather has to rely on the Commission to propose legislation. He believed these issues, combined with the precedence of EU legislation over national law, created a "crisis" of democracy (interview 11).

Others specifically linked further national parliamentary involvement to Euroscepticism and public acceptance of the EU. For example, an EU-focused staff member for one German *Land* argued that parliaments had been particularly important during the Euro crisis. She argued that, because the *Bundestag* was given such a substantial role, the public felt "they had a foot in the door." She believed public opinion would have been much more negative otherwise, even if the outcome did not change much. She thought the national parliaments could and should continue to be involved in order to make the people feel represented and argued this was why even the heads of government were promoting the national parliaments' involvement (interview 21). A German MP echoed the importance of the *Bundestag*'s involvement, discussing how she thought public tools like debates could potentially enhance the opinion of the EU (interview 22).

The second broad set of reasons legislators gave for interest in more involvement had to do with their role over policy. Many legislators spoke about how much national legislation comes from the EU—most who offered a number said somewhere between 50 and 80 percent. For example, one Polish senator discussed a proliferation of European legislation, such that the national parliament's legislative activity was slowly disappearing. If they still wanted to affect policy, they would have to be more involved with EU policy-making (interview 11). Another MP mentioned that the Eurozone crisis had highlighted the importance and urgency of EU involvement. During this period, working on EU policy was a "more demanding process, but also a more worthwhile one" (interview 1).

Legislators also thought they had a substantial added value, since they are "on the ground." They could relate practical experiences with legislation back to the EU and exchange experiences with one another (interview 17).

This experience was especially important for potential reforms to existing legislation. One staff member argued that the EP "does not have a clue" about the implementation of EU legislation and does not have enough staff to find out about it. Therefore, national parliaments' knowledge was necessary for them to make the best reforms and the parliaments did need to be involved (interview 21).

Legislators also thought there had been increased interest in recent years and that this would continue. For example, a Belgian senator discussed how interest in both the EU and EU-focused debates had increased over the past ten or twenty years, and "people in the parliament have learned to care about Europe" (interview 8). Similarly, a staff member for a German *Land* explained that the national parliaments, including the *Bundesrat*, are increasingly important in EU policy-making, because of both increased self-awareness and realizations of the EU's importance. She said that even Germany's regional parliaments want more information and influence in Brussels, so parliaments at every level are aware they have to play a role (interview 19). Members of the subnational Flemish Parliament expressed a similar desire for a greater role.

OPTIMISM AND PESSIMISM ABOUT INVOLVEMENT

The other main dimension of opinion was how optimistic or pessimistic legislators were about the practicality of involvement in European policy-making. All legislators recognized some challenges to involvement, including the amount of work, knowledge, and time required to be properly informed about both EU and national issues, as well as the lack of electoral incentives for EU involvement. However, those who were more optimistic had reasons for why these could potentially be overcome and suggestions for what practical involvement could look like. Legislators' country or parliamentary chamber did seem to factor into their optimism, since it affected the resources they had at their disposal as well as their sense of efficacy on EU matters. For example, legislators from Germany and Denmark often provided some of the most tangible future steps, and theirs are some of the parliaments with the greatest resources and the highest institutional strength on European affairs (Auel, Rozenberg, and Tacea 2015b).

Almost all legislators mentioned some challenges to parliamentary involvement, either as a reason why the current role was probably the most that was practical or as obstacles to overcome. Some of these challenges were fairly general, such as the difficulty of coordinating with other national parliaments due to linguistic and cultural differences (interview 16). There is also a general problem of time and organization (interview 16), or a question of "bandwidth" (interview 33), as legislators already have a lot of national-level work. This is especially true since many legislators emphasized the need to get involved earlier in the EU's legislative process in order to have more influence and catching things early requires even more effort.

Earlier and greater involvement also often requires institutional changes within the parliament. One Belgian MP described their role as "practically, quite limited," not because the EU level forbids it, but rather because their own parliament had not sufficiently changed its working habits (interview 4). One of his fellow MPs echoed these ideas, explaining how the ministers come to them after Council meetings but consultation beforehand would allow them to "have a say" in Belgium's position. However, the Belgian parliament was not "structurally" set up for this arrangement (interview 5).

Some challenges were practical, such as difficulties finding agreement between two chambers of a bicameral parliament (interview 32). This problem is magnified in federal states with subnational parliaments, like Belgium, and certainly across the EU, given the total number of chambers (interview 31). Involving more chambers can also cause delays. In Belgium, the subnational parliaments are involved in ratifying treaties. This was cited as a reason why, in June 2013, Belgium had still not ratified the Fiscal Compact[5] over a year after its signature (interview 6). Belgium did not ratify the treaty until March 28, 2014 and was the final Eurozone member to do so (Finance 2016).

Other challenges were more fundamental, such as getting the media to cover European matters, which is necessary to communicate information to the public (interview 24). This lack of media interest may be a main reason why some legislators are not motivated to spend time on European issues (interview 2). One parliamentary advisor on EU issues expressed that legislators cannot deal with local, national, and European affairs simultaneously, and people do not care whether their representatives are active on Europe. Such involvement "doesn't pay off at the national level, so you have to be a really well-known politician who will win reelection anyway" (interview 6). The relative unimportance of European matters, due to the lack of electoral connection on these issues, can then get institutionalized. One Belgian senator mentioned how other members often miss EU committee meetings but not just because of personal disinterest. Rather, the committee counts as an "extra" committee beyond their other obligations and its meetings are often held "at impossible days and hours" (interview 9).

The media attention problem is magnified by timing and coordination problems. Parliaments have the most potential to modify legislation early in the process. At this point, the media often shows no interest, since it would

---

5 Formally, the Treaty on Stability, Coordination and Governance in the Economic and Monetary Union, also known as the Fiscal Stability Treaty, was signed on March 2, 2012.

need to report on Commission proposals and/or EU negotiations. However, by the time the media does get interested, the legislation is often already finalized and it is too late for the national parliament (or even the government) to change things (interview 28).

The problem may be even greater in the United Kingdom. One British MP discussed how for many citizens, the EU had become a "proxy for racism," especially around this time, when migration was a major issue. When they try to explain the truth and benefits of Europe to citizens, they "simply aren't listening." However, "this is probably our fault" because of the establishment's tendency to blame Europe for unpopular policies (interview 38). A Danish MP also mentioned the British press: "There the press is horrible; the people know very little and they will believe ridiculous things." While he thought the "Danish press cannot really be blamed, as they still cover the EU more than the public wants them to," public apathy was a serious concern. He said that when he plans to talk about the EU, he does not announce the subject ahead of time because he does "not want people to stay away." He thought the two main reasons MPs do not get involved in European affairs are that people do not want to hear about it and that most parties are split internally over EU affairs (interview 29).

Another concern is that Europe and its issues are difficult for many legislators to understand (interview 20). Even an EU policy advisor discussed how the complexity of EU legislation makes it harder for legislators to understand it and be fully involved (interview 25). Another EU advisor complained that MPs were sometimes like "bad students" in that they did not care and always had a complaint—that the information the advisors sent was "too late, too technical, too little info, etc." More broadly, EU issues are "not sexy" (interview 6). Many or most legislators do not know enough about the EU, while "a very little group knows a hell of a lot" (interview 26). Based on similar reasoning, another MP called the EU committee the "committee of the nerds" (interview 2). One Danish MP desired a mechanism that would force every MP to do some sort of EU-based internship so they would all be more familiar with it (interview 24).

Just as those individual legislators who were more focused on Europe often expressed frustration with fellow legislators who were not, those from some of the more involved parliaments, such as in Denmark and Germany, were also frustrated by the lack of involvement from other national parliaments. Uneven involvement across parliaments makes cooperation more difficult. For example, when they have tried to contact other national parliaments, they are often not as prepared. The Germans spend a lot of money on EU involvement (primarily via staff, in both Brussels and Berlin) and others do not (interview 18). A member of the House of Lords expressed a similar concern, and suggested some of the bigger countries could help some of the smaller ones with fewer resources. For example, the United Kingdom could help Cyprus and Malta as Commonwealth countries (interview 37).

Legislators also cited the difficulty of making a substantial impact as a reason for not getting more involved. For example, one of the most tangible powers the national parliaments have is the Early Warning System. However, even this step was arguably "only a little step, not a big step" (interview 12). Similarly, a senator who had attended a policy meeting in Brussels expressed frustration that the EU still made the final decision. While he thought the meeting had opened the debate, he had no impression they could have a real impact. He feared attempts to fix this might make the relationship too complicated (interview 11).

Such meetings are also often seen as inefficient. A German MP argued that interparliamentary meetings are just talking, accomplish nothing, and there is no benefit. She thought they needed to be more focused, that there "should be three topics, not one hundred" and that they do not need to "discuss if the world is round." She was also frustrated because she wanted more informal exchanges that might produce real developments rather than just the formal discussions (interview 20). A Polish senator agreed these meetings were "superficial" and said he wanted them to "stop talking and say something" (interview 13).

Another challenge is that the EU's legislative process takes too long and there is a mismatch between the EU and national timelines. The EU's legislative process sometimes takes years, and "politics of whole countries may change in that time" (interview 11). A Danish MP remarked that the national parliamentary terms are short compared to the EU's legislative process. All legislators want to show they have accomplished something, and this may be difficult to do in European affairs, especially if legislation takes longer than the parliamentary term. The length is another reason why it is difficult to keep legislators interested in European issues (interview 24).

These mismatched timelines also limit coordination between national legislators and MEPs. One Danish MP said each of these groups felt "the other doesn't really care about the things they're working on" or the other group is "discussing things at a weird time when they are not relevant" (interview 1). To the extent there is coordination, it often occurs within parties. For example, an MP from the New Flemish Alliance said they had intraparty talks with MEPs on a weekly basis and their assistants had good access to the party's MEP's assistants (interview 7). However, if this coordination is occurring at the party level, it creates the potential for quite a lot of within-country variation as well as across countries.

Despite these challenges, some legislators still found reason to be optimistic about a greater future role and offered a number of options for what forms it could take. One of these began with a complaint about the current role: the

Early Warning System was seemingly ineffective and only a negative power. At the far end of the spectrum, one MP said it was "a waste of time" and was a "pacifier" that was "a way of keeping us busy and quiet" that "doesn't bring us anywhere." She also thought it was "wrong in the whole sense" because their role should be more proactive. She suggested that they could do this through more formalized and substantial contributions on the content of proposed legislation as well as via the introduction of a "green card" that proposed new legislation (interview 26). The idea of such a green card was raised in the *Folketing*'s report on twenty-three recommendations for further national parliamentary involvement (European Affairs Committee of the Danish Parliament 2014) and the House of Lords led an effort at introducing an informal green card encouraging the Commission to propose food waste legislation, which EU committee chairpersons in sixteen other parliamentary chambers co-signed.[6]

A consistent theme from many legislators, especially in Denmark and Germany, was the need to get involved earlier in the process when there was still more room for debate and negotiation. One Danish MP spoke about how they initially tried to resolve this by getting involved when legislation is on the Council agenda. However, by this point, much of the debate has already occurred in working groups and COREPER. Therefore, they have now instituted an "early mandate system," where the minister comes to the European Affairs Committee to get a mandate for the ministry's bargaining position as soon as working group meetings start, rather than just before the Council meeting (interview 25).

This step was a clear improvement and the Danish parliament already has some of the strongest institutions for EU affairs, but legislators still spoke about continued improvements to this system. For example, one MP who had both been on the Danish EU committee and had been a minister needing to get a mandate from it said one reality of the early mandate system was that it ended up giving ministers a broader mandate and therefore giving the committee (and parliament) less say. At the beginning, this makes sense, since it is not clear where negotiations will go and the EU-level actors need more room to maneuver. Then, the minister is supposed to return to the committee to get a stronger, more specific mandate as negotiations progress. However, in reality, they rarely return and end up retaining the broad mandate. She suggested tightening up this process and having ministers return would make oversight more effective (interview 26).

Another main area legislators discussed as an option for further involvement was to get the sectoral committees (i.e., those focused on policy areas

---

6 Submitted by the House of Lords to the Commission as a political dialogue opinion on July 22, 2015.

such as education or agriculture) more involved in monitoring EU legislation. This process is called "mainstreaming," since it treats EU legislation more like any other "mainstream" legislation, rather than as a separate domain reserved for the EU committee. Such a process would help integrate EU issues into national politics. One MP, when she was the EU spokesperson, took steps toward this by working with sectoral spokespeople on EU issues (interview 24). There has been some increased involvement, at least in the Danish *Folketing*, from those committees whose policy areas see a lot of EU policies, such as Agriculture and Fisheries (interview 26). Mainstreaming has the potential to increase the quality of parliamentary involvement, since the EU committee members tend to be "generalists" (interview 27), while sectoral committee members provide more expertise in their policy areas (interview 25). Such a process would also reduce the EU committee's work-load, allowing it to focus on broad changes, like treaty revisions (interview 10). One MP even said the ideal model would be to abolish the EU committee (interview 30). Mainstreaming would also help institutionalize the process of the parliament giving the government opinions on EU legislation and would help inform all legislators about EU issues (interview 10).

Yet another area of recent improvement, and potential future improvement, was cooperation between parliaments and with the EP. For example, a Polish senator discussed the "important strategic discussions" they can have with other legislators at COSAC (a meeting of representatives of all national parliaments and the EP), which can help them find a common position the EP can express at the European level and national parliaments can bring back to their governments (interview 14). However, others were less satisfied. One MP commented, "We have COSAC and the Early Warning System—that is ok;" they overall function well but much more was needed (interview 30). Others discussed that MEPs should be able to observe proceedings in the national parliaments (which they can in some countries) and offer suggestions (interview 12). A staff member thought the national parliaments could step in (by influencing their ministers) when the EP cannot or when its role is being diminished. For example, she cited "shenanigans" around the Euro crisis where the EP was being left out of policy-making as an instance when national parliaments might have been able to defend its rights (interview 23).

Others had ideas for more formal roles for the national parliaments. One MP suggested a united session of national parliaments as an alternative to the EP (interview 15), although this would be more like the earliest forms of the EP before its members were directly elected. Others raised the idea of parliamentary vetoes. One British MP argued that it was wrong that something could still pass in the Council even if the House of Commons unanimously voted against it (interview 35). A Belgian MP also wanted a veto but did acknowledge that this was not workable (interview 3). Another MP thought treaties the EU signs should be "mixed," so every national parliament would approve the final treaty, in addition to the Commission and the third-party country (interview 15).

Others thought it was not so much a matter of specific challenges or improvements but rather that it was a slow process and would take time. One MP acknowledged, "We need to strengthen the national parliamentary role, we need to develop this . . . but when you look at how well national parliaments are fulfilling their current role, they will need time to follow up on an expanded role." She added that "even in Denmark," which is considered more active on EU issues, they still have things to work on, such as involving the sectoral committees (interview 30).

Types of Legislators

Returning to the earlier typology, the disinterested pessimist is on the low ends of both dimensions. One example of this type of legislator is the Belgian senator who did not think the national parliaments were "really playing a role," and that doing so was for MEPs. He also discussed a number of the challenges facing involvement, such as how long the process can take, especially if Belgium's regional parliaments also need to vote, as well as the difficulty of understanding EU legislation if one is not a specialist (interview 8). This group was most common in Belgium and Poland, especially among those legislators without a strong interest in Europe or a policy specialization that sees much EU legislation.

Legislators with low interest but at the optimistic end of the practicality dimension are disinterested optimists. This category probably has the fewest legislators, as it does not make a ton of sense to spend time thinking about the practicality of additional involvement if one is uninterested in it. One potential example of a legislator of this type was the one who thought Europe was already too dependent on national interests and therefore was "skeptical" of a greater role. However, he did also speak about improving the system via mainstreaming, at least when the government asked for an opinion on legislation. He thought the current system was part of why he was not more informed about EU issues generally. In contrast, he was much more knowledgeable about the Fiscal Compact, since that had gone through the Budget Committee he served on (interview 10).

The third group is the interested pessimists—those interested in a greater role but who are pessimistic about achieving it. For example, one German MP thought the *Bundestag* was doing well with its own role but was very interested in more cooperation with other parliaments. She thought a more efficient and complete exchange would include not just final opinions but also the thinking behind them and the process for getting stuff done. However, she thought interparliamentary meetings ended up being "just talking" and "accomplished nothing." She cited disinterest among MPs, differences of language and culture, infrequent meetings, general inefficiencies, and a lack of a focused agenda as things that kept them from capitalizing on these exchanges (interview 20). This group seemed to be particularly common among those Belgian legislators interested in Europe but who questioned whether their parliament could really play a greater role.

Finally, the fourth group is the interested optimists, who both desire an increased role and think such a role is practical. One Danish EU Committee member was a prime example of this group. She thought the *Folketing* was already "one of the parliaments scrutinizing the government the best" but this was still "not sufficient," primarily because the sectoral committees needed to be more involved. She also argued for having the ministers come back to the EU committee to seek updated mandates, for a stronger relationship with the EP, and for a proactive role in EU legislation via the proposed green card. She emphasized the recommendations they had put out as constructive progress toward some of these changes, as well as a letter twenty-four parliaments had sent the Commission calling for a working group on the role of national parliaments (interview 26). This type of legislator also seemed to be quite common in the House of Lords, likely because they have a lot of resources, making it seem practical, and they also had a lot of interest in EU affairs, in part because the number of Lords allows for more specialization and because their national role is more limited. They were also quite common in Germany and Denmark.

CONCLUSION

One of the main reasons legislators offered for their interest in EU involvement was that they wanted to have a greater impact on European policy-making. The integration process led to issues of deparliamentarization and executive bias, as national parliaments lost power to the supranational level and to executives who do most EU negotiations (Raunio and Hix 2000; Marks, Wilson, and Ray 2002). At the highest level, this stems from the treaties themselves: "Treaties are negotiated by executives, even though they are ratified by legislatures. Because the Community was created through treaties, then, not only are national governments entrenched but the executive branch is strengthened in comparison with their respective national legislatures" (Sbragia 1992b, 273–274). It also is reflected in the predominant role of the Council in basic legislation and the leadership of the European Council, especially throughout the crisis period. If the national parliaments want to respond and reverse the "executive shift," as one German MP put it (interview 15), they need to get more involved with the EU.

The other main reason legislators cited for their interest in involvement was to increase the democratic representation of their constituents in the EU. European citizens are represented at the European level in two ways: directly in the EP and indirectly by their governments in the Council. "The indirect link between the individual citizen and the directives approved by the Council of Ministers troubles those who believe that the link between voter and policy-maker should be more direct, more robust" (Sbragia 1992b, 278). National legislators see themselves as an answer to this concern, since they can help make this link more direct and robust. Doing so will be important for as long as the Council remains such an important legislative body. Since the Council's importance seems unlikely to dissipate, democratizing this link will likely continue to affect the EU's democratic legitimacy. In fact, the combination of continued Council importance and its legitimacy may be fundamental to continued EU integration. Sbragia (2005, 288) cites the importance of member state representation as key to making continued integration feasible: "Representation of territorially based governments does provide a method of facilitating integration, of achieving federalism, without submerging the interests of the constituent units. It does offer the possibility of federalization through indirect rather than direct representation." If the parliaments can help strengthen and shorten this indirect link, it presents a possible way to provide additional democratic representation without treaty changes and completely restructuring the EU's institutions, for which there does not seem to be much current appetite.

Despite these reasons for further involvement, many of the challenges to increased national parliamentary involvement are real and cannot be simply overcome. However, recently added or improved tools for involvement (such as the changes made under the Lisbon Treaty) and the interest expressed by many legislators suggest that there is potential for an increased future role. There also seems to be a potential positive feedback loop, where those legislators and parliaments who are more interested and involved were also more optimistic about involvement. For example, legislators in Denmark and Germany were generally more involved than those in other countries, and members of the House of Lords were generally more involved than members of the House of Commons, and the more involved groups had a more optimistic outlook.

While the process of involving the national parliaments in European affairs has not necessarily been smooth or consistent, it has generally been in the direction of further involvement. Given the desire of many MPs to be more involved and the continually increasing importance of EU policy-making, it seems this trend is likely to continue. Some further involvement may come via additional roles and powers, but the more immediate path forward seems to be that parliaments would make more use of the tools they already have. They are also likely to find better, more efficient ways to use these tools, especially by learning from one another and sharing best practices. Their role will likely become decreasingly similar to that of most subfederal parliaments, but comparisons of these differences may improve our understanding of how legislatures can function across multiple levels of governance.

These differences will be particularly important for scholars to keep in mind when comparing the EU to federal systems. In 1992, Sbragia (1992a, 2) noted that the influence the national governments had in the EU's legislative process was an "immeasurable" difference between the EU and the United States (and most federal systems). Since then, the role of national parliaments has increased sufficiently, which is another important distinction between these systems. What she wrote about the relationship between the European Community of the time and the national institutions can now also be applied to the national parliaments and their members: "National leaders, institutions, and political experiences influence both politics and policy within the Community, but they in turn are influenced by the dynamic of Community politics" (interview 4). Thus, scholars should also consider this interplay when studying the Council or the national parliaments themselves. Since one goal of parliamentary oversight is to influence ministerial action at the Council, we need to consider how parliamentary action may be influencing its policy-making. For the national parliaments, especially in comparison to other, non-EU legislatures, EU oversight provides an additional space for parliamentary activity. As the earlier evidence demonstrates, many legislators see this EU-related activity as being quite important to their role as national legislators in today's Europe.

INTERVIEW REFERENCES

1. MP, Danish *Folketing*, Copenhagen, May 21, 2013.
2. MP, Danish *Folketing*, Copenhagen, May 21, 2013.
3. MP, Belgian *Chambre des Représentants*, Brussels, June 5, 2013.
4. MP, Belgian *Chambre des Représentants*, Brussels, June 6, 2013.
5. MP, Belgian *Chambre des Représentants*, Brussels, June 6, 2013.
6. EU Advisor, Belgian *Chambre des Représentants*, Brussels, June 7, 2013.
7. MP, Belgian *Chambre des Représentants*, Brussels, June 11, 2013.
8. Senator, Belgian *Sénat*, Brussels, June 11, 2013.
9. Senator, Belgian *Sénat*, Brussels, June 12, 2013.
10. MP, Polish *Sejm*, Warsaw, September 9, 2014.
11. Senator, Polish *Senat*, Warsaw, September 11, 2014.

12. Senator, Polish *Senat*, Warsaw, September 24, 2014.
13. Senator, Polish *Senat*, Warsaw, September 24, 2014.
14. Senator, Polish *Senat*, Warsaw, September 25, 2014.
15. MP, German *Bundestag*, Berlin, October 9, 2014.
16. MP, German *Bundestag*, Berlin, October 9, 2014.
17. MP, German *Bundestag*, Berlin October 10, 2014.
18. Staff Member, German *Bundestag*, Berlin, October 13, 2014.
19. Staff Member, German *Land* Representation, Berlin, October 16, 2014.
20. MP, German *Bundestag*, Berlin, October 20, 2014.
21. Staff Member, German *Land* Representation, Berlin, October 21, 2014.
22. MP, German *Bundestag*, Berlin, October 21, 2014.
23. Advisor, *Land* Representation to the Federal Government, Berlin, October 23, 2014.
24. MP, Danish *Folketing*, Copenhagen, October 28, 2014.
25. EU Advisor, Danish *Folketing*, Copenhagen, October 29, 2014.
26. MP, Danish *Folketing*, Copenhagen, October 29, 2014.
27. MP, Danish *Folketing*, Copenhagen, October 30, 2014.
28. MP, Danish *Folketing*, Copenhagen, November 5, 2014.
29. MP, Danish *Folketing*, Copenhagen, November 6, 2014.
30. MP, Danish *Folketing*, Copenhagen, November 7, 2014.
31. Senator, Belgian *Sénat*, Brussels, November 13, 2014.
32. MP, Belgian *Chambre des Représentants*, Brussels, November 14, 2014.
33. MP, UK House of Commons, London, November 20, 2014.
34. MP, UK House of Commons, London, November 25, 2014.
35. MP, UK House of Commons, London, December, 8, 2014.
36. MP, UK House of Lords, London, December 8, 2014.
37. MP, UK House of Lords, London, December 11, 2014.
38. MP, UK House of Commons, London, December 12, 2014.

BIBLIOGRAPHY

Auel, Katrin and Oliver Höing. 2014. "Scrutiny in Challenging Times—National Parliaments in the Eurozone Crisis." *European Policy Analysis*, 2014 (1): 16.

Auel, Katrin and Oliver Höing. 2015. "National Parliaments and the Eurozone Crisis: Taking Ownership in Difficult Times?" *West European Politics*, 38 (2): 375–395.

Auel, Katrin, Olga Eisele, and Lucy Kinski. 2016. "From Constraining to Catalysing Dissensus? The Impact of Political Contestation on Parliamentary Communication in EU Affairs." *Comparative European Politics*, 14 (2): 154–176.

Auel, Katrin, Olivier Rozenberg, and Angela Tacea. 2015a. "Fighting Back? And, If So, How? Measuring Parliamentary Strength and Activity in EU Affairs." In *The Palgrave Handbook of National Parliaments and the European Union*, edited by Claudia Hefftler, Christine Neuhold, Olivier Rozenberg, and Julie Smith, 60–93. London: Palgrave Macmillan UK.

Auel, Katrin, Olivier Rozenberg, and Angela Tacea. 2015b. "To Scrutinise or Not to Scrutinise? Explaining Variation in EU-Related Activities in National Parliaments." *West European Politics*, 38 (2): 282–304. https://doi.org/10.1080/014023 82.2014.990695.

Bergman, Torbjörn. 1997. "National Parliaments and EU Affairs Committees: Notes on Empirical Variation and Competing Explanations." *Journal of European Public Policy*, 4 (3): 373–387.

Bergman, Torbjörn. 2000. "The European Union as the Next Step of Delegation and Accountability." *European Journal of Political Research*, 37 (3): 415–429.

Cooper, Ian. 2012. "A 'Virtual Third Chamber' for the European Union? National Parliaments after the Treaty of Lisbon." *West European Politics*, 35: 441–465.

Damgaard, Erik and Henrik Jensen. 2005. "Europeanisation of Executive—Legislative Relations: Nordic Perspectives." *The Journal of Legislative Studies*, 11 (3–4): 394–411.

Dimitrakopoulos, Dionyssis G. 2001. "Incrementalism and Path Dependence: European Integration and Institutional Change in National Parliaments." *JCMS: Journal of Common Market Studies*, 39 (3): 405–422.

European Affairs Committee of the Danish Parliament. 2014. *Twenty-Three Recommendations—to Strengthen the Role of National Parliaments in a Changing European Governance*. Copenhagen: Folketinget.

Finance, Stanislas de. 2016. "Fiscal Compact Treaty: Scorecard for 2015—How Far Are EU Member States Meeting Their European Council Commitments?" PE 581.403. Brussels: European Parliamentary Research Service.

Hamerly, Ivy. 2007. "The Timing of EU Membership and Its Effects on National Legislative Oversight of European Affairs." Paper presented at the Biannual Meeting of the European Union Studies Association. Montreal, Canada, May 2007. http://aei.pitt.edu/7895/1/hamerly-i-04h.pdf

Karlas, Jan. 2012. "National Parliamentary Control of EU Affairs: Institutional Design after Enlargement." *West European Politics*, 35 (5): 1095–1113.

Kietz, Daniela. 2006. "What Accounts for National Divergence: The Baltic Parliaments and EU Affairs." Paper presented at the EU-Consent PhD Summer School. Budapest, Hungary, April 29–May 5, 2006. https://www.researchgate.net/publication/242506699_What_accounts_for_national_divergence_The_Baltic_Parliaments_in_EU_Affairs.

Marks, Gary, Carole J. Wilson, and Leonard Ray. 2002. "National Political Parties and European Integration." *American Journal of Political Science*, 46 (3): 585–594.

Martin, Lisa. 2000. *Democratic Commitments: Legislatures and International Cooperation*. Princeton, NJ: Princeton University Press.

Maurer, Andreas and Wolfgang Wessels. 2001. *National Parliaments on Their Ways to Europe. Losers or Latecomers?* edited by Andreas Maurer and Wolfgang Wessels. Baden-Baden: Nomos Verlag. http://aei.pitt.edu/1476/.

Neyer, Jürgen. 2012. "What Role for National Parliaments? European Integration and the Prospects of Parliamentary Democracy." In *National Parliaments and Their Electorates in EU Affairs*, edited by Katrin Auel and Tapio Raunio, 29–46. IHS Political Science Series 129.

Norton, Philip. 1996. "Conclusion: Addressing the Democratic Deficit." In *National Parliaments and the European Union*, edited by Philip Norton, 177–193. London: Frank Cass.

O'Halpin, Eunan. 1996. "Irish Parliamentary Culture and the European Union: Formalities to Be Observed." In *National Parliaments and the European Union*, edited by Philip Norton, 124–135. London: Frank Cass.

Pahre, Robert. 1997. "Endogenous Domestic Institutions in Two-Level Games and Parliamentary Oversight of the European Union." *Journal of Conflict Resolution*, 41 (1): 147–174.

Raunio, Tapio. 2005. "Holding Governments Accountable in European Affairs: Explaining Cross-National Variation." *The Journal of Legislative Studies*, 11 (3–4): 319–342.

Raunio, Tapio. 2009. "National Parliaments and European Integration: What We Know and Agenda for Future Research." *The Journal of Legislative Studies*, 15 (4): 317–334.

Raunio, Tapio and Matti Wiberg. 2000. "Does Support Lead to Ignorance? National Parliaments and the Legitimacy of EU Governance." *Acta Politica*, 35 (2): 146–168.

Raunio, Tapio and Simon Hix. 2000. "Backbenchers Learn to Fight Back: European Integration and Parliamentary Government." *West European Politics*, 23 (4): 142–168.

Rozenberg, Olivier. 2002. "The Involvement of National Parliaments in European Union Affairs: An Empirical Test of Two Variables." Paper presented at the ECPR Joint Sessions of Workshops. Turin, Italy, March 2002.

Saalfeld, Thomas. 2005. "Deliberate Delegation or Abdication? Government Backbenchers, Ministers and European Union Legislation." *The Journal of Legislative Studies*, 11 (3–4): 343–371.

Sbragia, Alberta M. 1992a. "Introduction." In *Euro-Politics: Institutions and Policymaking in the "New" European Community*, edited by Alberta M. Sbragia, 1–22. Washington, DC: The Brookings Institution.

Sbragia, Alberta M. 1992b. "Thinking about the European Future: The Uses of Comparison." In *Euro-Politics: Institutions and Policymaking in the "New" European Community*, edited by Alberta M. Sbragia, 257–291. Washington, DC: The Brookings Institution.

Sbragia, Alberta M. 2005. "Post-National Democracy as Post-National Democratization." In *Democracy and Federalism in the European Union and the United States: Exploring Post-National Governance*, edited by Sergio Fabbrini, 167–182. New York: Routledge.

Winzen, Thomas. 2013. "European Integration and National Parliamentary Oversight Institutions." *European Union Politics*, 14 (2): 297–323.

Chapter 7

Is There a European Union Administrative Style?

Administrative Traditions and the European Commission

B. Guy Peters

The fundamental question in this chapter is whether there is a distinctive administrative style within the European Commission. The institutions of the European Union (EU) have now been in existence in some form for six decades and there seemingly has been ample time for a distinctive pattern of administration to emerge. Although the European Commission is to some extent a public bureaucracy unlike any other, it is still a public bureaucracy and as such should be expected to have developed routines and a particular style for performing its tasks. But what sorts of routines? And what sort of style?

One possible outcome of the continuing development of the EU is that the Commission would have developed its own distinctive style of doing business. There are good reasons for assuming that such a distinctive style or tradition would have emerged, but there are equally good reasons to assume that the style might be a somewhat unpalatable stew of the numerous patterns of administration coming from the member states and of different internal subdivisions. One should expect the routinization and institutionalization of patterns of behavior within the structure over this time (Silberman 1993), but that institutionalization could be itself fragmented, given the internal structures of this and other bureaucracies.

An alternative perspective would be that the administrative practices within the EU are composed of an amalgam of the traditions of one or more of the constituent "families" of nations. This alternative, and indeed the first alternative of a distinctive style, are potentially impacted heavily by the changing fads and fashions in the practice of public administration. In particular, beginning in the later 1970s and continuing (at least to some extent) to the present, the New Public Management (NPM) (see Hood 1991; Christensen and Laegreid 2011) has been a continuing source of pressures for changing public administration within the EU and within the member nations (Ellinas, and Suleiman 2008).

Understanding the administrative style or tradition is in part an academic enterprise, attempting to identify and categorize the pattern(s) of administration within an organization. But this exercise may have a somewhat more practical dimension, as it can help to predict how the organization will perform when faced with different types of public policy and management challenges. In this chapter, I will almost certainly raise more questions than I can answer in any definitive manner, but I do hope that raising the questions can advance our understanding of how the Commission and other administrative bodies function.

THE CONCEPT OF ADMINISTRATIVE STYLE OR ADMINISTRATIVE TRADITION

This chapter is based on the notion that there are underlying administrative styles and traditions that despite, in most cases at least, having their roots in the past continue to influence contemporary public administration. These traditions about what constitutes appropriate administrative structures and behavior are embedded in the DNA of organizations and tend to replicate themselves even when contemporary theories about public management appear to contradict and undermine those traditions. Various waves of change in administrative theory and practice may come and go but some aspects of the traditions will persist.[1]

The administrative styles that one may observe in contemporary governments may have several sources. One is the more general political culture of the country or family of countries. Public administration is rather obviously part of the political system so ideas about what government should do, and how it should do those things, will inevitably help to shape public administration. For example, countries in which the state has been a major actor in economic development will tend to accept a stronger economic role for the public bureaucracy than would more *laissez-faire* economic systems. Further, a contractarian as opposed to organic conception of the state (Dyson 1980) will also shape the latitude of action available to bureaucracy.

Ideas about public administration may also be affected by more general ideas about organizations and management within the economy and society. Scholars such as Geert Hofstede (Hofstede, Hofstede, and Mirkov 2010) and

---

1 For example, after the widespread adoption of the NPM ideas mentioned earlier, older more formal and legalistic patterns of public administration have reasserted themselves.

the GLOBE group (House et al. 2006) have studied patterns of organization and management across cultures for some years and have developed a set of reliable indicators of internal organizational cultures (but see Jones 2007). While these differ most significantly across broad cultural areas (see appendix 1), they also differ within those areas and even within the same country. The basic point here is that although public administration is public, it still faces the same management issues as any other organization in the society and must be largely isomorphic with the general institutional and management patterns in the society (Dimaggio and Powell 1983).

Finally, there may be some factors affecting public administration, which are peculiar to the public bureaucracy within individual countries. For example, administration in France continues to be affected by the style of administration developed during the Napoleonic period (Peters 2008); modernization and regime change in some aspects in administration can be traced back to the centralized and developmental administrative style associated with the Napoleonic state (but see Dreyfus 2013). Likewise, some scholars have argued that German administration remains heavily influenced by earlier Prussian approaches (Derlien 1991).

Given the earlier facts, we can see readily that contemporary public administration represents the confluence of a number of specific national patterns. But it also represents the impact of major trends in administrative theory, notably the NPM. Although somewhat diffuse (Hood 1991), that set of ideas primarily stressed making public administration more like management in the private sector, reducing the policy advice role of public administrators, and also fragmenting the public sector into numerous autonomous or quasi-autonomous entities usually referred to as agencies. The emphasis on efficiency was to replace the more traditional emphasis on probity and effectiveness.

Although the NPM was a virtually universal phenomenon, it was accepted differently in different national settings. The heartland for NPM reforms was in the United Kingdom, the Antipodes, and Finland. Other countries such as Germany and France made very modest reforms, especially at the central government level (Reichard 2003). The ideas of NPM were more compatible with some administrative styles than with others, and even when implemented in some settings, they appeared to have little or no effect on governing patterns. But contemporary public administration, including that within the EU, is conducted with a backdrop of the NPM.

DIMENSIONS OF ADMINISTRATIVE TRADITIONS

To help understand the administrative patterns within the EU, I will present briefly several important dimensions of administrative traditions in EU countries. This list is not exhaustive (see Peters, forthcoming) but does provide information on some of the more important factors shaping the ways in which administration is conducted. While the discussion here is for European countries, these traditions also have relevance for public administration in other types of public bureaucracies.

Law versus Management

One dichotomy that is crucial for understanding differences among administrative systems is the relative importance of law and management in defining the roles of public servants. Having mentioned the importance of the NPM earlier, it is important to recognize that some administrative systems have an "old public management." Although the older concern with public management is most apparent in North America, in the European context, in the United Kingdom and Ireland, there has been a significant emphasis on the management role of civil servants. For the majority of the European administrative systems, however, the dominant approach to the task is law, and many if not most civil servants will describe their role as that of a lawyer. This is not to say that the managerialist approach is not concerned with law but only that law is not the first thing that springs to the mind of a civil servant.

Distinctiveness of the Career

Second, there is a question of the extent to which being a civil servant is a career, as argued by Weber, to be essential to a proper bureaucracy. In contemporary thinking about careers in public administration, the question is the extent to which political appointees—whether hired for expertise or for simply political reasons (see Panizza, Ramos, and Peters 2019)—occupy positions in the public sector that might be held by permanent officials. Further, do public officials leave the public sector and reoccupy positions in the private sector?[2]

Movements among levels of government represent another aspect of the distinctiveness of public sector careers. In Germany, for example, there is a good deal of movement among the levels of government, facilitated by the common legal foundation for public sector employment. Although less formalized, movement among levels of government is common in the Nordic countries. In other countries in Europe such as the United Kingdom and Italy, however, movement among levels is rare.

---

2 Prominent examples of this link between state and society would be *pantouflage* in France and *amakudari* in Japan.

State and Society

A third element of administrative traditions is defined by the relationship between the state and society and more precisely by the role that the public bureaucracy plays in those interactions. The simple dichotomy here is between pluralist systems in which interest groups vie for access and corporatist arrangements in which interest groups are legitimate participants in the political process. The reality is significantly more complex than that dichotomy, but the basic question of the openness of administrative systems to interest groups and bargaining among multiple groups as opposed to one-on-one symbiotic relationships is important for understanding the nature of public administration (Peters 2018, chapter 5).

The relationship between state and society may also be considered in terms of the power and autonomy of the state relative to social and market actors. While not focusing on the EU per se, Alberta Sbragia (2000b) has discussed the changing role of the state in providing (presumably) public services. As she points out, the relationship between state and society has been becoming more complex and hence administrative patterns have had to adapt to be capable of controlling the delivery of public services, as well as to find relationships between social actors and government.

Uniformity

A fourth distinction in patterns of public administration, and public policy, is the extent to which there are expectations of uniformity of public service provision throughout the territory of the state. On the one end, one would find countries in the Napoleonic tradition in which centralization and the use of instruments such as the prefectoral system are used to create high levels of uniformity for citizens. At the other end, federal regimes, and those with significant social cleavages, tend to accept greater diversity and even permit alternative forms of public law, for example, Scotland in the United Kingdom.

Alberta Sbragia's interest in the EU as, in essence, a federal system (1993) raises the point about uniformity in policy and administration rather clearly. One of the virtues, as well as one of the problems, of federal governance arrangements is that they do not demand uniformity and hence can accommodate political and cultural differences. But, as she points out, this can be a balancing act between equality and difference, as is true for any federal system.

Administration and Politics

The fifth dimension of administrative traditions relevant in this case is the relationship between politics and administration. The Anglo-American tradition, in particular, has argued for a rather strict separation between politics and administration, with the assumption that the task of public administrators is to follow the directions from their political "masters." The pattern of administrative behavior in most European countries, despite some theory to the contrary, is a much closer integration of politics and administration. Civil servants are more likely to play political roles (Braendle and Stutzer 2010) and individuals with strong political connections are more likely to be involved directly with public administration in these systems (see Rouban 2004).

Accountability

A continuing challenge for all political systems is in finding ways of restraining the power of bureaucracies and holding them accountable for their actions. In democratic systems, enforcing accountability is a central function for the legislature, but there is also a range of alternative forms of accountability. The most important of the alternatives is using law, and especially *ex-ante* legal controls over administration to prevent actions that are *ultra vires*. As noted earlier in some administrative systems, individual civil servants may function in a legal role but may also develop legal institutions and procedures that can be used for control, for example, the *Conseil d'Etat* in France and its analogues in Italy and Spain.

The degree of personal responsibility constitutes another important facet of accountability in administrative systems. While all public administrations hold individuals responsible for malfeasance and violations of laws and regulations, they may still differ on the extent to which individuals as opposed to working groups are made responsible for action. Accountability is usually discussed in terms of punishing misdeeds, but it can also be directed at encouraging, or demanding, performance on the job.

THE FOUR TRADITIONS

Some scholars have argued for the existence of a common European administrative culture (Beck and Thedieck 2008), I am arguing for the existence of at least four distinct administrative traditions among the European countries. Although inevitably simplifying the complexity of national patterns and peculiarities, I will be arguing that there are indeed four broad patterns of public administrative among the members of the EU: Anglo-American, Napoleonic, Germanic, and Scandinavian. These patterns of administration have developed over an extended period of time and despite many pressures for change do persist.

Table 7.1.   The Four Traditions

Attribute	Anglo-American	Napoleonic	Germanic	Scandinavian
State and society 1	Contract	Organic	Organic	Mixed
Law versus management	Management	Law	Law	Mixed
State and society 2	Pluralist		Corporatist	Corporatist
Career distinctiveness	High—falling[3]	Low	High	Low
Uniformity	Low	High	Medium	Medium
Administration and politics	Separate	Compatible	Somewhat compatible	Compatible
Accountability	Ex post legislative	Ex ante legalistic	Parliament and courts	Ex post parliamentary

These four patterns of administration, characterized by the six dimensions discussed earlier, are presented in Table 7.1. There are other dimensions of administrative systems that could be used to characterize these administrative systems. In particular, the Scandinavian systems are defined significantly through their patterns of interest intermediation and the very strong linkages between a wide range of interest groups and administration. This second pillar of democracy (Rokkan 1968) has become weaker in recent years, but the corporate-pluralist connections between state and society remain strong.

The information in Table 7.1 is largely presented as dichotomies or simple rankings. This obviously makes presentation easier but also obscures some more subtle differences among these styles of public administration. For example, although both are labeled as more legalistic than managerial, there are also significant differences between the Napoleonic and the Germanic styles in this regard.[4] Still, this presentation does point out the distinctiveness of the traditions and raises questions about how these styles can be blended into a single administrative style within the European Commission.

In the presentation of the four administrative traditions, the Anglo-American is the most distinctive. It is much more oriented toward management than the others and was so even before the advent of the NPM. The Scandinavian approach to public administration has had some emphasis on management but not to the extent of the United Kingdom or Ireland. Likewise, although all of these administrative systems certainly utilize parliamentary forms of accountability, the Anglo-American systems tend to rely more on this mechanism than do the others.[5]

---

3 In this case the reference is to the British and Irish patterns, given their relevance for the European Union. For the United States, the distinctiveness is much lower, with several thousand appointments available to the president.

4 A more complete and more nuanced account of these differences can be found in Peters (forthcoming) and Painter and Peters (2010).

5 The Scandinavian cases come close to the Anglo-American, given that some of their more distinctive features, for example, the *ombudsman*, are in essence parliamentary characteristics.

The Anglo-American and the Germanic traditions are also distinct from the other two in the distinctiveness of the administrative career. The assumption for both of these groups of administrative systems is that an individual will enter the civil service at a relatively early stage of the career and remain in the service until retirement. Especially in the Anglo-American cases, this assumption has been relaxed somewhat, given the claims for "generic management" in the NPM, but even then the general pattern is a career for the entire working life. In contrast, movement between the public and the private sectors is relatively easy in Scandinavia, and many members of the upper civil service in France leave the public sector for more lucrative careers in the private sector—*pantouflage* (Rouban 2010).

The emphasis on uniformity stands out as a special feature of the Napoleonic tradition. The highly centralized administrative system (even after significant efforts at decentralization; see Schmidt [1990]), as well as instruments such as prefectoral supervision, creates an administrative and policy system which provides highly uniform services across the territory of the states.[6] In contrast, the other systems allow substantial variations, even when they are formally unitary states. Indeed, some federal systems may be more uniform than the presumably unitary Scandinavian systems.[7]

THE EUROPEAN COMMISSION AS A PUBLIC BUREAUCRACY

As already noted, the European Commission is the bureaucracy, or at least one of them, for the EU. It is charged with performing at least some of the tasks expected of a bureaucracy in a national government. Although the European Commission is responsible for only a limited amount of implementation (Bauer 2006), it does perform other functions such as policy advice and the preparation of policy initiatives. And it does monitor implementation of EU policies by member governments. Although the question has been raised as to whether the Commission is a bureaucracy like all others (see Kassim 2018), there are a number of factors that make it function as such.

As noted, this chapter will focus on the role of the European Commission as the executive, and especially as the locus of public administration for the EU. This institution is in many ways a bureaucracy like any other (Wille 2013; but see Kassim 2018), but in other ways it is a distinctive organization, and that distinctiveness may be important for its capacity to legitimate the EU

---

6 The obvious exception is Spain after granting substantial and differential powers to the regions.

7 For example, the local governments have the capacity to set their own local tax rates, which would not be true in federal Germany or Austria.

and to perform the tasks usually associated with a public bureaucracy, and with the executive branch of government more generally. There are several important features that distinguish the Commission from the executive in other governments.

First, the Commissioners, the rough equivalent of ministers in a national government, are appointed on the suggestion of national governments and approved by the European Parliament for a fixed period. And this level of the executive is representative in a sense, with each of the member states having at least one commissioner, although this does give disproportionate representation to smaller member states. There has tended to be some specialization among the countries, with, for example, the Northern European countries frequently having responsibility for the environment and social issues, and France and Spain have dominated agriculture.

Second, a very large proportion of the staff of the Commission is on secondment from national governments. Thus, rather than having its own staff, the Commission is heavily influenced by temporary employees who are presumably good Europeans while in Brussels (or at one of the various European agencies scattered around the Union) but also expect to return to their national bureaucracies. Because their career paths may be more determined by officials at the national level, they may be reluctant to become too much the creatures of Brussels (Trondal, Murdoch, and Geys 2015). Further, the temporary nature of their involvement may make them less easily socialized into a common administrative culture.

Third, unlike most bureaucracies, the European Commission actually does very little implementation (Hofmann and Türk 2006). European regulations and directives are implemented largely through the national governments, with the Commission assuming a monitoring role, rather than performing the implementation directly itself. The Commission is therefore relatively small when compared to national public administrations (some 33,000 employees [many of whom are translators] compared to some 200,000 in the Belgian national civil service).[8]

In most national bureaucracies, implementation is the principal task, while in the Brussels bureaucracy it is secondary to other tasks such as policy advice and formulation and monitoring national implementation of policies. The tasks assigned to the European Commission, therefore, may reduce some of the differences found among national bureaucracies. The upper echelons of those national bureaucracies may be more similar than are the structures as a whole, given that the upper echelons in all systems tend to be more in touch with political leaders and to be more "hybrids" and "amphibians"

---

8 And because of the rather extreme form of federalism, the national civil service of Belgium is relatively small on a per capita basis when compared to other European countries.

between those two worlds of politics and administration. Further, this level of the administration may be experts, more concerned with designing effective policy than with the political issues arising from the implementation of those policies.

These factors may combine to make the Commission less European than might be expected from the formal emphasis on eschewing nationality in favor of a European identity. That said, survey evidence does indicate that a significant majority of the members of the Commission do join that organization because of a commitment to Europe (Kassim et al. 2013, 55–57). But much of that commitment exists prior to joining the Commission rather than as a function of socialization after joining.

Jarle Trondal (2010) provides another set of lenses for examining the European Commission and the executive apparatus of the EU more generally. He argues that there are four alternative and potentially competitive images of the officials within the Commission. These four images must be considered when attempting to understand how individual public servants in the Commission perform their tasks, and how the institution as a whole performs. These images are directed more specifically at the particularities of the Commission and the EU than other analyses of administrative culture and values.

The first two of these images—the supernational and the intergovernmental—focus on the attitudes of the Commission employees toward the role of the EU relative to the powers of the constituent national governments. These images are important for the commitment of European civil servants to the relative power of the Commission and other European institutions. This normative commitment to the European project is an important, if variable, component of the working lives of members of the Commission (see Christensen, Bekerom, and Voet 2007). While largely independent of the national administrative cultures mentioned earlier, differential commitments to supernationalism may be influenced by different levels of national commitments to that value.

The third of the images presented by Trondal emphasizes the importance of membership in a particular Directorate General (DG) or agency within the Commission. The implicit argument here is that there are departmental cultures or operating routines that may dominate other allegiances or values.[9] Within the national administrative cultures described earlier, there may be strong internal cultures within individual organizations. These generally represent the nature of the policy domain they administer (Goodsell 2011)

---

9 This perspective is analogous to the argument of institutionalists who argue that behavior within institutions is determined by "myths, symbols, routines" that constitute a "logic of appropriateness" (see March and Olsen 1989).

but may be more simply about the way in which they do business internally. Within the EU, the member of the Commission can be seen defending and representing his or her own DG in the usual policy battles of governing (see Peters 1992).

Other scholars have emphasized the importance of organizational involvement in shaping the behavior of officials in the EU. Morten Egeberg (1996, 2004), for example, has emphasized the role of structure along with nationality in explaining the performance of this organization, and the structures—the DGs—within it. Despite some of its singular characteristics, the Commission is just one more public sector organization (or institution) and can be understood as such.

Finally, there is an image of the executive order that Trondal described as "epistemic." By this, he referred to the varying patterns of connections which members of the executive have with actors within society and their role as gatherers and sorters of information. This perspective may be similar in some ways to the departmental view, but it also represents connections with interest groups within society and hence may be a more political, albeit not partisan, perspective on the role of administration. Although perhaps not as clear within the EU as in national governments, public administration constitutes the major interface between state and society (see Zacka 2017), and these connections may define their perspective on policy, as well as their own roles as administrators.

This epistemic lens developed by Trondal links with the literature on networks within the European Commission itself and between the Commission and social actors.[10] There is a substantial literature on the role of networks in the EU, pointing to the importance of these connections in making and implementing EU policies (Börzel 1997). These networks appear in the formulation of policy as well as in their implementation and the use of seconded experts helps to bring those networks directly and legitimately into the proceedings of the Commission.

Interestingly, however, Trondal does not mention the Weberian professional bureaucrat as one of the alternative visions for the Commission. This image may not be relevant for the commissioners who are the analogues of ministers but the image can certainly apply to the other public employees who work in the Commission. Liesbet Hooghe (1999), for example, contrasted Weberian and consociational styles among higher-level commission bureaucrats. She focused on the contrast between the bureaucracy as a legal, technocratic policy-making organization and the European bureaucracy representative institution for nationalities (see also Nagel and Peters 2018).

---

10 For a more general discussion of epistemic communities involved in policy-making, see Zito (2001).

UNTANGLING THE PUZZLE

The aforementioned discussion of the available literature provides three alternative ways to see the administrative style of the European Commission. One is that it is *sui generis* and has developed an internal administrative culture that pervades it and its members, so that the Commission functions somewhat like the unitary actor of administrative legend—an animal rarely found in the real world of administrative and governance. Some studies of the Commission (Cini 1996, 2000; Schön-Quinlivan 2011) have tended to argue, even if implicitly, that this institution is indeed a rather well-integrated organization that has been able to create its own style of making and administering policy. That style may depend in part on the leadership at the time, but the institution still marches to a single drummer, or at most, to a very small number of drumbeats.

Although stressing the internal fragmentation of the Commission, Kassim et al. (2013, 77ff) also stress its distinctive features as an administrative body. As well as its multinational nature and its extensive use of non-career officials, the Commission can be distinguished from other bureaucracies in several other ways. It has an ensemble of tasks and a central role in the policy process that distinguishes it from other bureaucracies. Its pattern of handling cross-cutting issues is more reminiscent of the Soviet Union than of a contemporary European administrative system, given the need to move issues to the top of hierarchies before engaging in any significant attempts at coordination.

The second perspective is that the Commission is an amalgam of the various national traditions that comprise it or even that it has become dominated by one tradition to the possible exclusion, or at least diminution, of others. Making the argument on behalf of this version of the Commission would require identifying certain aspects of the structure of the Commission and the behavior of its members that had clear connections to the styles of national administrations. While that connection may be visible, demonstrating the etiology behind the appearance of those patterns is more difficult.

The third possible pattern is that the structure of the Commission produces a more highly differentiated and segmented organization. That fragmentation may occur first on the basis of the policy domains for which the various DGs are responsible. The fragmentation may also be a function of the national administrative styles of the Commissioners and the *cabinets* that serve those Commissioners (Egeberg and Heskestad 2010).[11] And finally, the Commission may be fragmented on the basis of linkages with the society. These

---

11 The conventional wisdom at this time is that the *cabinets* have become less shaped by national patterns than in the past. See Kassim (2018).

linkages may reinforce the fragmentation produced through policy domains but may also create their own divisions within the organization.

The internal fragmentation of the European Commission, as well as the politics over policy within the institution, remains an important perspective on administration within this system. The bureaucratic politics within the system (Peters 1992) appears to continue unabated or perhaps even has increased. The agencification of the EU, following the pattern established by the NPM, obviously exacerbates the internal divisions within the executive order and can create yet another source of internal bureaucratic politics (see Williams 2005).

THE EVIDENCE, SUCH AS IT IS

In this penultimate section of the chapter, I will present some arguments for each of the visions of the nature of the Commission bureaucracy. While I am primarily interested in the legacies brought into the Commission from the member states and their public bureaucracies, the other two perspectives should be considered carefully. The evidence available here is hardly of the type that could be used to test any hypotheses, but even these "data" can provide some inklings about the complex internal workings of the institution and the relative strengths of the alternative visions.

It is important in this analysis of administrative cultures not to equate the importance of those cultures with the role of nationalism in EU decision-making. There are numerous studies that question any significant role of nationality in the behavior of Commission officials (see Gravier and Roth 2016) and that is not the argument here. Rather, the question is whether there are still issues of administrative styles, and of different understandings of the ways in which organizations in the public sector should and do function that shape behaviors. Some of these elements of culture may have little to do with the public sector *per se* but may be more conceptions of how management within organizations should be conducted.[12]

The question of nationalism in administration is reinforced by the large number of officials on secondment to the Commission from their national governments (see Suvarierol, Busuioc, and Groenleer 2013). As noted earlier, this secondment is a distinctive feature of the EU administrative system and can be conceptualized as a means of training national administrators in EU procedures and socializing them into EU values. But it can also be seen as putting cuckoos in the nest, given that these officials retain their primary

---

12 This is obviously related to the research of Hofstede, House, and the like mentioned earlier.

career path within their national governments and hence may not want to in any way undermine the interests of their home country.

The Distinctive Nature of the Commission

Some elements of the distinctive nature of the Commission were discussed earlier, notably its relatively small size, its composition coming from many national backgrounds, and its absence of significant implementation work as compared to a national bureaucracy. The role of secondments mentioned earlier raises one point about the distinctiveness of officials within the EU, as well as providing a mechanism for the transmission of national styles of administration into the EU.

The dossier system is one of the most distinctive features of the European Commission as an administrative system. Administrative action, whether concerned with policy formulation or with implementation, is delegated to an individual within a DG. He or she is then responsible for managing the dossier until some resolution is achieved. This administrative procedure is in marked contrast to practices in most administrative systems where the file would be moved up the hierarchy and the initiator would soon shed responsibility for managing it. This administrative pattern may especially impact the coordination of activities.

Legacies from the Member States

The above having been said, the administrative style of the EU does contain some of the elements of the member countries. For example, the administrative style within the Commission does appear more legalistic than managerial. This legalism is perhaps to be expected for an organization whose function is primarily to make and monitor law rather than to manage programs itself. But beyond the tasks required of members of the Commission, the emphasis has been on compliance perhaps more than on designing programs that can be efficient and effective (Treib 2006; König and Mäder 2014). Internally, even after attempts at reform such as those introduced by Neil Kinnock (see Ban 2013), the management of the Commission as an institution does not appear to be the principal concern of the central "management."

Given that the European Commission is not a partisan government, as would be true of the executive in one of the member countries, one might expect the issue of politics and administration to be of little or no concern.[13] However, there is an increasing body of literature on the Commission that

---

13 The *Spitzenkandidat* system may be making the selection of the president of the Commission more directly political.

argues for the existence of a role conflict for EU administrators between political and Weberian understandings of their role (see Bauer and Ege 2013). In this case, the "political" sense of their role is both institutional and defending the European project against national interests.

For those officials who occupy permanent positions in the Commission bureaucracy, the career is rather distinctive, although many will have had administrative careers in national governments prior to coming to the EU. Further, the agencification of the EU may be affecting career patterns somewhat, certainly by making them more specialized and increasing the internal fragmentation of the structures (Flinders 2004). The creation of so many specialized structures has also created more posts for seconded national experts to provide the technical expertise that more generalist EU administrators may lack.

Also, there appears to be a significant concern with creating uniformity throughout the territory of the EU, putting the EU administrative system more in the Napoleonic style. This is true even though the EU is a proto-federal state structure (Fabbrini 2010). The assumption since the inception of the Union has been that, for the single market to function, it was necessary to create uniform practices throughout the member countries. That said, implementing EU policies through the member states has meant that there will be variation, *de facto* if not *de jure*. Adding the national governments to the implementation process may have been politically necessary and has kept the Commission relatively small as a bureaucracy.

Finally, accountability has been something of a question within the EU, albeit less perhaps for the officials operating within the administrative structures than for the commissioners themselves (Bovens 2007). While the Lisbon Treaty and other changes to the system of responsibility of the Commission to the European Parliament have improved accountability, it does remain somewhat problematic. Further, the system of delegation in the implementation process also raises major concerns about the accountability and transparency of many processes within the Commission (Peers and Costa 2012).

Fragmentation and Internal Differences

The third alternative pattern of public administration within the European Commission would be defined by distinctive cultures and patterns of operation within the individual DG and agencies, rather than any more general pattern of administration within the institution as a whole. The available literature points out that the DG and especially the agencies do develop their own internal cultures. These cultures are based in part on the subject matter for which they are responsible. The cultures are also based in part on the "colonization" of various organizations by particular national groups who import their own styles of practice (Ellinas and Suleiman 2012). But those internal administrative styles can also be influenced by individual leaders (Ban 2013, 45–47) and hence change when the leadership does.

While there are the aforementioned background features affecting the internal cultures of components of the Commission, including the agencies, there may be more political reasons for fostering a distinctive pattern of commitment and beliefs within these organizations. Building an internal culture and a commitment to programs can be used to promote the interests of the DG or the agency in the inevitable conflicts with other organizations over policies and budgets (Wayneberg 2017).

Finally, I should point out that although this chapter has been concerned primarily with the effects of national patterns of administration on the Commission, the more common concern for European scholars has been the flow of influence in the opposite direction. That is, the creation of a "European Administrative Space" (Olsen 2003; Trondal and Peters 2013) has been a means for the Commission to influence policy-making across Europe more generally. As such, public administration has been an often underrated mechanism for European policy steering (Sbragia 2000) and for advancing European integration.

CONCLUSION

As promised, this chapter has opened more strands of inquiry than it has closed. The precise nature of the Commission as an executive organ for the Union has been a question since its inception but continues to arise even after some decades of the existence of the Union. This question continues, in part, because the EU and the Commission continue to change and those changes expose new facets of the institution and its membership. Some of the changes, for example, enlargement, have been more internal to the EU, while others, for example, the spread of an ideology of managerialism, have been exogenous, but all have had an influence on the way in which the Commission functions.

The primary interest I had when beginning the chapter was uncovering the administrative traditions that may reside within the Commission, given that it represents something of a composite of administration. As noted earlier, some elements of all the underlying traditions among European administrative systems can be found within the Commission. That said, the administrative system appears to be something of a hybrid, as indeed are other European administrative systems such as the Netherlands and Switzerland. This hybridity appears as layers within the organization, reflecting the development of the EU and of the Commission.

But these underlying traditions are not the only way of understanding the administrative style of the Commission. To some extent, it is *sui generis*, having developed its own ways of coping with the unique policy-making and administrative challenges it must confront. And like most organizations, assuming it is a unitary actor is an excessively heroic assumption so that the various components of the institution may have developed their own internal values and ways of doing business.

As is true for any attempt to examine an institution or a decision process through multiple lenses, each of the three approaches—national traditions, unique style, or fragmentation—provides some insights into the subject of the inquiry. This triangulation creates a problem of the overdetermination of outcomes, but it also permits an enhanced understanding of the nature of this institution and the role that the bureaucracy plays in the EU. Any one view may obscure some of the nature of the organization but the three together can facilitate understanding of this important institution.

BIBLIOGRAPHY

Ban, Carolyn. 2013. *Management and Culture in an Enlarged European Commission: From Diversity to Unity?* Basingstoke: Palgrave Macmillan.

Bauer, Michael W. 2006. "Co-Managing Programme Implementation: Conceptualizing the European Commission's Role in Policy Execution." *Journal of European Public Policy*, 13, no. 5: 717–735.

Bauer, Michael W. and Jörn Ege. 2013. "Commission Civil Servants and Politics: De-Politicized Bureaucrats in an Increasingly Political Organization." In *Civil Servants and Politics: A Delicate Balance*, edited by Christine Neuhold, Sophie Vanhoonacker, and Luc Verhey, 173–205. Basingstoke: Palgrave Macmillan.

Beck, Joachim and Franz Thedieck. 2008. *The European Dimension of Administrative Culture*. Baden-Baden, DE: Nomos Verlag.

Börzel, Tanja A. 1997. "What's So Special about Policy Networks? An Exploration of the Concept and Its Usefulness in Studying European Governance." *European Integration online Papers EioP*, 1, no. 16. http://eiop.or.at/eiop/texte/1997-016a.htm.

Bovens, Mark. 2007. "New Forms of Accountability and EU-Governance." *Comparative European Politics*, 5, no. 1: 104–120.

Braendle, Thomas and Alois Stutzer. 2010. "Public Servants in Parliament: Theory and Evidence on Its Determinants in Germany." *Public Choice*, 145, no. 1/2: 223–252.

Christensen, Johan, Petra van den Bekerom, and Joris van der Voet. 2007. "Representative Bureaucracy and Specialist Knowledge in the European Commission." *Public Administration*, 95, no. 2: 450–467.

Christensen, Tom and Per Laegreid. 2011. *The Ashgate Research Companion to the New Public Management*. Burlington, VT: Ashgate Publishing.

Cini, Michelle. 1996. *The European Commission: Leadership, Organisation and Culture in the EU Administration.* Manchester: University of Manchester Press.

Cini, Michelle. 2000. "Administrative Culture in the European Commission: The Cases of Competition and Environment." In *At the Heart of the Union: Studies in the European Commission,* edited by Neill Nugent, 73–90. Basingstoke: Palgrave Macmillan, 2nd edition.

Derlien, Hans-Ulrich. 1991. "Historical Legacy and Recent Development in the German Higher Civil Service." *International Review of Administrative Science,* 57, no. 3: 385–401.

Dimaggio, Paul J. and Walter W. Powell. 1983. "The Iron Cage Revisited: Institutional Isomorphism and Collective Rationality in Organizational Fields." *American Sociological Review,* 48, no. 2: 147–160.

Dreyfus, Françoise. 2013. "Far beyond the Napoleonic Model: Richness of the French Administrative History." In *La France et ses Administrations: Un état des saviors,* edited by Jean-Michel Eymeri-Douzans and Geert Bouckaert, pp. 45–68. Brussels: Editions Bruylant.

Dyson, Kenneth H. F. 1980. *The State Tradition in Western Europe: A Study of an Idea and an Institution.* Oxford: Oxford University Press.

Egeberg, Morten. 1996. "Organization and Nationality in the European Commission Services." *Public Administration,* 74, no. 4: 721–735.

Egeberg, Morten. 2004. "An Organizational Approach to European Integration: Outline of a Complementary Perspective." *European Journal of Political Research,* 43, no. 2: 199–219.

Egeberg, Morten. 2006. "Balancing Autonomy and Accountability: Enduring Tensions in the European Commission's Development." In *Multi-Level Union Administration: The Transformation of Executive Politics,* edited by Morten Egeberg, 31–50. Basingstoke: Palgrave Macmillan.

Egeberg, Morten and Andreas Heskestad. 2010. "The Denationalization of Cabinets in the European Commission." *Journal of Common Market Studies,* 48, no. 4: 775–786.

Ellinas, Antonis and Ezra N. Suleiman. 2008. "Reforming the Commission: Between Modernization and Bureaucratization." *Journal of European Public Policy,* 15, no. 5: 708–725.

Ellinas, Antonis and Ezra N. Suleiman. 2012. *The European Commission and Bureaucratic Autonomy: Europe's Custodians.* Cambridge: Cambridge University Press.

Fabbrini, Sergio. 2010. *Compound Democracies: Why the Europe and the United States Are Becoming More Similar.* Oxford: Oxford University Press.

Flinders, Matthew. 2004. "Distributed Public Governance in the European Union." *Journal of European Public Policy,* 11, no. 3: 520–544.

Goodsell, Charles T. 2011. *Mission Mystique: Belief Systems in Public Agencies.* Washington, DC: CQ Press.

Gravier, Magali and Camille Roth. 2016. "Practices of Representative Bureaucracy in the European Commission." Paper presented at 74th Annual Conference Midwest Political Science Association. MPSA 2016. Chicago, IL, USA. http://perg-tamu.com/documents/2016/6/GravierAndRoth_MPSA2016.pdf.

Greenwood, Justin. 2017. *Interest Representation in the European Union.* London: Palgrave, 4th edition.

Hofmann, Herwig C. H. and Alexander H. Türk, eds. 2006. *EU Administrative Governance.* Cheltenham: Edward Elgar Publishing, Inc.

Hofstede, Geert, Gert Jan Hofstede, and Michael Mirkov. 2010. *Culture and Organizations: Software of the Mind.* New York: McGraw-Hill, 3rd edition.

Hood, Christopher. 1991. "A Public Management for All Seasons?" *Public Administration*, 69, no.1: 3–19.

Hooghe, Liesbet. 1999. "Consociationalists or Weberians? Top Commission Officials on Nationality." *Governance*, 12, no. 4: 397–424.

House, Robert J., Paul J. Hanges, Mansour Javidan, Peter W. Dorfman, and Vipin Gupta, eds. 2009. *Culture, Leadership and Organization: The GLOBE Study of 62 Countries.* Thousand Oaks, CA: Sage Publications, Inc.

Jones, Michael L. 2007. "Hofstede—Culturally Questionable?" Paper presented at Oxford Business and Economics Conference. Oxford, UK, June 24–26, 2007. https://ro.uow.edu.au/commpapers/370/.

Kassim, Hussein. 2018. "The European Commission as an Administration." In *The Palgrave Handbook of Public Administration and Management in Europe*, edited by Edoardo Ongaro and Sandra van Thiel, 783–804. London: Palgrave Macmillan.

Kassim, Hussein, John Peterson, Michael W. Bauer, Sara Connolly, Renaud Dehousse, Liesbet Hooghe, and Andrew Thompson. 2013. *The European Commission of the Twenty-First Century.* Oxford: Oxford University Press.

König, Thomas and Lars Mäder. 2014. "The Strategic Nature of Compliance: An Empirical Examination of Law Implementation in the European Union." *American Journal of Political Science*, 58, no. 1: 246–263.

March, James G. and Johan P. Olsen. 1989. *Rediscovering Institutions: The Organizational Basis of Politics.* New York: The Free Press.

Minkov, Michael. 2011. *Cultural Differences in a Globalizing World.* Bingley, UK: Emerald Group Publishing Limited.

Nagel, Maximilian and B. Guy Peters. 2018. "Representative Bureaucracy and the European Union: Promise and Pitfalls." Paper presented at conference on "Community in Crisis?" Zeppelin University. Friedrichshafen, Germany.

Olsen, Johan. 2003. "Toward a European Administrative Space?" *Journal of European Public Policy*, 10, no. 4: 506–531.

Painter, Martin J. and B. Guy Peters, eds. 2010. *Tradition and Public Administration.* Basingstoke: Palgrave Macmillan.

Panizza, Francisco, Conrado Ramos, and B. Guy Peters. 2019. "Party Professionals, Programmatic Technocrats, Apparatchiks and Agents: A Typology of the Modalities of Patronage." *Public Administration*, 97, 141–161. forthcoming.

Peers, Steve and Marios Costa. 2012. "Accountability for Delegated and Implemented Acts after the Treaty of Lisbon." *European Law Journal*, 18, no. 3: 427–460.

Peters, B. Guy. 1992. "Bureaucratic Politics and the Institutions of the European Community." In *Euro-Politics: Institutions and Policymaking in the New European Community*, edited by Alberta M. Sbragia, 75–122. Washington, DC: The Brookings Institution.

Peters, B. Guy. 2008. "The Napoleonic Tradition." *International Journal of Public Sector Management*, 21, no. 2: 118–132.

Peters, B. Guy. 2018. *The Politics of Bureaucracy: An Introduction to Comparative Public Administration*. London: Routledge, 7th edition.

Peters, B. Guy. Forthcoming. *Administrative Traditions and Administrative Reform*. Oxford: Oxford University Press.

Reichard, Christoph. 2003. "Local Public Management Reforms in Germany." *Public Administration*, 81, no. 2: 345–363.

Rokkan, Stein. 1968. "Norway: Numerical Democracy and Corporate Pluralism." In *Political Oppositions in Western Democracies*, edited by Robert A. Dahl, 70–115. New Haven, CT: Yale University Press.

Rouban, Luc. 2004. "Politicization of the French Civil Service: From Structural to Strategic Politicization." In *Politicization of the Civil Service in Comparative Perspective: The Quest for Control*, edited by B. Guy Peters and Jon Pierre, 81–100. London: Routledge.

Rouban, Luc. 2010. "L'Inspection générale des Finances 1958–2008: Pantouflage et reneouveau des stratéegies élitaires." *Sociologies Pratiques*, 2010/2, no. 21: 19–34.

Sbragia, Alberta M. 1993. "The European Community: A Balancing Act." *Publius: The Journal of Federalism*, 23, no. 3: 23–38.

Sbragia, Alberta M. 2000a. "The European Union as Coxswain: Governance by Steering." In *Debating Governance: Authority, Steering, and Democracy*, edited by Jon Pierre, 219–240. Oxford: Oxford University Press.

Sbragia, Alberta M. 2000b. "Governance, the State and the Market: What Is Going On?" *Governance*, 13, no. 2: 243–250.

Schmidt, Vivien A. 1990. *Democratizing France: The Political and Administrative History of Decentralization*. Cambridge: Cambridge University Press.

Schön-Quinlivan, Emmanuelle. 2011. *Reforming the European Commission*. London: Palgrave Macmillan.

Silberman, Bernard S. 1993. *Cages of Reason: The Rise of the Rational State in France, Japan, the United States and Great Britain*. Chicago: University of Chicago Press.

Suvarierol, Semin, Madalina Busuioc, and Martijn Groenleer. 2013. "Working for Europe?: Socialization in the European Commission and the Agencies of the European Commission." *Public Administration*, 91, no. 4: 908–927.

Treib, Oliver. 2006. "Implementing and Complying with EU Governance Outputs." *Living Reviews in European Governance*, 1, no. 1: 1–24.

Trondal, Jarle. 2010. *An Emergent European Executive Order*. Oxford: Oxford University Press.

Trondal, Jarle and B. Guy Peters. 2013. "The Rise of the European Administrative Space: Lessons Learned." *Journal of European Public Policy*, 20.2: 295–307.

Trondal, Jarle, Zuzana Murdoch, and Benny Geys. 2015. "On Trojan Horses and Revolving Doors: Assessing the Autonomy of National Officials in the European Commission." *European Journal of Political Research*, 54, no. 2: 249–270.

Wayneberg, Ellen. 2017. "Framing en Belied." *Beliedsonderzoek Online*.

Wille, Anchrit C. 2013. *The Normalization of the European Commission: Politics and Bureaucracy in the EU Executive*. Oxford: Oxford University Press.

Williams, Garrath. 2005. "Monomaniacs or Schizophrenics?: Responsible Governance and the EU's Independent Agencies." *Political Studies*, 53, no. 1: 82–99.

Zacka, Bernardo. 2017. *When the State Meets the Street: Public Service and Moral Agency*. Cambridge, MA: Harvard University Press.

Zito, Anthony. 2001. "Epistemic Communities, Collective Entrepreneurship and European Integration." *Journal of European Public Policy*, 8, no. 4: 585–603.

Appendix 1

Dimensions of Organizational Culture

a. **Hofstede**
  Means-oriented versus goals-oriented
  Internally oriented versus externally oriented
  Easy-going versus strict work discipline
  Open versus closed system
  Local versus professional
  Employee-oriented versus work-oriented

B. **GLOBE**
  Performance orientation
  Future orientation
  Assertiveness orientation
  Social collectivism
  In-group collectivism
  Humane orientation
  Power distance
  Gender egalitarianism
  Uncertainty avoidance

C. **Minkov**
  Industry versus indulgence
  Monumentalism versus flexutility
  Hypometria versus prudence
  Exclusionism versus universalism

Sources: Hofstede, Hofstede, and Minkov (2010); House (2011); Minkov (2011).

Chapter 8

The Leadership Deficits of Surplus Germany

Wade Jacoby and Elizabeta Jevtic-Somlai

How can economic and political integration take place among states with varying levels of wealth? This perennial research question in European Union (EU) studies is often framed around regulatory politics (Egan 2014; Newman and Posner 2018). Indeed, Alberta Sbragia (2000, 316–321) framed clashes of regulation among "rich and poor" EU member states as a central issue twenty years ago.[1] In that work, which drew on her expertise on trade regimes and Southern Europe, Sbragia emphasized EU enlargement—then taking shape for Central and Eastern Europe (CEE)—as an important new locale for researching this tension. Emphasizing enduring "tradeoffs" rather than one-time "bargains," Sbragia (2000, 321) stressed the need for "thinking seriously about the tradeoffs intrinsic to enlargement."

This chapter foregrounds two sharp trade-offs that have since emerged in full force: one between trade flows inside the Single Market and the difficulties that can arise from the complementary net capital flows that always accompany net trade flows and another a trade-off between the desire to respond humanely to massive refugee flows into Europe and the practical challenges to integrating refugees into national life. Both sets of trade-offs often pit "rich" Germany against "poor" CEE states. German policy, we will show, forces often-painful adjustment in neighboring states, among which are the four "Visegrád" states of Poland, Hungary, the Czech Republic, and Slovakia.[2]

Our core claim is thus a response to Sbragia's injunction, showing that rich Germany's policies do pose deep challenges to the poorer Visegrád societies.

---

1 Also Sbragia (2010).
2 This chapter's empirical focus is Visegrád; nevertheless, we occasionally use the term CEE to underscore trends that clearly hold for the wider region.

We analyze two cases that initially may appear unrelated. The first case is of a persistent imbalance between Germany's surging production and lagging domestic consumption and investment. This generated capital flows that Germany *externalized* to the rest of the world. The second case is of refugee flows that Germany, we argue naively, helped *internalize* to the member states of the EU.

We selected these cases not only because they fit Sbragia's rich-poor dichotomy but also because Germany is the highest profile and perhaps most extreme of a cluster of northern European member states with similar policies that pose stiff challenges for Visegrád states. A few of these northern states have run high current account surpluses (the Netherlands, Luxembourg, Denmark, and, until recently, Sweden), while others took essentially the same position on refugees as Germany (Austria and Sweden). Further, both cases are crucial for debates on the rise in populism, and both are in areas of traditional member state competence but in which the EU recently has gained some authority. The cases also differ: while one (trade) was slow-developing, focused on the economy, and nearly invisible to Visegrád publics, the other (refugees) came on faster, focused on human rights and political institutions, and was highly visible in Visegrád.

Both sets of policies have forced adjustment in Visegrád and sparked a backlash there. We show that nationalism in Visegrád states is partly a response to becoming a counterpart to German capital flows.[3] To be sure, German (and other West European) capital initially was crucial for rebuilding Visegrád economies after the collapse of communism (Appel and Orenstein 2018). But, pace Mae West, too much of a good thing is not always "wonderful." Foreign capital—particularly portfolio inflows—in excess of plausible investment opportunities inflates bubbles and creates debt. Yet in the European Single Market, member states cannot stop capital inflows. Free capital mobility is a major EU feature and, in some quarters, a highly prized accomplishment, even if capital inflows in non capital-constrained economies can be immensely disruptive.[4]

And if the economic growing pains were not enough for the Visegrád region, Germany's sudden 2015 shift on refugee policy—however nobly motivated—created another huge challenge. Germany's *fait accompli* further undermined the EU's Dublin Regulation, and its subsequent push for an EU-wide quota system helped internalize this pressure to Visegrád member

---

3 Later, Southern Europeans found these same flows disruptive, and they have been a key factor in U.S.-German tensions under both Obama and Trump.

4 A point the International Monetary Fund (IMF) and other international organizations have recognized (Stone 2002; Pistor 2009; Buszko and Krupa 2015).

states, which soon proved reluctant to harbor refugees. We show that Germany's welcoming policy toward refugees during 2015–2016 exacerbated and inflamed populist sentiments in Visegrád, creating more space for illiberal parties. German policy dealt several cards that helped such illiberal parties— including the *Alternative für Deutschland* (AfD)—boost their popular vote. Moreover, illiberal parties in the region also banded together in a rare show of Visegrád consensus.

We are sympathetic to Angela Merkel's decision to accept around one million refugees in 2015–2016.[5] But the administrative, fiscal, and social capacity required to manage this inflow mandates skepticism that Visegrád states could have taken remotely similar numbers in proportion to their own populations. Without excusing the embarrassing performance of those Visegrád states taking essentially zero refugees (Scheppele 2015), these states could never hope in per capita terms to match the German effort. German policies—especially when demonized by Visegrád populists—helped inflame public opinion in the region.

The negative externalities of Germany's refugee policies thus compounded older negative economic externalities. German policy has long shifted shares of national income away from households and to firms and government. These shifts have increased national savings and decreased both consumption and public and private investments. Such policies tighten skilled labor markets and turbocharge export surpluses by undermining consumption and imports while subsidizing exports. German capital in excess of domestic investment must then flow abroad. But if it flows to countries where growth is not capital-constrained, it eventually must spark malinvestment, consumption booms, or unemployment (or all three in sequence, as in Spain) (Pettis 2013; Jacoby 2020).

With this sketch of our broad concerns, we turn now to two case studies and investigate the links between Germany and the Visegrád region. Each policy—refugees and macroeconomic policies—has contributed to the illiberal pushback from individual Visegrád states. By linking these two "problems," we follow and contribute to an emerging theoretical and empirical literature that sees populist politics as either pitting native citizens and elites against migrants (to produce right-wing populism around identity cleavages) or pitting native citizens and migrants against national elites (to produce left-wing populism around class cleavages) (Dancygier 2010; Mukand and Rodrik 2017). We show that both impulses are present in Visegrád today.

---

5 Even if smaller number eventually applied for asylum. We acknowledge that some migrants were immigrants and not refugees but follow convention in using the latter term.

PROBLEM 1: GERMANY'S GOODS SURPLUS NOW FORCES PAINFUL ADJUSTMENTS ABROAD

Foreign capital from a rich state can be a lifeline for a poor state, but in the wrong circumstances, it can also be an anchor weighing them down. The very German capital inflows that were crucial for rebuilding CEE economies after 1990 could also, in extreme amounts, become an economic danger to the region. In this, the experience of the CEE and Visegrád states was not unique. These dynamics are poorly understood in political science and in economics, let alone among elected politicians and voters. The resulting confusion is *one* important root of populism.

To see these roots, we need to go back to German behavior before the European Monetary Union (EMU). Germany's central economic problem of the 1990s and early 2000s was unemployment. Pre-EMU, Germany's traditional response already had been to subsidize its manufacturing export sectors and keep wage increases below inflation (Bibow 2017). But this technique was limited by the tendency of the national currency to appreciate as soon as export surpluses rose. As foreign buyers chased German goods, their demand for the D-Mark increased, and this higher demand pushed up the value of the currency. The stronger currency would stimulate German imports (and consumption) and hurt German exports, generally keeping the German goods surplus in a modest range.

The Euro broke this feedback mechanism because a single currency can't adjust to multiple member countries' current account movements. So when the Social Democratic Party (SPD)-Green government of the early 2000s loosened labor protections and cut welfare benefits (the so-called Hartz reforms), the Euro did not adjust upward when exports surged. Meanwhile, German consumption could not increase because the wage share of national income was declining—between 2003 and 2016, German final consumption fell from nearly 77 percent of GDP to about 73 percent, even as unemployment *fell*. As German growth continued to outstrip consumption for several years in the early and mid-2000s, German savings necessarily rose. Since national savings was simply the difference between (rising) national production and (falling) national consumption, German savings *had to* go up. German investment, however, remained flat (private) or even fell (Germany's public investment is among the lowest in the Organisation for Economic Co-operation and Development [OECD]). Therefore, this German savings surge flowed out into the rest of Europe, which had few institutional tools for managing capital inflows. After all, free movement of capital had become a major emphasis of the post-Maastricht EU.[6]

---

6 Directive 361/88 abolished capital controls for all EU members.

In the early years of strong German net capital outflows after 2003, recipients in (Eurozone) Southern Europe and in (mostly non-Eurozone) CEE[7] could generally find investment opportunities. Foreign direct investment (FDI) (especially in the auto sector), infrastructure, housing, and tourism were all areas in which investment from Germany (and other northern surplus countries) could generate reasonable returns for their savers and—given higher inflation rates in the South and East—very low real rates for borrowers. But the outward surge of German capital—which as Figure 8.1 shows soon reached between 4 and 6 percent of German GDP—soon satisfied the most productive investment possibilities in what is often called "peripheral Europe" (Bruszt and Vukov 2017).

In a nutshell, these large and sustained capital movements, because they were driven much more by the supply of capital from Germany than by the demand for capital from peripheral Europe, tended to end in investment and consumption bubbles. In the intervening years, of course, the unemployment that was Germany's central problem in the early 2000s largely abated—a mere 3.1 percent in February 2019. The new German problem is the resulting persistent imbalance between surging domestic production and lagging consumption and investment. Germany, we argue, has *externalized* that problem, first to Southern and Eastern Europe and much later to the rest of the world, including the United States, where it has sparked anger from both the Obama and Trump administrations. This is because any country exporting capital is also exporting more or less exactly the same amount of goods and services, a point we develop next.

The *fact* of Germany's large current account surplus is not in doubt but only its causes and implications. Figure 8.1 shows that Germany's current account moved from negative territory—where it had been through much of German reunification—into large surpluses by 2004.[8] In recent years, the surplus has been around 7 to 8 percent of GDP and is driving much of Germany's growth. Why? Put broadly, any national economy in an open international order has three primary sources of growth: total consumption, total investment, and net trade. Because Germany now has both low consumption and low investment, it has come to depend on exports for growth.

Export-led growth is not new, of course. Post–World War II Germany used an export-led growth model, and yet the resulting surpluses were generally

7 Only Slovenia joined EMU prior to the crisis onset, followed later by Slovakia (the only Visegrád state in EMU) and the Baltic states.

8 The current account is more than the goods trade. It is a country's net balance in traded goods *and services*, net income on its overseas investments, and net "transfers" (especially remittances). Of these components, the trade portion is, by far, the largest. Germany's (in)famous goods trade closely approximates its overall current account since the other components (small deficits in trade in services and remittances and a modest surplus in secondary investment income) usually balance each other out.

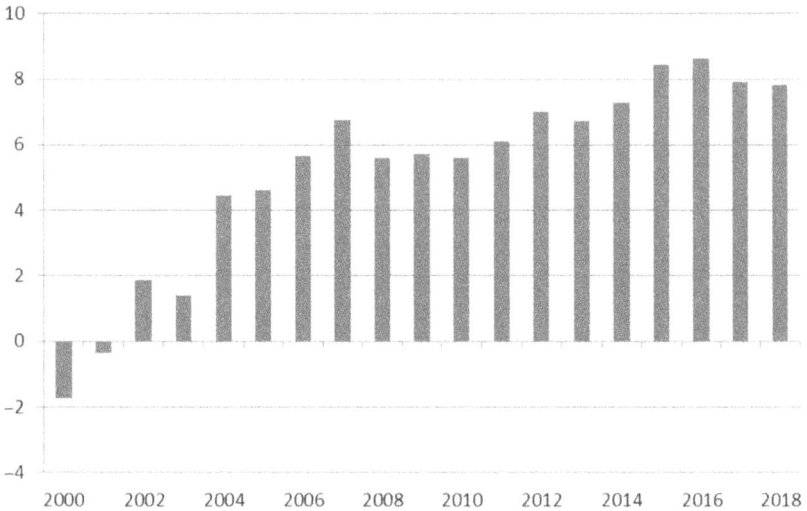

Figure 8.1   Germany's Current Account, 2000–2018 (percentage of GDP)

low (often under 1 percent of GDP) with surges short-lived (e.g., the late 1980s). What have changed are Germany's demographics; Germany's wage and wealth distribution; and, crucially, a number of its policies in the labor, welfare, and fiscal domains. Germany got older—among major economies, only Japan and Italy are similarly aged—and it has far more inequality than it used to (Fratzscher 2016). Both factors lead to higher national savings— mature workers earn more, while high earners spend a lower percentage of their incomes. Both factors also depressed investment, primarily through lower consumption expectations. Since extra savings not used domestically are, by definition, exported, this shifts demand abroad, which is reflected in a trade surplus (Jones 2009; Pettis 2013; Kollmann et al. 2014). As noted, the Euro exacerbated these trends, because the usual mechanism to restore balance had been the appreciation of the currency of surplus countries. More-over, Germany also raised taxes on consumption, cut taxes on business, and constitutionalized balanced budgets. These policy choices further depressed domestic incomes and/or increased reliance on demand from abroad. The result is a country that leans very hard on external demand.[9]

   German policy-makers and their apologists in the German media gener-ally account for the recent export surplus with reference to superior German engineering (Jacoby 2020). But it is hard to account for something new—and surpluses of this magnitude are clearly new—with an old causal factor like German engineering. There is no evidence of a sharp increase in German

---

9 Exports account for nearly half of Germany's GDP. The OECD average is just under 30 percent.

product quality in recent years. Instead, Germany's trade surpluses are not primarily the result of cost control and great products alone but the necessary complement of capital outflows, whose causal weight can "dominate" the trade balance in the age of financial globalization (Temin and Vines 2013; Baldwin et al. 2015; Pettis 2015; Jones 2009; Shin 2011). Trade surpluses are not a sign of a country "winning," as the annual celebratory "export world champion" stories in the German press often imply. They are, instead, usually a sign of major mismatches between a country's savings and investment rates.

The indicator that best captures this change in Germany is national savings, which grew from roughly 21 to 28 percent of German GDP during the period in question (2003–2018). To be clear, (poorer) German households didn't change their savings behavior very much; rather, the increased savings came from firms—corporate profits, a form of savings, reached record levels (see Figure 8.2)—and the government, which has been running surpluses at all levels. Why should it matter to other countries, including those in Visegrád, how much Germany saves? Because national savings don't just sit in banks. Rather, they are invested, either at home or abroad. And since global savings and investment *must* equal one another by definition, savings *increases* in one place logically *must* be matched either with investment growth (there or somewhere else) or by savings *declines* somewhere else (Pettis 2013, 29–32, 50–52). Germany is one of a number of countries, including China, the Netherlands, Japan, and South Korea, that are now saving far more than they are either consuming or investing.[10]

Thus, where German officials tend to claim Germany's trade surplus is simply the aggregate result of free consumer choices abroad, it is actually at least as much the result of Germany's capital outflows changing consumption and investment decisions abroad. These capital outflows are the result of policy choices that shift national income from German consumers to firms (as profits or capital subsidies) or to the government (as big budget surpluses, which reached 1.75 percent of German GDP in 2018). Global capital flows have their own logic and have now grown to dwarf trade flows. Countries that persistently save more than they invest often generate concerns among their commercial partners, either regionally or globally or both (Pettis 2013, 128–135, 142–149).

All of this brings us back to Visegrád. Germany's excess savings—that is, in excess of domestic investment—often flowed to places with higher inflation rates since it meant reduced real costs for borrowers there. As EU membership became more probable in the early 2000s, political risks seemed

---

10 To put it slightly different, a country's GDP is the sum of its consumption and investment, and, since all GDP is income for the nation's residents, GDP must therefore be the sum of consumption and savings—the only two things people can do with their income.

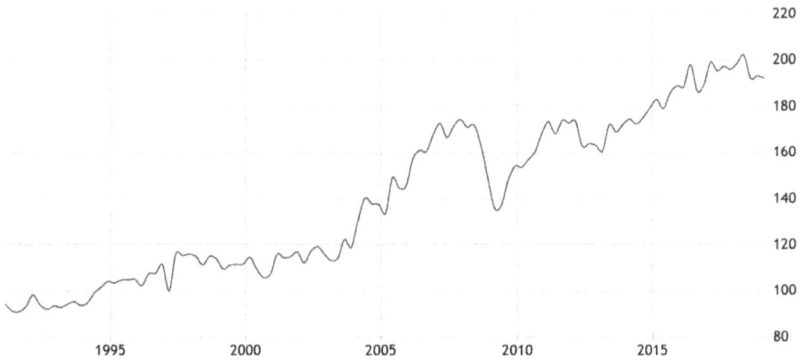

Figure 8.2   German Corporate Profits, 1990–2018 (Billions of Euros)

to decline in Visegrád and capital poured in. Some of this capital found very productive uses in a region with high skills and low wages, and the so-called wealth effects produced demand for even more capital (Pettis 2013). As savings flowed in from abroad, investment thus could rise for a time to keep up. Over time, however, Visegrád savings had to fall to compensate for the vast amounts coming in from Northern Europe (Germany was not the only country to figure out this game, particularly when EU macroeconomic policy pointed the way) (Jacoby and Hopkins, forthcoming). Malinvestment in unproductive outlets (often in housing and real estate) was one short-term result, and debt-fueled consumption (the opposite of savings) was another (Bohle 2018). When liquidity sharply contracted after 2007, CEE's need to pay back German savers resulted in a brutal mix of internal depreciation and currency depreciation.[11]

Could these negative externalities have been avoided? Once German policy shifted aggressively in the early 2000s to dampen internal consumption, it would have been very difficult. With free capital flows a part of Single Market rules, there are few mechanisms for stopping such inflows. Arguably, the EU's 1999 Financial Services Action Plan (FSAP) incentivized cross-border portfolio flows and contributed to the upward spike in German capital outflows after 2003.[12] At this point, CEE and Visegrád states were in the final stretches of membership negotiations, which would have made capital controls quite difficult even if the full extent of the danger had been widely recognized.[13]

---

11 In CEE, depreciation was used by Hungary and, to an extent, Poland, but not Romania, the Czech Republic, Bulgaria (which pegged), or Slovakia (which joined the Euro). Southern Europe, which could not depreciate, tried to restore balances with internal depreciation alone (e.g., "austerity") (Blyth 2013).

12 FSAP also increased speculative flows, which later made more difficult EMU states' efforts to manage legacy debts. See Piattoni and Notermans (this volume, chapter 9).

13 Only Poland's central bank worked actively to limit domestic indebtedness.

International banks were willing to lend, and many citizens in poorer transformational countries can hardly be blamed for accessing freely extended capital at historically good rates. It would have been hard for Visegrád states to stop them. Sadly, few Visegrád central banks even tried (Buszko and Krupa 2015).

Thus, the borrowing binge in both Visegrád and Southern Europe is connected with a prior German savings binge that generated capital well beyond Germany's investment needs, which remained roughly flat over the period (Jacoby 2020). Given EU rules, foreign borrowers had weak legal alternatives to accepting Germany's imported capital. Germany, thus, imports consumer demand from abroad precisely because it has taken policy steps to deny itself the capacity to consume its own product (or an equivalent amount of foreign products). Relatively low German wages become problematic not primarily because they "undercut" other states but because they are part of a whole range of policies that depress German consumption and imports and, instead, import demand from other states (Johnston, Hancké, and Pant 2014; Hassel 2017).

While parts of the Visegrád region have seen incomes grow through industrial FDI, other parts of the region have suffered from access to cheap capital that could not be (or at least was not) used productively. Because the mechanisms at work are both extremely powerful *and* quite hard for ordinary citizens or even ordinary policy-makers to understand, they generate a backlash that is ferocious—because it's driven by the nearly inescapable need to repay debt—but not coherent—because the role of German policy shifts is mostly invisible. In something like the way American politics has generated a fierce but economically illiterate response to massive and sustained inflows of foreign capital in an environment where capital is already plentiful, Visegrád regimes have also generated half-coherent, angry nationalist economics with a focus on foreign banks more than on foreign manufacturing firms (Hawkins et al. 2019).[14]

Excellent scholarship documents different facets of this dualism (Bálint 2014; Bruszt 2008; Drahokoupil 2008; Bohle and Greskovits 2012; Podkamincr 2013; Johnson and Barnes 2015; Bohle and Jacoby 2017b; Epstein 2017; Medve-Bruszt and Vukov 2017; Bohle 2018). Global input-output data that decompose industrial value chains show that upskilling in Visegrád is real and that returns to higher skills are growing from already high levels (though not as fast as returns to capital). However, low- and medium-skilled workers have lost income shares (Timmer et al. 2014).

---

14 Traditional parties in the region made plenty of mistakes. Such "representational failures" are central to the emerging consensus on populism and complement our analysis, which does not try to make "economics" the only cause of populism (e.g., see our next case study).

Our intent is not to make such dualist trends a monocausal explanation for rising Visegrád populism or European reform blockades. Instead, we stress simply that Germany's economic preferences are both deeply rooted at home and disruptive abroad. Germany can import an outsized share of currently scarce global demand, but it can only do this by venting corporate and government savings to other states. Such states, in turn, have relatively few options outside policies that restrain the demand for foreign goods among substantial sectors of the population. After all, foreign capital obviously has to be paid back. Between 2007—the year the crisis began in the region—and 2017, the average swing in the current account of the eleven CEE EU members has been 15 percent of GDP.[15] Bulgaria went from −23.9 percent of GDP in 2007 to +6.5 percent in 2017. In 2007, *every* state in CEE ran a deficit. By 2017, only Slovakia (−2.0) and Romania (−3.2) did. Moreover, these debts had to be managed in a situation of very low inflation, meaning the real value of debt remained high.

Increasingly, then, we see CEE and Visegrád states following the path blazed by Germany and other northern creditor states (and indeed the path taken by Asian countries after the current account crisis there in the late 1990s): reduce labor's share of national income, subsidize capital in exporting sectors, and hope the resulting inequality can be managed politically. But whereas Germany has a robust social state that redistributes market income quite aggressively, no such social state is available in Visegrád. The more modest social programs they have are stretched to capacity, and conventional parties of center, right, and left have been damaged by the policy package just sketched.

The resulting political mess is *not* "all Germany's fault"—after all; Visegrád societies face many difficulties, including demographic contraction and severe political corruption. Visegrád central banks and finance ministries certainly could have tried harder to stem excessive inflows. Yet we insist that any effort to understand political tensions there cannot make analytical headway without understanding Germany's economic externalities. Sadly, any hopes that the (presumably) final Merkel-led government might operate differently with an SPD Minister of Finance have been dashed by a bland coalition agreement and defiantly *status quo* thinking on most issues related to the European economy (Coalition Agreement between the CDU-CSU and SPD 2018). In office, SPD finance minister Olaf Scholz's official statements are largely in line with those of his long-time CDU predecessor in the office, Wolfgang Schäuble.

---

15 Unweighted average based on Eurostat data. Author calculations.

PROBLEM 2: GERMANY'S REFUGEE POLICY ALSO FORCES ADJUSTMENT IN VISEGRÁD

It is no secret that the EU's refugee policy since fall 2015 has forced adjustment and caused a pushback by its Visegrád members. Contrary to the first case study, where the economic disruptions happened slowly and were hard for both Visegrád elites and voters to connect to German behavior, no such difficulty existed when connecting refugee policy to Germany's response to it (irrespective of its reality) (Bohle and Jacoby 2017a).

Skeptical Visegrád politicians—led by not only Orbán but also Fico and, since the October 2015 elections, Polish politicians—cleverly used existing anti-refugee sentiments to further inflame public opinion across the Visegrád states (Hegedűs et al. 2016). Since Visegrád public opinion already saw both refugee inflows and German power as major concerns,[16] very little official fear-mongering was required to lead many citizens to make the connection from an anti-refugee to an anti-Germany position. A full 94 percent of Visegrád respondents told pollsters that their governments were not "supporting Angela Merkel's policy" (Krastev 2015; Hegedűs et al. 2016, 8). Though Merkel acted in rough concert with Austrian and Swedish leaders, it was her decision that was most seized upon by Visegrád leaders to turn nationalist sentiments into a vote-winning cause. This move furthered the "basic schism between the Visegrád countries and Western European countries," and legitimized populist movements in the Visegrád bloc (Gábor 2016, 10). That the immigration discussions continue to be used as a slogan to justify any populist actions is evident in the continued squabbles between Visegrád countries and EU, as well as their unwillingness to comply with EU quotas (McKenzie 2018).

While the economic case saw Germany *externalize* a traditional problem in its domestic political economy over a longer period of time, the refugee case saw Germany attempting to address a global issue in fairly short span of time and by default *internalize* it to the EU context. To be sure, the refugees—some of whom had been in flight for months or even years—were headed for Europe, and the EU's inflexible and underfunded "Dublin Regime" was in no way prepared to deal with the massive inflow or Germany's reaction

---

16 Pew Research Center, "Post-Brexit, Europeans More Favorable toward EU," June 2017, p. 20. While most Europeans view Germany favorably, Visegrád respondents feel it has too much power over EU decisions (e.g., 54 percent in Poland; 49 percent in Hungary).

to it (Alexander 2017).[17] But few doubt that Merkel's surprising decision on September 2, 2015, made in conjunction with the then-Austrian chancellor Werner Faymann, not to close the so-called Balkan Route into Central Europe, injected an important new dynamics in the overall events. In particular, Visegrád politicians have stressed the role of German state policy and its associated *Wilkommenskultur* in civil society in sending a signal to refugees not yet in Europe (Hegedűs et al. 2016, 17). In the Visegrád states, these acts were interpreted as evidence that they lacked voice and were expected to adjust to EU decisions (or in this case, Berlin's directives). Merkel's policy shift not only failed to grasp the broader consequences of openness but also (perhaps given the time constraints) disregarded the caution lights coming from Visegrád officials (Stevulova 2017). It is possible that Merkel never intended to internalize the global problem but to absorb the vast majority of the shock alone. After all, Germany had labor market shortages, and no one could say how many refugees and immigrants would come (Alexander 2017). But opening its borders and pushing others to do the same internalized a cross-regional issue to the national politics of states with wildly varying levels of wealth. Germany's stellar fiscal situation combined with its much larger economy contributed to a financial response that no Visegrád state could hope or was willing to match.

German Efforts to Integrate Refugees

Of the 1.3 million refugees arriving in Europe, Germany registered around 890,000 formal applications for political asylum by the end of 2015 (Trines 2017). In 2016, the number of asylum seekers dropped to 280,000 (Trines 2017). In just two years, Germany was gearing up to shelter and take care of more than 1.1 million people (see Figure 8.3). That number declined in 2017 to 186,644 registered applicants in Germany (OECD 2017; Chase 2018).

While these numbers meant an increase of more than 1 percent of Germany's total population, the number alone is not the actual challenge (Trines 2017). The real challenge is threefold: (1) how well can Germany integrate the refugees it takes in; (2) can it manage skeptical populist responses; and (3) what should be done with the refugees arriving in Europe that Germany is unable or unwilling to take in?

IMF estimates show that Germany's fiscal investment into asylum seekers ran at €3.1 billion in 2014 (0.08 percent of GDP), increasing to €12.1 billion by 2016 (0.35 percent of GDP) (Katz, Noring, and Garrelts 2016, 16). Germany's Ministry of Finance estimates are much higher, suggesting that Germany

---

17 The *causes* of Merkel's decision are beyond the scope of this chapter. See Alexander (2017).

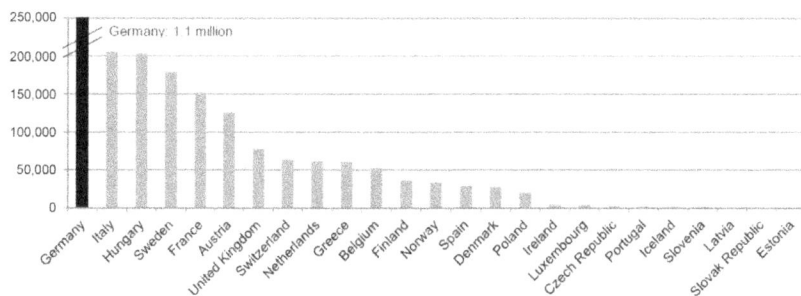

Figure 8.3 Asylum Applications in 2015–2016: (European OECD Countries, Germany Highlighted)

has invested €21.7 billion in 2016, with an additional €21.3 billion envisioned for 2017 (Finanzministerium Deutschland 2017).[18] Trines concludes that this "amount, which includes preventive measures like humanitarian aid in crisis countries, as well as financial aid to countries like Turkey and Greece, represents more than half of the country's current annual defense budget of €37 billion" (Trines 2017). More recent estimates put total German spending on refugees at between €70 and €80 billion between 2015 and 2022 (Focus Online 2018; Zeit Online 2018).

These initial estimates provide a *prima facie* case that adequate refugee integration means financial responsibility that Visegrád states might find too costly. Moreover, the right-wing response within Germany makes it harder for it to integrate the refugees, despite the availability of funds and greater experience (going back to the Yugoslav Wars) integrating refugees into labor markets. Anti-refugee sentiments almost cost Merkel her government and were a sore point during the coalition negotiations with both the CSU and the SPD (Spiegel Online 2018). Thus, the caution of Visegrád leaders might be understandable. However, Orbán has gone farther, widening the rift with Germany by making the country a focal point for Hungarian grievances that are far more visible than the trade and investment issues covered in the chapter's first half (Kubicek 2019).

And unlike the trade and investment case, the refugee crisis has seen the Visegrád states more in line with one another (and at odds with Germany). Moreover, they have gained traction with their reservations among other (including older) EU member states (Dennison and Janning 2016). Yet these reservations cannot excuse the paltry efforts that have been undertaken so far in cases like the Czech Republic (with its asylum acceptance rate of

---

18 This would mean an annual investment of €11,000 per person for 2016 (or an average of €30/person/day).

1.3 percent (8 out of 1,096 in 2017) (WorldData.info 2019) or Poland (with its 2018 rejection rate of 85.6 percent) (Helsinki Foundation for Human Rights 2019). Meanwhile, Hungary's acceptance rate is 6.8 percent, with about two asylum applications accepted a day (Bariagazzi 2017; European Parliament 2017, 60–61; Nelson 2018).[19] With financial assistance repeatedly offered by the EU, it is clear that the monetary burden is not the only reason for Visegrád states' refusal to accept refugees.

Managing Skeptical Populist Responses

There are many reasons why CEE voters and elites might reject German exhortations to accept refugees. Ivan Krastev (2017, 44–59) attributes what he calls "Eastern Europe's compassion deficit" to a number of overlapping factors: fear of a return to multiethnic societies associated with the harshest and most insecure periods of the twentieth century; anxiety in ethnically homogenous nations about population decline, falling birth rates and outmigration; the CEE societies' prior failure to integrate Roma minorities (see also Maas, this volume, chapter 4); fear of labor market competition; the residue of Soviet-era anti-cosmopolitan campaigns; an enthusiasm for the nineteenth-century German idea of the nation as ethnically homogenous; and the lack of a colonial history and thus no sense of guilt towards peoples of Asia and Africa.

Against this backdrop, Germany, nevertheless, spearheaded a fixed-quota scheme at the EU level and engineered an ugly EU deal with semi-authoritarian Turkey (Becattoros 2014). Both were electoral gifts to Visegrád populist leaders, who were able to argue to their voters that they were simply the victims of EU diktats and hypocrisy.[20] That the quota was subject to a qualified majority vote in the Council of Ministers seems not to have undercut the force of this political argument.[21] Efforts to implement the quotas have further inflamed Visegrád public opinion, and the rejectionist position of the Visegrád states also allowed other EU countries to hide behind their "recalcitrance" (Dennison and Janning 2016, 2). Where pressure on Visegrád countries is

---

19 Hungary spent virtually nothing from the central government budget on refugee support between 2015 and 2017 (European Parliament 2017).

20 Orbán argues that Hungary is "defending Europe despite the West," quoted in Korkut (2019). See also "Orbán Viktor sajtónyilatkozata az Európai Tanács rendkívüli ülését követően az M1 Híradónak," October 2016, http://www.miniszterelnok.hu/orban-viktor-sajtonyilatkozata-az-Europai-tanacs-rendkivuli-uleset-kovetoen-az-m1-hiradonak/.

21 Romania joined Hungary, Slovakia, and the Czech Republic in voting against the measure in the European Council. Poland voted for the measure while still ruled by Civic Platform. Under the subsequent PiS Government, Poland (like Hungary) has refused any refugees under the European system.

exercised, German officials must step back and let the EU lead. Any other steps will be perceived as Germany imposing its will through the EU.

Moreover, the Visegrád countries' decision to not follow German preferences over refugee issues is not only an issue of economic costs, there is also a matter of perceptions—of being seen as an equal within the EU and as a defender of EU's culture and national identity. These concerns go to the core of Sbargia's integration trade-off (2000; see also Ruiz Jiménez et al. 2004; Örkeny 2005–2006).[22] As a result, Hungary, which has had among highest number of refugees transiting through, and Slovakia, which has seen only a few, both rejected Germany's approach to refugees.

Germany's attempt to show solidarity with refugees also became a point of contention at home, with the resurrection of the nearly dead AfD in fall 2015 (Moulson 2018). Merkel's unanticipated policy shift also tested European security strengths (e.g., the Berlin Christmas market attack was perpetrated by an asylum seeker), likely pushed Brexit from a losing electoral proposition to a winning one, and revealed striking gaps in European solidarity. While improving hundreds of thousands of refugee lives, it came at a high cost, one that the newly elected leadership across Europe might not be willing to pay in the long term.[23]

Policy Considerations Going Forward

How might Germany begin to move Visegrád skeptics back toward a common EU position? First, there is a need for a diplomatic "reset," a moratorium on leading German officials commenting caustically on Visegrád reluctance to follow Germany's lead (Jovanovic 2018). Criticism from Berlin, however justified, has often been counterproductive. Germany's leadership is perceived in Visegrád as self-serving, so it is little wonder that Visegrád countries resist it. Worse, while individual Visegrád states often have been angered by German policy since becoming EU members, the refugee crisis seems to have unified the Visegrád states much more than, say, divisive bailout politics in the wake of the economic crisis. "Visegrád cooperation" used to be an oxymoron. More recently, however, we've seen more coordinated Visegrád action. Visegrád countries' vocal reluctance to share the refugee burden also strengthened other far-right and populist movements across Europe, including the AfD in Germany. AfD pressure was clearly visible

---

22 Visegrád public opinion data show that while these countries feel close to the EU, emotional attachment to country prevails over emotional attachment to Europe. See Kubicek (2019).

23 Pew data show that while the majority of Europeans do not hold anti-refugee sentiments, most disprove of how EU is handling the issue (September 19, 2018). http://www.pewresearch.org/fact-tank/2018/09/19/a-majority-of-Europeans-favor-taking-in-refugees-but-most-disapprove-of-eus-handling-of-the-issue/.

during the building of the German coalition in the first half of 2018, and the Coalition Agreement's new annual refugee ceiling cemented the fact that Merkel had to sacrifice her open-door policy in order to save the CDU/CSU alliance and the grand coalition with the SPD (Huggler 2018). The annual cap of 200,000 refugees proved a victory for the skepticism of the AfD and the Visegrád bloc.

Second, Germany will need to tread carefully in its own traditional use of migrant workers from CEE. Germany has a long track record of employing skilled workers from the CEE and Visegrád countries. It has continued to do so in 2014 and 2015, to compensate for the lack of labor force, employing on average 533,000 foreigners annually (Der Spiegel 2015). Germany's eagerness now to integrate many refugees into the labor market both fulfills a pressing need and implies less German dependence on skilled workers from the CEE countries. This need not be a source of tension if carefully managed. As their own populations decline, CEE countries will be eager to keep their skilled workers at home. However, remittances, long a source of increased consumption at home, would then decline as well (Bohle and Jacoby 2017b).

Finally, future reform debates need to better address the relationship between loyalty to European humanitarian values, rule of the law, and security. The proposed restructuring of regional funds, such as the European Regional Development Fund, to support member states that host migrants and refugees in order to pay for new housing, language courses, and skills training is a step in the right direction and might be an alternative way to tackle the challenges faced by the current (clearly inadequate) Dublin system of distributing asylum seekers (Kleist 2018). As Dullien (2016, 10) suggests, creating a unified system could help the EU continue its humanitarian effort in a more unified manner, without giving up its security. However, any effort would need to be instigated and built with Visegrád countries' ideas, approval, and assistance.

Given the current state of affairs between the Visegrád and other EU members, it remains to be seen if such development is possible. It strikes us as likely only if the numbers of refugees assigned to Visegrád states for the near future is little more than symbolic. Of course, even if the new German leadership practices skillful diplomacy and gradually distances itself from the impression that Germany would try to absorb nearly unlimited numbers of refugees, the highly visible aftereffects of the policy will reverberate in Visegrád. If, over time, Germany manages the complex labor market, cultural, educational, and domestic security implications of a substantial refugee population, it is conceivable that Visegrád states may make more efforts in that direction. For now, Germany's decision to internalize a global problem has been met with fierce and, we think, durable resistance in Visegrád.

CONCLUSION

This chapter has looked at two different policy domains: trade/investment and refugees. It argues that Germany has been predictable in one area, erratic in the other, and mostly dangerous for Visegrád in both. In turn, the externalities—seen and unseen, visible and invisible—have helped drive Visegrád politics in a more national-populist direction. The externalities have not always been intended by Germany—or even very well understood by German elites—but the consequences for the European regionalism at the center of Alberta Sbragia's work are quite negative, nevertheless. To be sure, the forces we document exist alongside other forces driving populism. Illustrative evidence has helped us explore ideas seldom linked together in the European reform debate.[24] Our analysis points an accusing finger at Germany, but in no way is this meant to excuse the abhorrent behavior of many of the Visegrád region's most high-profile leaders. The shredding of constitutional norms and undermining of democratic institutions is a cause for great concern, and that is not Angela Merkel or Wolfgang Schäuble or Olaf Scholz's fault.

At the same time, the dynamics we emphasize are both important and linked: we have showed how the widespread movement toward export-oriented manufacturing in Visegrád tends to widen disparities in economic returns to skills. In turn, this trend away from decent returns to low skills not only exacerbates domestic inequality, but also, of course, is likely to pit whatever refugees might achieve residency in Visegrád against native workers in the low wage service sectors.[25] Thus, if a key governance task for Visegrád states was to learn to benefit from foreign capital without being swamped by it, their techniques for doing so—emphasizing FDI for higher value-added manufacturing—have tended to make them even less capable of integrating refugees into their national labor markets. Their defense against the German capital export machine was to make their own attenuated version of it (generating small rather than large surpluses). Meanwhile, their states and civil societies clearly lack the resources being devoted to refugees in Germany, Austria, or Sweden.

At some level, Visegrád elites and voters know this. They also seem to feel—and fear—the tensions that result from even small numbers of refugees. While it is tempting to regret this parochialism in the context of tragedies in Syria and Iraq, these fears are also understandable. As Dancygier's work on the United Kingdom shows, there is a recipe here for substantial conflict, either *migrant/refugee versus native conflict* (in

---

24 For an exception, see Matthijs (2016).
25 Were refugees able to acquire the skills to compete for jobs in advanced manufacturing sectors in Visegrád, this judgment would have to be revised.

the less likely event that Visegrád parties defend migrant access to public goods like housing, education, or public employment) or *migrant versus state conflict* (in the more likely case that they do not) (Dancygier 2010). Meanwhile, even if labor markets are relatively open, if refugees in Visegrád have high reservation wages—the amount required to move an individual into a job—the resulting reliance on the already-modest Visegrád social states will likely breed more resentment. That these tensions exist in many states outside Visegrád helps us understand that while the Visegrád states are poster children for their current reluctance to take refugees, they are hardly alone.

While this chapter framed an important EU dilemma around Alberta Sbragia's twenty-year-old insight about the difficulties of rich and poor states integrating, we conclude it with reference to her 2010 article in the *Journal of European Public Policy* in which she drew attention to U.S.-EU trade frictions. Subsequently, Germany's policies have angered the Obama administration and, as the EU overall goes more and more into current account surplus (now over 3 percent), have also generated major frictions with the Trump administration. To be sure, neither U.S. administration has clearly understood the full roots of the problem of capital flow dynamics, but even if misdiagnosed, the problems emanating from Germany are real and give a new dimension to the inter-regional trade rivalry analyzed by Sbragia. And while Obama generally welcomed the Merkel refugee policy, Trump has criticized it. Our point is not that he is right to do so but that he mirrors Visegrád's use of German policy as a kind of antimodel in appealing to his popular base. After calling her refugee policy "insane" during his campaign, he later tweeted, "We don't want what is happening with immigration in Europe to happen with us!" (Posener 2018).

What is to be done? The road to a better-functioning EU is hard, but we think it begins in Berlin simply because Berlin is calling so many of the shots (Bulmer and Paterson 2019). Of the three usual sources of economic growth—total consumption, total investment, and net trade—Germany now relies too much on the latter and uses policy to restrict the other two. This must change. The EU Commission and European Central Bank have already been distancing themselves from Germany's preferred austerity-heavy policy mix for crisis-hit countries. Europe should now strengthen the macroeconomic imbalance procedure (MIP)—its main instrument for national macroeconomic policy—by disallowing large current account surpluses. It should consider allowing member states—who are now generally much more vigilant—to also slow or stop capital inflows on macroprudential grounds. And Germany and other northern creditor states should embrace these difficult changes—or risk seeing the Euro collapse and return to trade adjustment through exchange rates.

We are more ambivalent in our prescriptions on the refugee challenge. On the one hand, Merkel may be right that "Germany can do it."[26] Certainly, many poorer states nearer the chaos in the Middle East have taken far more refugees per capita than Germany and Sweden. A million refugees should not overwhelm a union of 500 million (Dullien 2016, 6–12). On the other hand, more will eventually come. And any popular *perception* of sustained, uncontrolled refugee inflows would likely generate enough anxiety to swamp even the most stable European democracy (Krastev 2017). Reform of EU-wide regulations on refugee inflows that acknowledge economic and public order concerns while respecting the human rights of those fleeing violence thus seem to us justifiable on pragmatic grounds. More and better spending on refugees' education, training, housing, and health care (including psychological health) is also critical, and it is to Germany's credit that it has done so. This helps with both dilemmas in this chapter, internalizing problems rather than externalizing them. It increases domestic demand and domestic investment and reduces reliance on net exports.

But Europe needs Germany to pursue other policies as well. It urgently needs to slash taxes on labor and consumption (especially the value-added tax), move public investment from the low end of the OECD to the higher end,[27] and find ways to reduce soaring national savings and improve firms' investment climate. Special investment funds—already envisioned for transportation—might also be established for schools and hospitals. Minimum pensions could be established. Moving to the European level, Germany, along with other persistent surplus states, could more aggressively take the lead in continent-wide initiatives in defense, refugee integration, border protection, and research and development.

Germany's fiscal situation would worsen, as has that of every country obliged or inclined to accept savings inflows in excess of what can be profitably invested. This would be politically contentious, so why should Germany bother? Because Germany helped cause these problems and absent significant reform in Berlin, the chances of addressing Europe's underlying problems are slim. For a country that defines its long-term interests as European, the stakes are high. As long as German public culture insists its surpluses are unproblematic for others, it will understandably refuse to change policy.

Alberta Sbragia was right to emphasize the distinction between trade-offs and bargains. Germany, in recent years, has bargained well. It helped design a Euro system that allowed both tight money and big trade national surpluses—two historical German preferences that rarely fit well together before the Euro. It later helped convince the EU to push austerity and saw the resulting flight to

---

26 *Wir schaffen das.*
27 For one of the periodic flickers of hope on public investment, see Randow (2019).

safety lower its debt service by perhaps €100 billion. It resisted EU's efforts to limit its own surpluses in the MIP negotiations. Under duress in 2015, it may even have found a partial fix for its coming labor shortages while still limiting the resulting backlash by pushing an EU bargain with Turkey (and follow up deals with human smuggling networks in North Africa). But short-term bargains are different from long-term trade-offs, and German policy now needs to see this difference and act on it. If it refuses, the forces of disintegration will continue to gather strength not only in Europe but also across the Atlantic.

BIBLIOGRAPHY

Alexander, Robin. 2017. *Die Getriebenen: Merkel und die Flüchtlingspolitik: Report aus dem Innern der Macht*. Munich: Random House.

Appel, Hilary and Mitchell Orenstein. 2018. *From Triumph to Crisis: Neoliberal Economic Reform in Postcommunist Countries*. New York: Cambridge University Press.

Baldwin, Richard, Thorsten Beck, Agnès Bénassy-Quéré, Olivier Blanchard, Giancarlo Corsetti, Paul de Grauwe, Wouter den Haan, Francesco Giavazzi, Daniel Gros, Sebnem Kalemli-Ozcan, Stefano Micossi, Elias Papaioannou, Paolo Pesenti, Christopher Pissarides, Guido Tabellini and Beatrice Weder di Mauro. 2015. "Rebooting the Eurozone: Step 1—Agreeing a Crisis Narrative." Vox.eu, November. https://voxeu.org/epubs/cepr-reports/rebooting-eurozone-step-1-agreeing-crisis-narrative.

Bariagazzi, Jacopo. 2017. "Brussels Takes on (Most of the) Visegrad Group over Refugees." June 13. *Politico*. https://www.politico.eu/article/brussels-takes-on-most-of-the-visegrad-group-over-refugees/.

Becattoros, Elena. 2014. "3 Years on, What's Become of the EU-Turkey Migration Deal?" *AP News*. https://www.apnews.com/2eb94ba9aee14272bd99909be2325e2b.

Bibow, Jörg. 2017. "How Germany's Anti-Keynesianism Has Brought Europe to Its Knees." Levy Institute Working Paper. www.levyinstitute.org/publications/how-germanys-anti-keynesianism-has-brought-Europe-to-its-knees.

Blyth, Mark. 2013. *Austerity: The History of a Dangerous Idea*. New York: Oxford University Press.

Bohle, Dorothee. 2018. "The Political Economy of Housing Booms and Busts in Europe's Periphery." *Studies in Comparative International Development*.

Bohle, Dorothee and Bela Greskovits. 2012. *Capitalist Diversity on Europe's Periphery*. Ithaca, NY: Cornell University Press.

Bohle, Dorothee and Wade Jacoby. 2017a. "Dynamic Europeanization." Working Paper. European University Institute.

Bohle, Dorothee and Wade Jacoby. 2017b. "Lean, Special, or Consensual? Vulnerability and External Buffering in the Small States of East-Central Europe." *Comparative Politics*, 49(2): 191–212.

Bruszt, László. 2008. "Multi-Level Governance—the Eastern Versions: Emerging Patterns of Regional Developmental Governance in the New Member States." *Regional and Federal Studies*, 18(5): 607–627.

Bruszt, László and Visnja Vukov. 2017. "Making States for the Single Market: European Integration and the Reshaping of Economic States in the Southern and Eastern Peripheries of Europe." *West European Politics*, 40(4): 663–687.

Bulmer, Simon and William Paterson. 2019. *Germany and the European Union: Europe's Reluctant Hegemon?* London: Palgrave.

Buszko, Michal and Dorota Krupa. 2015. "Foreign Currency Loans in Poland and Hungary: A Comparative Analysis." *Procedia Economics and Finance*, 30: 124-136.

Chase, Jefferson. 2018. "Refugee Numbers in Germany Dropped Dramatically in 2017." *DW News*, January 16. https://www.dw.com/en/refugee-numbers-in-germany-dropped-dramatically-in-2017/a-42162223.

Coalition Agreement between the CDU-CSU and SPD, 2018. "Ein neuer Aufbruch für Europa, eine neue Dynamik für Deutschland, ein neuer Zusammenhalt für unser Land." https://www.cdu.de/system/tdf/media/dokumente/koalitionsvertrag_2018.pdf?file=1.

Dancygier, Rafaela. 2010. *Immigration and Conflict in Europe*. New York: Cambridge University Press.

Dennison, Susi and Josef Janning. 2016. "Bear Any Burden: How EU Governments Can Manage the Refugee Crisis." *European Council on Foreign Relations*. http://www.ecfr.eu/page/-/Bear-Any-Burden_Dennison-Janning.pdf,.

Der Spiegel. 2015. "Deutscher Arbeitsmarkt braucht mehr Ausländer." March 27. http://www.spiegel.de/wirtschaft/soziales/zuwanderung-deutscher-arbeitsmarkt-braucht-mehr-auslaender-a-1025834.html.

Drahokoupil, Jan. 2008. *Globalization and the State in Central and Eastern Europe: The Politics of Foreign Direct Investment*. Abingdon: Routledge.

Dullien, Sebastian. 2016. "Paying the Price: The Cost of Europe's Refugee Crisis." *European Council on Foreign Relations*, April.

Egan, Michelle. 2014. *Single Markets: Economic Integration in Europe and the United States*. New York: Oxford University Press.

Epstein, Rachel. 2017. *Banking on Markets: The Transformation of Bank-State Ties in Europe and Beyond*. Oxford: Oxford University Press.

European Parliament. 2017. "Country Case Study: Hungary." Tables 34–35, pp. 60–61. http://www.Europarl.Europa.eu/RegData/etudes/STUD/2017/614194/IPOL_STU%282017%29614194%28ANN02%29_EN.pdf.

Eurostat. 2017. "Asylum Statistics." *EUROSTAT*, June 21. http://ec.Europa.eu/Eurostat/statistics-explained/index.php/Asylum_statistics.

Finanzministerium Deutschland. 2017. "Flüchtlingskrise kostet Deutschland jährlich 22 Milliarden Euro." *Die Welt*, January 27. https://www.welt.de/politik/deutschland/article161565378/Fluechtlingskrise-kostet-Deutschland-jaehrlich-22-Milliarden-Euro.html.

Focus Online. 2018. "Die bisherigen Kosten der Flüchtlingskrise in Deutschland." May 18. https://www.focus.de/politik/deutschland/aufnahme-und-integration-bericht-die-bisherigen-kosten-der-fluechtlingskrise-in-deutschland_id_8949358.html.

Fratzscher, Marcel. 2016. *Verteilungskampf: Warum Deutschland immer ungleicher wird*. Munich: Carl Hanser Verlag.

Gábor, Győri. 2016. The Political Communication of the Refugee Crisis in Central and Eastern Europe. *Budapest: Policy Solutions*.

Hassel, Anke. 2017. "No Way to Escape Imbalances in the Eurozone? Three Sources for Germany's Export Dependency." *German Politics*, 26(3): 360-379.

Hawkins, Kirk, Rryan Carlin, Levente Littvay, and Cristóbal Kaltwasser. 2019. *The Ideational Approach to Populism: Concept, Theory and Analysis*. Abingdon: Routledge.

Hegedűs, István, et al. 2016. "The Refugee Crisis and the Reactions of the Visegrad Countries." Working Paper, *Hungarian Europe Society*, September 26.

Helsinki Foundation for Human Rights. 2019. Statistics: Poland. https://www.asyluminEurope.org/reports/country/poland/statistics.

Huggler, Justin. 2018. "German Coalition Talks Falter Again over Refugee Rights." *The Telegraph*, January 29. https://www.telegraph.co.uk/news/2018/01/29/german-coalition-talks-falter-refugee-rights/.

Jacoby, Wade. 2020. "Surplus Germany." *German Politics* 29(1).

Jacoby, Wade and Jonathan Hopkin. Forthcoming "From Lever to Club? Comparing Conditionality in EU Enlargement and the Eurozone Crisis." *Journal of European Public Policy,* 27.

Johnson, Juliet and Andrew Barnes. 2015. "Financial Nationalism and Its International Enablers: The Hungarian Experience." *Review of International Political Economy*, 22(3): 535–569.

Johnston, Alison, Bob Hancké, and Suman Pant. 2014. "Comparative Institutional Advantage in the European Sovereign Debt Crisis." *Comparative Political Studies*, 47(13): 1771–1800.

Jones, Erik. 2009. "Shifting the Focus: The New Political Economy of Macroeconomic Imbalances." *SAIS Review*, 29(2): 61–73.

Jovanovic, Dragana. 2018. "Germany's Merkel and Hungary's Orban Get Testy in Public over How to Handle Refugees." *ABC News*, July 6. https://abcnews.go.com/International/germanys-merkel-hungarys-orban-testy-public-handle-refugees/story?id=56406032.

Katz, Bruce, Luise Noring, and Nantke Garrelts. 2016. "Cities and Refugees: The German Response." *Brookings*, September 18. https://www.brookings.edu/research/cities-and-refugees-the-german-experience/.

Kleist, J. Olaf. 2018. "Will Finance Policies Solve the EU 'refugee crisis?'" *Netzwerk Flüchtlingsforschung*, February 28. http://fluechtlingsforschung.net/will-finance-policies-solve-eu-refugee-crisis/.

Kollmann, Robert, Marco Ratto, Werner Roeger, Jan in't Veld, and Lukas Vogel. 2014. "European Economy: What Drives the German Current Account? And How Does It Affect Other EU Member States?" European Commission, *Economic Papers*, vol. 516, April. http://ec.Europa.eu/economy_finance/publications/economic_paper/2014/ecp516_en.htm.

Korkut, Umut. 2019. "Migration Controls in Italy and Hungary: Institutionalised and Discursive Means of Audience-Making." European Union Studies Association Paper, Denver, CO, May.

Krastev, Ivan. 2015. "Eastern Europe's Compassion Deficit." *New York Times*, September 8. https://www.nytimes.com/2015/09/09/opinion/eastern-Europes-compassion-deficit-refugees-migrants.html.

Krastev, Ivan. 2017. *After Europe*. Philadelphia: University of Pennsylvania Press.

Kubicek, Paul. 2019. "Liberal Cosmopolitanism, Illiberal Nationalism, and the Backlash against the European Union in Post-communist Europe." European Union Studies Association, Denver, CO, May.

Matthijs, Matthias. 2016. "Powerful Rules Governing the Euro: The Perverse Logic of German Ideas." *Journal of European Public Policy*, 23(3): 375–391.

McKenzie, Sheena. 2018. "European Parliament Votes to Punish Hungary for Erosion of Democracy." *CNN.com*, September 12. https://www.cnn.com/2018/09/12/Europe/hungary-orban-eu-vote-intl/index.html.

Medve-Bálint, Gergő. 2014. "The Role of the EU in Shaping FDI Flows to East Central Europe." *Journal of Common Market Studies*, 52(1): 35–51.

Moulson, Geir. 2018. "Germany: Merkel Seeks to Heal Divisions after Migrant Influx." *The Washington Post*, March 21. https://www.washingtonpost.com/world/Europe/germany.merkel-pledges-that-2015-migrant-influx-wont-recur/2018/03/21/b13877d6-2d06-11e8-8dc9 3b51e028b845_story.html?utm_term=.9bb33025dd99.

Mukand, Sharun and Dani Rodrik. 2017. "The Political Economy of Liberal Democracy." Harvard Kennedy School of Government, April. https://drodrik.scholar.harvard.edu/files/dani-rodrik/files/the_political_economy_of_liberal_democracy_27march2017.pdf.

Nelson, Soraya Sarhaddi. 2018. "Hungary Reduces Number of Asylum-Seekers It Will Admit to 2 per Day." *NPR.org*, February 3. https://www.npr.org/sections/parallels/2018/02/03/582800740/hungary-reduces-number-of-asylum-seekers-it-will-admit-to-2-per-day

Newman, Abraham and Elliot Posner. 2018. *Voluntary Disruptions: International Soft Law, Finance, and Power*. New York: Oxford University Press.

OECD. 2017. *Finding their Way: Labour Market Integration of Refugees in Germany*. Paris: OECD.

Örkeny, Antal. 2005–2006. "Hungarian National Identity: Old and New Challenges." *International Journal of Sociology*, 35(4): 28–48.

Pettis, Michael. 2013. *The Great Rebalancing: Trade, Conflict, and the Perilous Road Ahead for the World Economy*. Princeton, NJ: Princeton University Press.

Pettis, Michael. 2015. "Syriza and the French Indemnity of 1871–73." Carnegie Endowment for International Peace, February 4. http://carnegieendowment.org/chinafinancialmarkets/58983.

Pistor, Katharina. 2009. "Into the Void: Governing Finance in Central & Eastern Europe." SSRN Scholarly Paper 355. Columbia University Law and Economics Working Paper. http://papers.ssrn.com/abstract=1476889.

Podkaminer, Leon. 2013. "Development Patterns of Central and Eastern European Countries (in the Course of Transition and Following EU Accession)." Vienna Institute for International Economic Studies. Research Report #338.

Posener, Alan. 2018. "When It Comes to Germany, There's Method in Trump's Madness." *The Guardian*, June 19. https://www.theguardian.com/commentisfree/2018/jun/19/donald-trump-germany-immigration-angela-merkel.

Randow, Julia. 2019. "Deficit Conquered, Germany Is Finally Boosting Public Spending." *Bloomberg.com*, February 28. https://www.bloomberg.com/

news/articles/2019-03-01/germany-is-slowly-getting-on-board-the-investment-train.

Ruiz Jiménez, Antonia M., Jaroslaw Górniak, et al. 2004. "European and National Identities in EU's Old and New Member States: Ethnic, Civic, Instrumental and Symbolic Components." *European Integration online Papers*, 8(11). http://eiop.or.at/eiop/texte/2004-011a.htm.

Sbragia, Alberta. 2000. "'Trade-Offs Rather Than Bargains in Europe?' Symposium on Governing in Europe: Effective and Democratic?" *Journal of European Public Policy*, 7(2): 316–321.

Sbragia, Alberta. 2010. "The EU, the US, and Trade Policy: Competitive Interdependence in the Management of Globalization." *Journal of European Public Policy*, 17(3): 368–382.

Scheppele, Kim. 2015. "Orbán's Police State: Hungary's Crackdown on Refugees Is Shredding the Values of Democracy." *Politico*, September 14. http://www.politico.eu/article/orbans-police-state-hungary-serbia-border-migration-refugees/.

Shin, Hyun Song. 2011. "Global Savings Glut or Global Banking Glut?" *Vox.eu*, December 20. http://voxeu.org/article/global-savings-glut-or-global-banking-glut.

Spiegel Online. 2018. "Verhandlungen Dauren An: Immer Noch." *Der Spiegel*, July 2. http://www.spiegel.de/politik/deutschland/cdu-csu-und-spd-koalitionsverhandlungen-dauern-an-immer-noch-a-1192140.html.

Stevulova, Zuzana. 2017. "'Visegrad Four' and Refugees." *Confrontations Europe*, July 15. http://confrontations.org/interface-en/visegrad-four-and-refugees/?lang=en.

Stone, Randall. 2002. *Lending Credibility: The International Monetary Fund and the Post-Communist Transition*. Princeton, NJ: Princeton University Press.

Temin, Peter and David Vines. 2013. *The Leaderless Economy: Why the World Economic System Fell Apart and How to Fix It*. Princeton, NJ: Princeton University Press.

Timmer, Marcel, Abdul Erumban, Bart Los, Robert Stehrer, and Gaaitzen de Vries. 2014. "Slicing Up Global Value Chains." *Journal of Economic Perspectives*, 28(2): 99–118.

Trines, Stefan. 2017. "Lessons from Germany's Refugee Crisis: Integration, Costs, and Benefits." *World Education News+Reviews*, May 2. http://wenr.wes.org/2017/05/lessons-germanys-refugee-crisis-integration-costs-benefits.

WorldData.info. 2019. "Asylum Applications and Refugees in the Czech Republic." https://www.worlddata.info/Europe/czechia/asylum.php.

Zeit Online. 2018. "Scholz rechnet Kosten für Flüchtling https://www.zeit.de/politik/deutschland/2018-05/bundesfinanzministerium-olaf-scholz-fluechtlingspolitik-kosten-flucht.

Chapter 9

Legacy Debt, Financial Integration, Political Polarisation and Economic Divergence

Italy and the Euro

Simona Piattoni and Ton Notermans

In late summer of 2018, Italy became the first Eurozone country to be governed by a coalition of populist and Eurosceptic parties. The general election handed a majority to a coalition composed of the Lega, the oldest surviving party which had its roots in a mobilisation against the allegedly corrupt and self-referential elites that governed Italy from *Roma Ladrona*, and the upstart M5S, whose main theme similarly was the degeneration of the governing political caste. This mobilisation was directed in equal measure at Brussels and Rome. In a remarkable turnaround for a country whose identity was "fundamentally a European one" (Sbragia 2000b: 95), both elite consensus and popular support for Europe were shattered in a relatively brief period. By 2018, 63 per cent of Italians vehemently disagreed with the statement that Italian interest are well taken into account in the European Union (EU), 43 per cent felt that Italy would be better off outside the EU (European Commission 2018a), while 30 per cent thought having a common currency was a bad thing (European Commission 2018b).

Traditionally, European integration was seen in Italy as an anchor to stabilise its public debt, modernise its economy and secure its continuous catching up, but since the onset of the Eurozone crisis a substantial segment of the population and the political elites have come to see European economic governance as a source of crisis, divergence and inequality. As a result, the government seems bent on challenging the rules of macroeconomic governance, in particular threatening to ignore its commitments under the Stability and Growth Pact (SGP). Shortly after the British decision to leave, the EU hence faces another fundamental challenge to its rules and self-image.

The relevant EU institutions—the Eurogroup, the Euro Summit, the Commission and the European Central Bank (ECB) as well as the core countries of northern Europe, particularly Germany—vehemently disagree with this apportioning of the blame. Having its roots in the stagflationary dislocations of the 1970s and 1980s (Notermans and Piattoni 2017), the EU's economic governance is built on the neoliberal assumption that the economy needs protection from politics by means of the institutionalisation of protective rules as well as market-driven pressures. Yet the crisis that unfolded in 2008 was of a fundamentally different nature and therefore it required a different approach. It essentially consisted of a repetition of the crises that hitherto had been typical of emerging markets, driven by a build-up of massive macroeconomic imbalances that subsequently were unwound in a sudden stop. We contend that the policy recipes imposed in Europe after the crisis in fact did much to worsen its impact.

Italy's accumulated gross public debt has its roots in a decade of intense social and political polarisation in the 1970s and escalating debt service in the wake of the disinflationary policies of the early 1980s. Partially with the help of the external constraints of the requirements of EMU membership, which helped amplify domestic political change, fiscal policy was brought under control by the early 1990s, making the debt largely a legacy problem reflecting past political dislocations. That legacy, however, turned into a core economic vulnerability as the crisis, precipitated by the massive macroeconomic imbalances in the wake of financial integration and the creation of the single currency, exposed the country to financial contagion forcing it into a bad equilibrium. The EU's reaction to the crisis, following the recipe of the International Monetary Fund's (IMF) old Washington consensus, prescribed fiscal austerity in combination with labour and product market liberalisation, further served to intensify the debt problem. Austerity under the conditions of a financial crisis depressed GDP growth in both Italy and its trading partners.

The recommended strategy of running current account surpluses, by generalising the German mercantilist model to the peripheral Eurozone members, further depressed overall growth and led to the double-dip recession unique to the EU. It also set Italy again on a course of rising debt/ GDP ratios despite continuous primary surpluses. The EU's adjustment programme located the solution to anaemic growth in structural reforms to free the potential of the market. Italian governments during the past two decades have implemented a host of (microeconomic) structural reforms in line with the demands of Economic and Monetary Union (EMU) and intensified their efforts during the crisis. However, they failed to produce the hoped for recovery, as they involved an attempt to solve a macroeconomic crisis with microeconomic means. The political result of the crisis, and of the ensuing policies that exacerbated it, was that Italy joined the ranks of countries in which a growing segment of the electorate came to reject the EU's growth paradigm although its political history provided a particularly fertile ground for populist contestation.

In short, Italy's second decade in the EMU, the 2010s, points to the limitations of the assumptions underlying EU economic governance, in particular the view that excessive interference with markets is the primary threat to economic prosperity and that this threat is best countered by a combination of technocratic rule-bound governance insulated from political pressures and the disciplining force of integrated markets for goods, services and finance.

A NEOLIBERAL EU?

European economic governance is frequently held to be of a fundamentally (neo)-liberal character. The EU is seen to excel in negative integration, robbing the member states of essential policy tools while not creating any comparable regulatory capacity at the supranational level (Scharpf 2010). Indeed, the EU in this perspective might seem to approach Friedrich Hayek's dream of a federal construct that would protect the market by curtailing the competences of its member states (Slobodian 2018, chapter 3). Yet overall, this understanding of EU governance is inaccurate if one considers the many policy areas—for example, the common agricultural policy—in which the EU regulates and even over-regulates (Majone 2009, 90 ff).

As Alberta Sbragia (2000a) has shown, to understand EU governance in terms of the state vacating space in favour of the market is misleading. What distinguishes this regime from its predecessor is a set of different objectives in which control of inflation takes precedence at the macro-level while microeconomic policies are to increase firm-level profitability and productivity. Where the EU's governance style displays affinities with neoliberal ideas is in its conviction that democratic governance needs to be curtailed in order to prevent it from destabilising the economy, but that programme is not tantamount to deregulation but rather envisages regulation by means of tight rules and discrctionary policies entrusted to experts.

With the Maastricht Treaty, monetary management was entrusted to a politically independent and unaccountable central bank on the assumption of an inherent inflationary tendency of democratic politics. The outcome is decidedly illiberal in the sense that it hands a public monopoly in the creation of money over to a body of experts employing a host of tools in a discretionary manner to steer the market towards a numerical target of ±2 per cent inflation. To halt an (according to this view) equally inborn tendency of democratic politics to 'buy votes' through undue fiscal expansion that in the end only serves to undermine the dynamics of the market, debts and deficits were subjected to strict rules that, while partially ignored since the early 2000s, were immediately strengthened in response to the crisis. These implied introducing a balanced-budget rule, in many cases acquiring constitutional rank. Moreover, further integration of financial and goods markets was promoted in order to punish 'unsound policies' by means of capital flight and loss of competitiveness. Alongside fiscal austerity, the EU's main strategy for overcoming the crisis consisted of an emphasis on structural reforms that allegedly liberate markets from an—yet again presumptively—inborn tendency of democracies to yield to rent-seeking interest groups that undermine market dynamics, trade unions in particular.

Germany, which played an increasingly dominant role in the EU's economic governance given the shift to intergovernmental decision-making that characterised the crisis period, was held up as living proof of the correctness of this strategy, having morphed from the sick man of Europe in the 1990s to its star performer in the 2010s through politically painful but effective reforms of constitutionally enshrined fiscal rigour, competitiveness-boosting welfare reforms and flexibilisation of the labour market. From its perspective, Italian criticism of EU economic governance could only be pure and simple scapegoating. Italy's problems were entirely homemade: its escalating debt, currently at 132 per cent of GDP, signalled its lack of fiscal discipline, while its anaemic growth rate was proof of its inability to override special interests by implementing structural reforms. Political rejection of the 'sound policies' advocated for Italy constituted a vicious circle in which poor economic performance and Euroscepticism mutually reinforced each other, with potentially disastrous consequences for the coherence of the Eurozone and the EU as a whole.

Yet the North Atlantic financial crisis that had set in 2008 had causes fundamentally different from those that the structure of EU economic management was designed to address. The efficient market hypothesis undergirding the liberalisation of financial markets, as well as the benign neglect of issues of financial stability in monetary policy, had floundered in a boom-bust cycle driven by excessive indebtedness and risk-taking (Mohan 2019). The belief that fiscal austerity and a small state liberate the dynamics of the market has given way to a resurgence of the paradox of thrift in which spending cutbacks in the aggregate increase instead of reduce debt. That liberalised markets will lead to both cross-country and within-country convergence was increasingly hard to maintain in view of a polarisation within and across states.

LOSING AND REGAINING FISCAL CONTROL

Concerns that Italy's public debt might represent a threat to the cohesion of the Euro are not new. Already in the run-up to 1999—the beginning of phase three of the Euro—it was doubted that the country was actually suitable for EMU membership, especially in German circles.[1] The threat was seen to emerge from the apparent inability of Italian governments to live within their means. At an average 114 per cent of GDP between 1993 and 1998, gross public debt was very distant from the 60 per cent threshold established in Maastricht. The budget recorded continuous deficits, barely keeping under the 3 per cent limit just before the EMU cut-off date (Hosli 1998), with the improvement reflecting incidental proceeds from privatisations and an *ad hoc* Euro-tax, hence casting doubt about its sustainability. Debts and deficits, in turn, were feared to exert inflationary pressures, both directly through their effects on demand and indirectly as they might inhibit growth and put pressure on the ECB to desist from pursuing the interest rate policy deemed necessary to reach its inflation goal (Stark 2001). It was this fear of Italian fiscal irresponsibility that drove the German initiative to strengthen the fiscal constraints of the future EMU by means of the SGP.

Yet the Italian debt primarily was a problem dating back to the 1970s and 1980s. It is impossible to overestimate the difficulty of those two decades and the lasting legacy that they have had on the Italian economy and society. During the first two postwar decades, the debt to GDP ratio remained at roughly 34 per cent, but since the late 1960s it increased for two main reasons. First, debt-financed public spending increasingly was used in an attempt to mitigate escalating social tensions. Second, the strategy of monetary disinflation, which was gradually embarked upon after the second oil price shock, escalated the debt service due to high interest rates.

Unlike most West European countries, Italy did not succeed in concluding an encompassing social contract. Tensions were further stoked by the rapid industrialisation of what still was predominantly an agricultural society, accompanied by the migration of a substantial part of the labour force from South to North. Those tensions exploded in the late 1960s, first in the form of massive wildcat strikes, soon to be followed by left- and right-wing terrorism that seemed to push the country to the edge of civil war. Though this might have furnished the occasion for a more inclusive social contract along the lines concluded elsewhere in the late 1940s, the sense of national unity and purpose that marked the immediate postwar years had long evaporated. Italian business, deeply suspicious of the left, feared their subversive potential, while the fragmented unions with tenuous links between the leadership and

---

1 See, e.g., the interview with German finance minister Theo Waigel shortly before the decision on what member states would qualify for EMU membership ('Beten Hilft Immer' *Der Spiegel* 6/1998, 2 February) and Chancellor Kohl's scepticism with respect to PM Prodi's austerity efforts ('Mißtrauen gegen Italien', *Der Spiegel* 5/1998, 26 January).

the shop floor lacked the will and the organisational capacity to be tied into corporatist concertation.

The 1970s were the years during which a proper Italian welfare state was created, offering services that already were taken for granted in other European countries. This effort unfortunately took place right when the favourable economic conditions of the postwar period ended and the Italian industrial model was undermined by epochal increases in the prices of energy and raw materials. Additionally, large sums were spent on keeping failing firms alive in an effort to keep industrial peace, while overall the composition of public spending shifted away from investment and towards consumption.

As a result, the debt to GDP ratio more than doubled between 1970 and 1985, while general government budget deficits reached an average annual rate of 6.9 per cent of GDP in the 1970s and 10.8 per cent in the 1980s (Figure 9.1). Though this Keynesian spending spree yielded some results – the country performed better in terms of growth during the 1970s than most West European countries (Boltho 2013), while current accounts were prevented from deteriorating substantially by devaluations of the

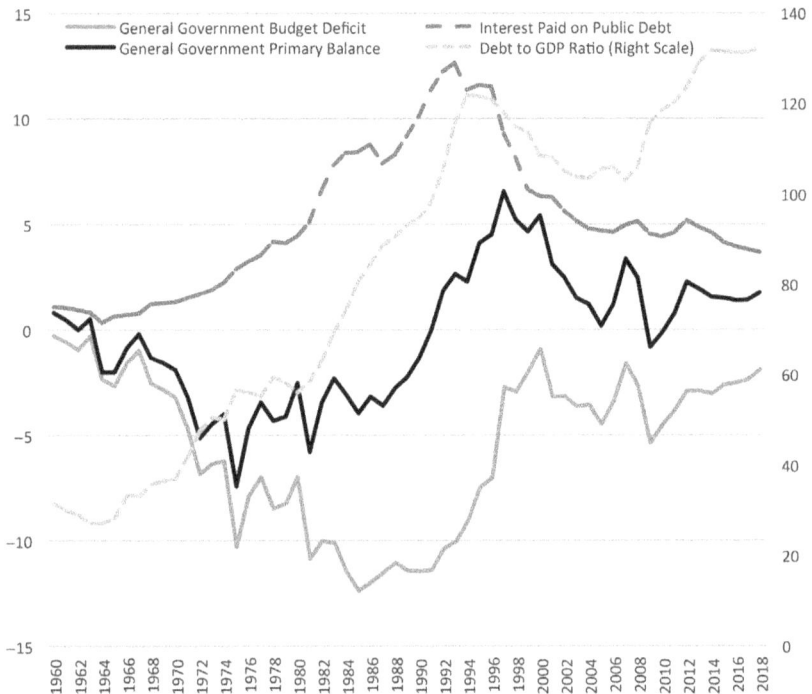

Figure 9.1 Debt, Deficits and Debt Service, Italy 1960–2018 (percentage of GDP).
Source: 1960–2011, Mauro et al 2013.

Lira—in the late 1970s, it became clear that this strategy was ultimately unworkable as Italy applied for IMF assistance in 1974 and 1977, the last Organisation for Economic Co-operation and Development (OECD) country to do so before the Eurozone crisis. Unable to implement a form of corporatist concertation, deficit-spending fuelled rampant inflation driven by a wage-price-wage spiral institutionalised by automatic wage indexation (*scala mobile*) and reinforced by an almost continuously depreciating currency. Since the late 1970s, macroeconomic policy, hence, gradually shifted towards bringing down inflation, stabilising the currency and containing spending.

A milestone in this strategy was the so-called divorce of the Banca d'Italia from the Treasury, meaning that the former no longer was required to mop up bonds that went unsold at the established minimum price at auctions. Despite this strong signal, apparently the Italian governments of the 1980s did not exert any greater prudence, as the Bank of Italy's future president, Mario Draghi, later remarked (Draghi 2011, 7). However, after the deep recession of 1982, primary deficits continuously declined to eventually move into positive territory in the early 1990s. That this trend-break initially was not reflected in a decline of overall deficits was due to the escalating interest rates that the disinflationary strategy of using the nominal exchange rate with the DM as the anchor implied.

While the need to bring the deficit under control had already moved to the top of the agenda in the 1980s (Della Sala 2004), Italy's decision to join EMU from the start was instrumental in reinforcing that process (Sbragia 2004: 57). The story of the progressive 'normalisation' of the Italian political economy and its efforts to be among the first states to adopt the common currency has been recounted many times (Scobie et al. 1996; Sbragia 2000b; Ferrera and Gualmini 2004). During the 1990s, the cross-party commitment to EMU supported by a pro-European electorate served to centralise the budget process empowering the executive at the cost of a traditionally fragmented Parliament, allowing for much tighter control of overall revenue and spending and turning what had been a European misfit in terms of fiscal policy into a 'normal' member state (Sbragia 2000b, 95–96). In particular, the role of the Council President was strengthened in order to lend greater coherence to the action of the executive and defuse the excessive intrusion of Parliament into budgetary policy. The pension system underwent a series of reforms placing it on a financially sustainable course by forcing Italians to retire later, thus redressing some of the excesses of the 1970s but also triggering the resentment of the prospective retirees and discouraging the hiring of the younger generations, and thus contributing to a high rate of youth unemployment. Taxes were almost continuously increased since Maastricht, but tax evasion has not been decisively countered.

Consequently, Italian budgets have shown a primary surplus since 1992, with only two exceptions – after the G20-coordinated reflation of 2009 and 2010 – a record unmatched by any other EMU country. Admittedly, budget discipline abated somewhat under the Berlusconi governments of the early years of the new millennium, yet the primary balance remained in surplus.

LEGACY DEBT IN INTEGRATED AND VOLATILE FINANCIAL MARKETS

Both the Italian deficit and debt/GDP ratio started to rise again with the onset of the North Atlantic Financial crisis, in 2008, and of its European component, the Eurozone crisis, in 2010. This time, though, both indicators did not signify a relapse into the political inability to balance the books but primarily reflected adverse market dynamics and the negative impact of the EU's crisis management strategies.

The groundwork for the crisis had been laid by the single currency and its accompanying Single Market in Financial Service (SMFS). By removing both exchange rate risk and the adjustment mechanism of exchange rate fluctuations, the common currency almost from its inception engendered massive macroeconomic imbalances in which large capital flows, primarily from Northern European countries, financed private and public expenditures in real estate, consumption and public debt in the southern periphery. This was reflected in a polarisation of current account positions with the northern member states running ever-higher surpluses matched by ever-deeper deficits in the southern and eastern member states. Those payment imbalances were crucially stimulated by the EU's programme of integrating European financial markets.

In part, integrated finance was considered a necessary complement to a stable Euro, as the EMU entrusted to market sanctions the disciplining of member states running high deficits and accumulating public debts.[2] This mechanism could only function if capital flows within the Union were unencumbered, which was achieved with Directive 361/1988. In part, though, the programme of integrating European finance was inspired by the desire to compete with and eventually even overtake the United States as the central player in global finance. As the United States deregulated financial markets in the 1990s, the EU also passed several pieces of legislation aimed at creating a large European financial market capable of competing with American investment and commercial banks. A number of directives were produced already

---

2 For a general statement of this strategy, see Borrás and Radaelli (2011).

in the 1970s and 1980s leading up to the creation of a SMFSs and culminating in the Second Banking Directive of 1989 (89/464/CEE of 15 December 1989) and the Financial Services Action Plan of 1999, which allowed European banks to use and create many of the 'innovative' financial instruments that eventually caused the sub-prime crisis in the United States. Moreover, financial industry appeared to be the new growth sector, so that promoting and integrating finance would also boost jobs and growth.

The programme of financial integration often is incorrectly understood as a strategy of deregulation. In fact, what changed was the mode of regulation. First, in an effort to catch up with the booming U.S. market in derivatives (that later came to be known as toxic assets), the EU passed a series of measures of positive integration promoting the trade in such instruments.[3] Second, nobody in Europe, not even the interest associations of the financial industry, ever seriously maintained that finance should go unregulated (Padoa-Schioppa 2004). The SMFS introduced supplementary legislation and a framework for banks' supervision (Epstein and Rhodes 2016). Based on the assumption, typical of liberal thinking, that the aggregate is the mere sum of its component parts, such that if each individual institution is financially sound then the system as such also will be sound, what changed instead was a discrediting of macro-prudential regulation, introduced after the Great Depression, in favour of micro-prudential regulation, which was supposed to be market-friendly and allow for a large role to the individual institutions themselves in risk assessment (Padoa-Schioppa 2004, chapter 4).

The outcome was a giant speculative boom, sometimes ironically called the Great Moderation (Bernanke 2004) that started to collapse first in the United States around 2007 but whose repercussions were soon felt in Europe as well. The U.S. crisis did directly affect the EU through the involvement of European financial intuitions in the U.S. derivatives trade, but more importantly, it exposed the fragility of Europe's model of finance that had been largely inspired by the United States. As the value of bank assets melted away and the interbank loan market froze because it had become impossible to asses risks with any confidence, financial flows to the periphery reversed as banking institutions in core countries sought to rebuild their balances. In Europe, the eastern member states were the first to run into such a sudden stop, experiencing an economic collapse that in several instances outdid what had been experienced at the height of the Great Depression in the 1930s (Åslund 2009).

---

3 For example, the Financial Collateral Directive of 6 June 2002, EU Settlement Finality Directive of 19 May 1998, Directive 2009/44/EC of 6 May 2009 amending Directive 98/26/EC, and Directive 2002/47/EC.

Finance allegedly had no fatherland as its ability to move across borders at will would force countries into a "golden straitjacket" (Friedman 2000), but faltering banks now became dependent on rescue by their home governments. The result was a potentially catastrophic vicious circle that was set in motion by the second European instalment of the crisis. With the sustainability of inflated public debt itself now coming under suspicion, interest rate differentials across countries soared with the effect of making the debt of the more heavily indebted countries increasingly less sustainable. As national sovereign bonds were downgraded, banks' assets position further deteriorated, intensifying an already-ongoing credit squeeze. The collapse of the real economy as a result of that squeeze was consequently further intensified by the downward spending adjustment provoked by the destruction of financial wealth on a massive scale (Farmer 2017). This, in turn, increased the incidence of Non-Performing Loans (NPLs) in the non-financial sector, further weakening banks' asset positions.

In line with European directives, Italy adapted its banking regulation, which had been fundamentally shaped by the vicissitudes of the Great Depression. Legislative decree no. 385 of 1 September 1993 (*Testo Unico delle leggi in materia bancaria e creditizia*) marked the end of the rigid separation between savings banks and commercial banks and reintroduced the model of the universal bank, which had been outlawed in 1936. In addition, through mergers and acquisitions, existing banks were encouraged to create larger banking companies which could, in theory, better balance the risk of collecting short-term deposits and lending long term, offer their clients better and more varied investment instruments and compete with the largest European banks. Yet unlike some other countries that had gone through the devastating financial crises of the 1990s, Italy took measures to reduce its vulnerability in Europe's integrated financial markets. Despite the changes in the regulatory framework, Italian banks remained both more conservative in their investment choices – limiting their leverage to around 14× instead of the European average of 24× – and perhaps more protected by a thick network of inter-relations (De Bonis, Pozzolo and Stacchini 2012). Moreover, they were not exposed to (foreign) toxic assets (Bologna, Caccavaio and Miglietta 2014).

In the integrated European financial markets, however, Italy could not protect itself against financial contagion, because of the relative size of its debt and the reputation for fiscal laxity that it had created (notwithstanding almost two decades of primary surpluses). Matters came to a head in the second half of 2011, when Greek debt restructuring seemed a possibility. Merkel and Sarkozy compounded the alarm by calling for private sector involvement in their meeting at Deauville in October. Suffering from a case of contagion, interest spreads started to increase rapidly, manifesting what De Grauwe and

Ji (2012, 866–867) have termed a 'bond price bubble' and creating not only financial but political panic. Whereas debt and deficit to GDP ratios were largely irrelevant before the crisis, higher debt and deficits now increased the spread (Klepsch and Wollmershäuser 2011). Yet markets did not switch to pricing what are considered the 'fundamentals'. Instead, expectations, based on reputation and therefore fundamentally of a self-fulfilling nature, now came to play a crucial role.

The sovereign debt market was turned into a Keynesian beauty contest in which market participants' expectations of other markets participants' expectations were decisive. As a result, in the wake of the crisis, interest rates spreads increased far beyond what fundamentals would justify, provoking a dramatic North-South divergence (Figure 9.2). Therefore, southern member states were consistently downgraded by credit-rating agencies beyond what fundamentals could justify (Nauhaus 2015). Although Germany had had to deal with the debt inherited from its reunification, in addition to a significant bill for bank rescues that did not have any counterpart in Italy, it could count on a reputation of creditworthiness, a complete and well-functioning welfare state, lower interest rates on its sovereigns and a lower accumulated public debt to pull itself out of the crisis. The effort to comply with the Maastricht parameters and the SGP criteria has, therefore, caught Italy and Germany at different points in their growth trajectories and has served to further amplify the distance between the two.

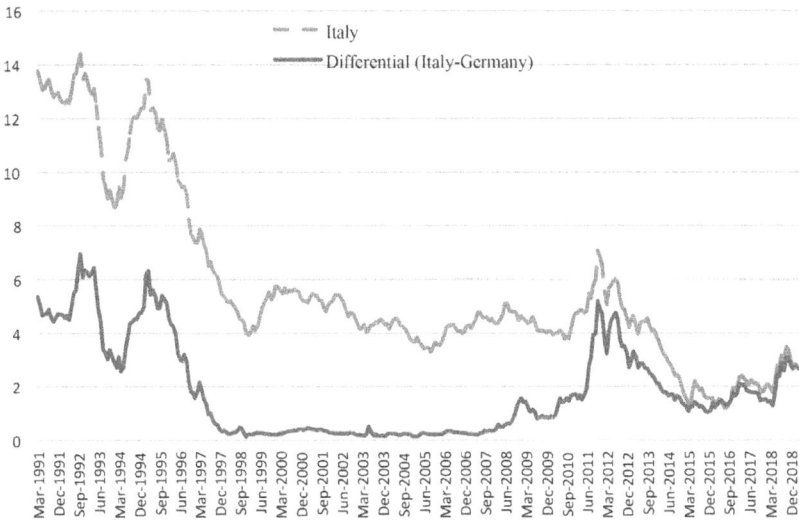

Figure 9.2   Long-Term Interest Rates (percentage per year).
Source: OECD.

DEEPENING THE CRISIS: THE EU'S
MERCANTILIST AUSTERITY

With Italy now considered the ticking time bomb under the common currency, the EU moved to impose conditionality on Italian governments. As the spread on Italian sovereigns escalated, under pressure from the EU and the ECB, on 12 November 2011, President Giorgio Napolitano nominated a former EU commissioner Mario Monti to head a technocratic government. The letter sent to the Italian government by the then ECB president Jean-Claude Trichet and *Banca d'Italia* governor Mario Draghi on 5 August 2011 indicated the policy mix that would supposedly allow Italy to prosper within the confines of the common currency: fiscal austerity and structural reforms aiming to flexibilise markets and improve the current account. A technocratic government operating under EU pressures might have appeared as way to overcome what were considered to be the deficiencies of Italian democracy, but the rescue policies failed to restore investors' confidence. Instead, it did decisively undermine popular support for the integration project while boosting the electoral fortunes of the Lega and M5S.

The recipe urged by the ECB and the Eurogroup and implemented by PM Monti followed the standard approach of radical budget austerity and structural reforms, in particular a further liberalisation of the labour market. As requested by the Eurosummit of 26 October 2011 (European Council 2011), Monti promised a balanced budget by 2013 and a structural surplus by 2014. Pension reform, introduced on 4 December 2011, would save about €30 billion within the next twenty years. An additional €26 billion in austerity measures were passed in the summer of 2012 followed by more measures in the stability law of October.

It was not immediately clear though how shrinking the public sector, especially in the midst of the crisis when the private sector was suffering from an acute credit crunch, would contribute to restoring growth. Indeed, after the U.S. crisis had erupted, the G20, supported by the EU Commission (2008), had resolved in 2008 for a fiscal stimulus to at least cushion some of the effects, but once the crisis hit the EU, the dominant thinking on this side of the Atlantic had become that shrinking the public sector would lead to a more than proportionate expansion of the private sector. This 'expansionary contraction' (Alesina and Giavazzi 2015) was strongly supported by Jean-Claude Trichet (2010) at the ECB, who did not shy from using the threat of withholding emergency liquidity assistance to banks in order to force countries into such a programme (Tooze 2018). Moreover, since much of the credit boom in the periphery had been financed with foreign funds, current account surpluses would be required to ensure repayment and such surpluses could be achieved only by depressing further the domestic economy, assuming that demand from the rest of the world would hold firm. Indeed, one notable outcome of the EU

Table 9.1. Growth, Debt and the Current Account

	2007	2008	2009	2010	2011	2012	2013	2014	2015	2016	2017	2018
GDP at constant prices (2007 = 110)												
Eurozone	100	100.5	95.9	97.9	99.5	98.7	98.4	99.8	101.9	103.9	106.4	108.4
Italy	100	98.9	93.5	95.1	95.7	93.0	91.3	91.5	92.3	93.3	94.9	95.7
United States	100	99.9	97.3	99.8	101.4	103.7	105.6	108.2	111.3	113.0	115.5	118.8
Current account balance (% of GDP)												
Eurozone	0.04	−1.47	−0.13	−0.06	−0.09	1.37	2.28	2.52	2.93	3.20	3.24	2.95
Italy	−1.39	−2.82	−1.89	−3.41	−3.00	−0.34	0.99	1.91	1.34	2.54	2.78	2.46
United States	−4.92	−4.63	−2.58	−2.88	−2.87	−2.64	−2.08	−2.08	−2.24	−2.31	−2.31	−2.38
General government debt to GDP ratio (%)												
Eurozone	65.00	68.74	79.22	85.03	87.57	91.85	94.10	94.38	92.27	91.36	89.11	87.13
Italy	99.79	102.41	112.55	115.41	116.52	123.36	129.02	131.79	131.56	131.40	131.36	132.16
United States	64.77	73.79	86.85	95.55	99.87	103.34	104.88	104.58	104.79	106.84	105.20	107.39

Sources: AMECO, authors' calculations.

crisis was that the pattern of internal current account polarisation under a more or less balanced current account for the Eurozone as a whole until 2011 was now replaced by generalised current account surpluses (Table 9.1).

The result was not growth but a renewed recession (the second dip of the double-dip crisis), this time unique to the Eurozone (Table 9.1). The aggregate again did not prove to be the sum of the component parts as the Keynesian 'paradox of thrift' re-emerged. The IMF (2012) had already warned against it, as the effort to cut deficits by each individual country would become self-defeating due to a collapse in GDP that in fact yielded increases in the debt to GDP ratios. After a slight recovery in 2010 and 2011, Italian GDP started to sag again in 2012 and did not manage to recover its 2007 level even by 2018 (Table 9.1); as a result, its debt to GDP ratio also started to increase again from around 100 per cent in 2007 to over 132 per cent in 2018. Declining growth prospects and a rising debt to GDP ratio led to repeated downgrades of the Italian public debt, further increasing the burden of debt service.[4] Moreover, the U.S. government increasingly came to object to its role of enabling generalised Eurozone current account surpluses by accepting the concomitant deficits, then also undermining the external element of what was supposed to be the EU's recovery strategy.

The EU adjustment programmes provoked increasing debt to GDP ratios and even necessitated a partial Greek default in 2012; thus, they did little to calm markets. Although the ECB had been slow to react to the crisis compared to the Federal Reserve, it now stepped in to prevent a potential collapse

---

4 Fitch downgraded Italian debt on January 27 from A+ to A−, S&P followed on 13 January, downgrading from A to BBB+ and Moody's on 13 February from A2 to A3.

of the debt accumulated by especially French and German banks that were heavily exposed to southern sovereigns. To the dismay of the German and Dutch central banks, the ECB had initiated its Securities Market Programme (SMP) already in May of 2010 alongside the first package for Greece, which had allowed it to purchase distressed private and public sector bonds on secondary markets, in practice mostly Southern European sovereigns. The intention of that programme was for the ECB to act as a buyer of last resort, propping up the price of bonds, lowering their yields and thereby breaking a self-fulfilling 'doom loop' (Draghi and Constâncio 2012).

This programme, however, had little or no effect on Italian rates, which peaked in late 2011 and early 2012, largely because Trichet now made purchases conditional on heightened austerity in Italy and repeatedly refused to intervene, considering such efforts insufficient. Mario Draghi's famous statement of 26 July 2012 that he would do 'whatever it takes to save the Euro', leading to the announcement of the Outright Monetary Transactions (OMT) programme on 6 September, did instead seem to set in train a gradual reduction in Italian sovereign bond yields. The ECB's mere announcement that it stood ready to buy potentially unlimited amounts of distressed bonds seemed to be enough to calm markets (De Grauwe and Ji 2013), without the OMT ever having to be employed.

However, the differential of Italian to German treasury bonds never returned to pre-crisis levels and started to increase again as of late 2017, with a peak after the coming into office of the M5S-Lega government in the spring of 2018. The main difference between the SMP and the OMT was that the latter was in principle unlimited, but its major potential drawback was that it was tied to a country requesting European Stability Mechanism (ESM) assistance, thereby subjecting itself to conditionality. And as the Greek experience had shown, conditionality implies severe austerity which in turn substantially increases the debt to GDP ratio. Accordingly, it would seem questionable whether making Italy a programme country under direct European control would solve its problems.

It has repeatedly been pointed out that such runs on sovereigns cannot happen in countries that manage their own currency because the central bank's ability to print money at will guarantees repayment (Pilkington and Mosler 2012; De Grauwe and Yi 2013). Yet that monetary sovereignty precludes debt runs may not be entirely accurate as a currency that is subject, or expected to be so, to persistent depreciation due to devaluing exchange rates and/or inflation may lose market confidence, eventually experiencing the impossibility of refinancing its debt in its own currency. Indeed, in the 1990s and 2000s, participation in the single currency project seemed to have the effect of lowering instead of increasing interest rate spreads; but in the constellation that occurred since 2008, it had the opposite effect. The solution of the ECB unconditionally backing sovereign debt instead proved out of reach in Europe, either because the ECB was sensitive to especially German and Dutch concerns about morals hazard, which would have required an intensification of the crisis in order to force the periphery into the structural reforms deemed necessary. Alternatively, the ECB itself may have been attached to the dogma that the cause of the crisis lay in the structural rigidities of the periphery instead of financial market malfunctioning.

Apart from halting panic, the key to recovery consisted of restoring credit to the real economy. Again, somewhat later than the Federal Reserve, the ECB sought to do so by means of providing unlimited liquidity of up to three years to the banks through various Long Term Refinancing Operations (LTRO) and Targeted Longer-Term Refinancing Operations (TLTRO) programmes as well as quantitative easing, which it started in March of 2015. The stated intention of those programmes was to counteract the credit squeeze and restart lending to the real economy, which indeed is the key to growth and recovery. Yet the programme largely proved ineffective in this respect in Italy. With the crisis, European financial markets fragmented as cross-border contracts were unwound and capital withdrew to its home base. Holdings of Italian public debt, which had internationalised in the wake of the SMFS programme, now again became more nationally concentrated. Moreover, with the yields on public debt increasing and investment in the real economy considered ever more risky, given the ongoing depression, banks used a substantial part of the liquidity provided by the ECB to increase their exposure to domestic sovereigns. As a result, Italy seemed to be moving into an additional trap.

What had started out as a banking system largely devoted to lending to the real economy and with little risk exposure came to accumulate ever larger amounts of NPLs to the real economy, curtailing its lending in favour of public debt, thus aggravating the crisis. At the same time the higher perceived risk implied that lending rates to the real economy, similar to and in part as a result of the divergence in sovereign yields, also increasingly diverged in the Eurozone. In the United States, in contrast, the FED seemed to have managed to avoid this trap through an aggressive programme that sought to clean up the balance sheets of banks[5] or resolve them, instead of the European strategy of keeping banks alive without restoring their lending capacity.

STRUCTURAL REFORMS TO ADDRESS MACROECONOMIC ISSUES

Given the economic difficulties that Italy has found itself in again since the onset of the Euro crisis, it has been almost universally concluded that

---

5 The so-called Troubled Asset Relief Programme.

the reform process set in motion in the 1990s under the pressure to qualify for EMU membership had obviously been relaxed and partially reversed as soon as the common currency had been introduced (De Cecco 2007; Culpepper 2014; Agostini and Natali 2016; Magone 2016: 94; Franks et al. 2018, 5). Brunazzo and Della Sala (2016, 223) diagnosed an "inability of Italian governments of all political stripes in the period since the Maastricht Treaty to carry out basic structural changes that should have been part of being in the single currency". Indeed, many scholars who have recounted the story of Italy's turnaround in the 1990s (Della Sala 1997; Sbragia 2000b; Radaelli 2002; Ferrera and Gualmini 2004) doubted whether the resolve of the technocrats could be maintained for long. In part the problem was a lack of credibility of Italian governments that, during the First and Second Republics, were blackmailed by their fractured constituencies and litigious coalitions and were therefore inevitably short-lived (both the first Berlusconi and Prodi governments were brought down by internal dissidents breaking off from the governing majority). In part, this scepticism was dictated by the observation that Italian society had been kept together during the troubled 1970s and 1980s by accommodating its many requests and that, therefore, a prolonged concerted effort at limiting such requests was highly unlikely. This is, in a way, precisely what appears to have happened. The prolonged effort at *risanamento* and the tax hike caused by the exceptional effort to meet the Maastricht criteria (not just the one-off tax applied by the Amato government on all savings deposits but the continuous ratcheting up of various taxes, such as the corporate income tax (IRES) and the regional production tax (IRAP), sent shockwaves through the Italian population that was adamantly opposed to the very idea of taxing wealth and religiously attached to its savings.

Yet the overall picture is not one of lack of structural reforms. In fact, significant measures were passed since the early 1990s in the field of industrial relations and labour legislation, encouraging concertation and enlisting trade unions' support in the recovery effort. Labour legislation had been progressively relaxed and the hiring and firing of workers made increasingly easier, which according to many swelled the numbers of temporary and poorly paid jobs probably without really contributing to improving overall labour productivity (Codogno 2009; Pinelli et al. 2017). A head start had been made in 1991 with law 223 of 23 July 1991, which relaxed the rules governing collective dismissals. Employment protection legislation was watered down in four main steps: the Treu reforms of 1997, the Biagi laws of 2003, the 2012 Fornero reform and the Jobs Acts of 2014. Wage indexation was dismantled and the Monti government succeeded in watering down the dismissal protection of article 18 of the *Statuto dei lavoratori*. The ability of political parties to obstruct reform, moreover, had been seriously weakened with the Biagi laws of 2002 that had effectively allowed the executive to bypass parliament in matters of labour market legislation.

Table 9.2. Labour and Product Market Reforms

	Strictness of employment protection regulation				Restrictiveness of economy wide product market regulation	
	Germany		*Italy*		*Germany*	*Italy*
	Regular contracts	*Temporary employment*	*Regular contracts*	*Temporary employment*		
1985	2.58	5.00	2.76	5.25		
1990	2.58	3.25	2.76	4.88		
1998	2.68	2.00	2.76	3.63	2.23	2.36
2003	2.68	1.50	2.76	2.00	1.80	1.80
2008	2.68	1.00	2.76	2.00	1.40	1.51
2010	2.68	1.00	2.76	2.00		
2013	2.68	1.13	2.68	2.00	1.28	1.29

Source: OECD.
Note: 0 very loose, 5 = very strict.

Table 9.2 shows the overall effects of these reforms on employment protection regulations. For regular contracts, protection has only been weakened marginally, but it remains at a level comparable to employment success stories such as Germany, the Netherlands and Sweden. Protection for temporary contracts has been radically reduced over the past two decades, though it remains slightly above average. At the same time, the incidence of such contracts has radically increased, with part-time contracts rising from 6.3 per cent of total employment in 1995 to 18.5 per cent in 2017 and temporary contracts rising from 5.2 to 12.1 per cent.[6] Protection was significantly higher in terms of additional restrictions on collective dismissals, but since 2013 – the latest available data – the Jobs Act also has provided for a significant relaxation here.

Product market liberalisation – the other pillar of structural reforms – involved privatisation of state-owned enterprises and the relaxation of regulations. The privatisation programme had started in the late 1980s and picked up steam after 1992. Most state-owned companies were sold between 1992 and 1998. Most importantly, the banking sector, which had been largely state-owned since the Great Depression, was privatised. Some privatisations may have been poorly handled – paramount examples are the recurrent rescues of Alitalia and the shameful sale of Taranto's ILVA for the nominal price of €1 to a private entrepreneur – but most were successfully implemented. Additional reforms have focussed on liberalising the professions, easing the

6 *Source*: Eurostat.

start-up of new firms, cutting red tape in general and simplifying insolvency regulation. As a result, the restrictiveness of product market regulations now is at a level comparable to that of Germany and Belgium, while still less strict than in the United States (Table 9.2).

In short, the data do not suggest that a lack of structural reforms can explain the Italian malaise. Empirically documenting the positive effects of structural reform has proven rather difficult not just for the Italian case. Such reforms may frequently have a negative short-term effect on employment, aggregate demand and public accounts (OECD 2016; Banerji et al. 2017; Piasna and Myant 2017), so that the claim for their beneficial effects must be projected into an unspecified distant future with the risk of turning the argument into an unfalsifiable dogma.

That structural reforms would prove largely ineffective cannot be all that surprising. The crisis did not have its origin in a sudden increase in labour and product market rigidities but was of a purely macroeconomic nature: a malfunctioning financial system had led to a severe credit squeeze on the real economy and a massive destruction of wealth, whose negative effects were further exacerbated by the EU's determined turn to austerity. To expect a solution from structural reforms, hence, involves a typical neo-liberal fallacy of composition of fighting macroeconomic problems with microeconomic solutions. Liberalising the labour market may reduce wage costs, but while an individual firm may increase output and employment by gaining an advantage over its competitors, it is unclear how general wage cost reduction would produce a macroeconomic effect. In fact, successive labour liberalisations have tended to promote a further drop in inflation as firms lowered their prices in order to stimulate demand, not only leading the ECB to undershoot its 2 per cent inflation target but also creating a potential problem of deflation that can only serve to further undermine financial stability. At best, labour market flexibilisation might succeed as a form of 'beggar-thy-neighbour' strategy – by increasing the export surpluses of one country at the expense of the trading partners' deficits – but becomes altogether dysfunctional when it is generalised to the entire Eurozone. To expect renewed growth from structural reforms that enhance productivity (rather than cutting costs) seems equally vain. Increased productivity merely means that the same level of output can be produced with fewer inputs. Under the present conditions, when the credit squeeze and the reigning fiscal austerity do not allow firms to harbour any hopes for growth, productivity gains only serve to reduce the amount of inputs employed (and therefore encourage lay-offs), as testified by the observed negative (short-term) correlation between such reforms and employment (Banerji et al. 2017; OECD 2016).

CONCLUSION

Italy's turnaround from a Euro-enthusiastic to a Eurosceptic country is fraught with potentially dramatic political and economic consequences for both Italy and the EU. The turnaround marks a break with the postwar political project of modernising the Italian economy and society by creating ever-closer ties with the other European states. By distancing itself from the EU project, Italy enters uncharted waters both politically and economically, but also the EU is affected as it is deprived of the unconditional support of one of its founding members and traditionally most Euro-enthusiastic populations. Politically, Italy now appears to draw closer to the illiberal democracies of Eastern Europe and Russia – an alignment that, paradoxically, not even the Italian Communist Party had pursued with as much determination during the Cold War period. Economically, it flirts with the idea of regaining monetary sovereignty in a context which is very different from that of the 1970s, during which the common currency project was first conceived, and of the 1990s, when it was implemented. In the current context of hypersensitive financial markets, even flaunting the possibility of a Euro Italexit imposes immediate costs in terms of reduced credit rating assessments and higher interest rates on sovereign bonds.

But the rise of populist scepticism with respect to the benefits of economic integration is not a phenomenon confined to Italy (Algan et al. 2017; Guiso et al. 2017; Dal Bó et al. 2018). In fact, a surge in populist voting has characterised virtually all North Atlantic economies, including Germany, where the new *Alternative für Deutschland* has its stronghold in the socioeconomically disadvantaged states of the former East Germany. That discontent has roots that reach back decades. The postwar trend of decreasing income inequality, a growing wage share in GDP and high levels of employment was reversed sometimes in the 1980s when the EU was laying the foundations for its current form of economic governance. But as long as competitiveness in international markets, particularly financial markets, was considered an immutable law of nature, dissatisfaction was more likely to translate into political apathy, cynicism and lower voter turnout. The Eurocrisis in the end seems to have provided the catalyst for this latent dissatisfaction to transform into a massive protest vote. After all, in this case the invisible hand of globalisation was replaced with the very visible hand of the EU, and that hand quite clearly seemed to operate in favour of the established elites, as banks and financial institutions that bore a major responsibility for the crisis were bailed out with dozen of billions to be financed by further cutbacks in public spending, in particular public sector wage and welfare spending.

The rise of M5S, which combined its criticism of the Italian political caste with criticism of the mounting socioeconomic inequalities from the start, started during the 2012 local elections (Bordignon and Ceccarini 2013). After the 2013 elections, it was the largest party in parliament with 108 out of 617 seats in the House of Deputies and 54/302 seats in the Senate. The newly formed *Scelta Civica* party of Mario Monti instead only obtained 8.3 per cent, and was disbanded shortly afterwards. In the national elections of 2018, the M5S surged to 32.7 per cent, the Lega to 17.5 per cent, which however translated into 36 and 20 per cent of the seats in parliament and allowed them to form the first all-populist government of the postwar period.

The EMU strategy of pursuing economic growth through monetary stability, structural reforms and current account surpluses proved better suited to Germany, which could weather a dramatic overhaul of its labour market in order to regain the competitiveness it had lost after reunification because it already had a fully formed and well-functioning welfare state which could absorb the connected social dislocations. It could further withstand the concerns of financial markets, thanks to a history of financial prudence that sustained markets' confidence in Bunds also in times of high public deficits and mounting debt. Having restored creditworthiness before the onset of the Eurocrisis, finally, Germany came to actually profit from it with as much as €100 billion dividend from the crisis (Dany et al. 2015). Through its weight in the European Council and the ECOFIN, Germany could impose timing and conditions of the Eurocrisis resolution which allowed its banks to divest themselves from the troubled southern periphery's bonds and actually end up gaining from it. Given these unique conditions, the 'German recipe' cannot be replicated in countries which are struggling to complete and defend a fledgling welfare state and in which, therefore, social endurance of economic hardship is not only more problematic but also more demanding.

To conclude, it is not structural reforms and fiscal prudence *per se* that explain Germany's success, and they consequently cannot be generalised to all EMU member states, which moreover lack Germany's initial conditions and resilience. Just as the liberalisation of trade is normally invoked by the strong exporting powers, so exhortations aimed at building a solid financial reputation and at gearing macroeconomic policies to the sole aim of appeasing global markets are common among strong financial market players but suffered by fledgling economies and troubled creditors. For these reasons, the generalised mercantilist recipe that is proposed for the entire Eurozone cannot succeed. Nobody in Europe seems to entertain the possibility that decent levels of income and growth could be achieved by the Eurozone mainly relying on its internal market and the demand that it generates. Until the crisis, the EMU and the Eurozone had a more or less balanced current account, but since the Eurocrisis a structural current account surplus has emerged which deprives Eurozone member states of the much-needed investment support and further creates problems for Europe's trading partners – particularly to the United States, which traditionally has been the consumer of last resort but no longer is willing to act as such – who now also tend to pursue the same strategy.

BIBLIOGRAPHY

Agostini, Chiara and Davide Natali. 2016. 'Italian Welfare Reforms: Missed Opportunities for a Paradigmatic Change?' In *Challenges to European Welfare Systems*, edited by Klaus Schubert, Paloma de Villota and Johanna Kuhlmann, 395–418. Cham: Springer.

Alesina, Alberto and Francesco Giavazzi. 2015. 'The Effects of Austerity: Recent Research.' *NBER Reporter* 2015, no. 3: Research Summary. https://www.nber.org/reporter/2015number3/alesina.html.

Algan, Yann, Sergei Guriev, Elias Papaioannou and Evgenia Passari. 2017. 'The European Trust Crisis and the Rise of Populism.' *Brooking Papers on Economic Activity*, 2017, no. 2: 309–382.

Åslund, Anders. 2009. 'The East European Financial Crisis.' *CASE Network Studies and Analyses* No. 395/ 2009: 1–30. Warsaw: CASE Center for Economic Research. https://papers.ssrn.com/sol3/papers.cfm?abstract_id=1527022.

Banerji, Angana, Valerio Crispolti, Era Dabla-Norris, Romain Duval, Christian Ebeke, Davide Furceri, Takuji Komatsuzaki and Tigran Poghosyan. 2017. 'Labor and Product Market Reforms in Advanced Economies: Fiscal Costs, Gains, and Support.' *IMF Staff Discussion Notes* 17/03: 1–32. Washington, DC: International Monetary Fund.

Bernanke, Ben S. 2004. 'The Great Moderation.' Speech, St. Louis, Missouri, 8 October 2004. Federal Reserve Bank of St. Louis, Conference on Reflections on Monetary Policy 25 Years after October 1979. https://www.federalreserve.gov/boarddocs/speeches/2004/20040220/.

Bologna, Pierluigi, Marianna Caccavaio and Arianna Miglietta. 2014. 'EU Bank Deleveraging.' *Questioni di Economia e Finanza QEF (Occasional Papers)* No. 235: 1–32. Rome: Banca d'Italia. https://www.bancaditalia.it/pubblicazioni/qef/2014-0235/QEF-235.pdf.

Boltho, Andrea. 2013. 'Italy, Germany, Japan from Economic Miracles to Virtual Stagnation.' In *The Oxford Handbook of the Italian Economy since Unification*, edited by Gianni Toniolo, 108–133. Oxford: Oxford University Press.

Bordignon, Fabio and Luigi Ceccarini. 2013. 'Five Stars and a Cricket. Beppe Grillo Shakes Italian Politics.' *South European Society and Politics*, 18, no. 4: 427–449.

Borrás, Susana and Claudio M. Radaelli. 2011. 'The Politics of Governance Architectures: Creation, Change and Effects of the EU Lisbon Strategy.' *Journal of European Public Policy*, 18, no. 4: 463–484.

Brunazzo, Marco and Vincent Della Sala. 2016. 'Italy between Transformismo and Transformation.' In *Core-Periphery Relations in the European Union Power and Conflict in a Dualist Political Economy*, edited by José M. Magone, Brigid Laffan and Christian Schweiger, 216–228. London: Routledge.

Codogno, Lorenzo. 2009. 'Two Italian Puzzles: Are Productivity Growth and Competitiveness Really so Depressed?' *Ministry of Economy and Finance Department of the Treasury Working Papers* No.°2—March 2009: 1–33. Rome: Ministry of Economy and Finance—Department of the Treasury. https://papers.ssrn.com/sol3/papers.cfm?abstract_id=1417456.

Culpepper, Pepper D. 2014. 'The Political Economy of Unmediated Democracy: Italian Austerity under Mario Monti.' *West European Politics*, 37, no. 6: 1264–1281.

Dal Bó, Ernesto, Frederico Finan, Olle Folke, Torsten Persson and Johanna Rickne. 2018. *Economic Losers and Political Winners: Sweden's Radical Right*. http://perseus.iies.su.se/~tpers/papers/Draft180902.pdf.

Dany, Geraldine, Reint E. Gropp, Helge Littke and Gregor von Schweinitz. 2015. 'Germany's Benefit from the Greek Crisis.' *IWH Online 7/2015*. Halle: Leibnitz Institut für Wirtschaftsforschung. https://www.econstor.eu/bitstream/10419/142208/1/io_2015-07.pdf.

De Bonis, Riccardo, Alberto Franco Pozzolo and Massimiliano Stacchini. 2012. 'The Italian banking system: Facts and Interpretations.' *Economics and Statistics Discussion Paper* No. 068/12. Campobasso, IT: University of Molise, Dept. EGSeI. http://web.unimol.it/progetti/repec/mol/ecsdps/ESDP12068.pdf.

De Cecco, Marcello. 2007. 'Italy's Dysfunctional Political Economy.' *West European Politics*, 30, no. 4: 763–783.

De Grauwe, Paul and Yuemei Ji. 2012. 'Mispricing of Sovereign Risk and Macroeconomic Stability in the Eurozone.' *JCMS: Journal of Common Market Studies*, 50, no. 6: 866–880.

De Grauwe, Paul and Yuemei Ji. 2013. 'From Panic-Driven Austerity to Symmetric Macroeconomic Policies in the Eurozone.' *JCMS: Journal of Common Market Studies*, 51, no. S1: 31–41.

Della Sala, Vincent. 1997. 'Hollowing Out and Hardening the Italian State: European Integration and the Italian Economy.' *West European Politics*, 20, no. 1: 14–33.

Della Sala, Vincent. 2004. 'The Italian Model of Capitalism: On the Road between Globalization and Europeanization?' *Journal of European Public Policy*, 11, no. 6: 1041–1057.

Draghi, Mario. 2011. 'L'autonomia della politica monetaria: Una riflessione a trent'anni dalla lettera del Ministro Andreatta al Governatore Ciampi che avviò il "divorzio" tra il Ministero del Tesoro e la Banca d'Italia.' 15 February 2011. https://www.bancaditalia.it/pubblicazioni/interventigovernatore/integov2011/AREL_150211.pdf.

Draghi, Mario and Vítor Constâncio. 2012. 'Introductory Statement to the Press Conference (with Q and A).' Speech, Frankfurt am Main, Germany, 6 September 2012. European Central Bank. https://www.ecb.Europa.eu/press/pressconf/2012/html/is120906.en.html.

Epstein, Rachel A. and Martin Rhodes. 2016. 'The Political Dynamics behind Europe's New Banking Union.' *West European Politics*, 39, no. 3: 415–437.

European Commission. 2008. 'COM(2008) 800 Final, Communication from the Commission to the European Council: A European Economic Recovery Plan.' Forwarded to the Council on 27 November 2008. *Eur-Lex* Document 52008DC0800. https://eur-lex.Europa.eu/legal-content/EN/ALL/?uri=COM:2008:0800:FIN.

European Commission. 2018a. Standard Eurobarometer 90. European Union. doi:10.2775/84355. http://data.europa.eu/euodp/en/data/dataset/S2215_90_3_STD90_ENG

European Commission. 2018b. Flash Eurobarometer 473—'the Euro Area'. European Union. doi:10.2765/013968. https://data.europa.eu/euodp/en/data/dataset/S2211_473_ENG.

European Council. 2011. 'Eurosummit Statement.' Statement, Brussels, Belgium, 26 October 2011. The European Council—Council of the European Union. https://www.consilium.Europa.eu/uedocs/cms_data/docs/pressdata/en/ec/125644.pdf.

Farmer, Roger E. A. 2017. *Prosperity for All: How to Prevent Financial Crises*. Oxford: Oxford University Press.

Ferrera, Maurizio and Elisabetta Gualmini. 2004. *Rescued by Europe? Social and Labour Market Reforms in Italy from Maastricht to Berlusconi*. Amsterdam: Amsterdam University Press.

Franks, Jeffrey, Bergljot Barkbu, Rodolphe Blavy, William Oman and Hanni Schoelermann. 2018. 'Economic Convergence in the Euro Area: Coming Together or Drifting Apart?' *IMF Working Paper* WP/18/10: 1–47. Washington, DC: International Monetary Fund. https://www.imf.org/~/media/Files/Publications/WP/2018/wp1810.ashx.

Friedman, Thomas L. 2000. *The Lexus and the Olive Tree: Understanding Globalization*. New York: Anchor Books.

Guiso, Luigi, Helios Herrera, Massimo Morelli and Tommaso Sonno. 2017. 'Demand and Supply of Populism.' *CEPR Discussion Paper* No. DP11871: 1–61. https://ssrn.com/abstract=2924731.

Hosli, Madeleine. 1998. 'The EMU and International Monetary Relations: What to Expect for International Actors?' In *The European Union in the World Community*, edited by Carolyn Rhodes, 165–192. Boulder, CO: Lynne Rienner Publishers, Inc.

IMF. 2012. 'Global Economic Prospects and Policy Changes.' Meeting of G-20 Finance Ministers and Central Bank Governors, Mexico City, Mexico, 25–26 February 2012. International Monetary Fund. https://www.imf.org/external/np/g20/pdf/022512.pdf.

Klepsch, Catharina and Timo Wollmershäuser. 2011. 'Yield Spreads on EMU Government Bonds—How the Financial Crisis Has Helped Investors to Rediscover Risk.' *Intereconomics*, 46, no. 3: 169–176.

Magone, José M. 2016. 'From "Superficial" to "Coercive" Europeanization in Southern Europe: The Lack of Ownership of National Reforms.' In *Core-Periphery Relations in the European Union Power and Conflict in a Dualist Political Economy*, edited by José M. Magone, Brigid Laffan and Christian Schweiger, 87–98. London: Routledge.

Majone, Giandomenico. 2009. *Europe as the Would-be World Power: The EU at Fifty*. Cambridge: Cambridge University Press.

Mauro, Paolo, Rafael Romeu, Ariel Binder and Asad Zaman. 2013. 'A Modern History of Fiscal Prudence and Profligacy.' *IMF Working Paper* No. 13/5: 1–52. Washington, DC: International Monetary Fund. https://www.imf.org/en/Publications/WP/Issues/2016/12/31/A-Modern-History-of-Fiscal-Prudence-and-Profligacy-40222.

Mohan, Rakesh. 2019. 'Finance and Monetary Policy beyond Neoliberalism: The Way Ahead for Emerging Markets.' In *Beyond Neoliberalism: Insights from Emerging Markets*, edited by Geoffrey Gertz and Homi Kharas, 48–60. Washington, DC: The Brookings Institution.

Nauhaus, Steffen. 2015. 'The Power of Opinion: More Evidence of a GIPS-Markup in Sovereign Ratings during the Euro Crisis.' DIW Berlin Discussion Paper No. 1501: 1–19. Berlin: Deutsches Institut für Wirtschaftsforschung. https://ssrn.com/abstract=2655947 or http://dx.doi.org/10.2139/ssrn.2655947.

Notermans. Ton and Simona Piattoni. 2017. 'Democracy and (Dis)integration: The Conditions for a Legitimate and Effective Economic and Political Organization.' *EUI Working Papers* RSCAS 2017/40: 1–27. Florence, IT: European University Institute—Robert Schuman Centre for Advanced Studies. https://cadmus.eui.eu/bitstream/handle/1814/47793/RSCAS_2017_40.pdf?sequence=1.

OECD. 2016. *OECD Employment Outlook*. Paris: OECD Publishing.

Padoa-Schioppa, Tommaso. 2004. *Regulating Finance: Balancing Freedom and Risk*. Oxford: Oxford University Press.

Piasna, Agnieszka and Martin Myant. 2017. *Myths of Employment Deregulation: How It Neither Creates Jobs nor Reduces Labour Market Segmentation*. Brussels: ETUI.

Pilkington, Philip and Warren Mosler. 2012. 'Tax-Backed Bonds—a National Solution to the European Debt Crisis.' *Levy Economics Institute of Bard College Policy Note* 2012/4. Annandale-on-Hudson, NY: Levy Economics Institute of Bard College. http://www.levyinstitute.org/pubs/pn_12_04.pdf.

Pinelli, Dino, Roberta Torre, Lucianajulia Pace, Laura Cassio and Alfonso Arpaia. 2017. 'The Recent Reform of the Labour Market in Italy: A Review.' *European Economy Discussion Paper* 072: 1–42. Luxembourg: Publications Office of the European Union. https://ec.Europa.eu/info/publications/economy-finance/recent-reform-labour-market-italy-review_en.

Radaelli, Claudio. 2002. 'The Italian State and the Euro: Institutions, Discourse, and Policy Regimes.' In *European States and the Euro: Europeanization, Variation, and Convergence*, edited by Kenneth Dyson, 212–237. Oxford: Oxford University Press.

Sbragia, Alberta M. 2000a. 'Governance, the State, and the Market: What Is Going On?' *Governance*, 13.2: 243–250.

Sbragia, Alberta M. 2000b. 'Italy Pays for Europe: Political Leadership, Political Choice, and Institutional Adaptation.' In *Transforming Europe: Europeanization and Domestic Change*, edited by Maria Green Cowles, James A. Caporaso and Thomas Risse, 79–96. Ithaca, NY: Cornell University Press.

Sbragia, Alberta M. 2004. 'Shaping a Polity in an Economic and Monetary Union: The EU in a Comparative Perspective.' In *Euros and Europeans: Monetary Integration and the European Model of Society*, edited by Andrew Martin and George Ross, 51–75. Cambridge: Cambridge University Press.

Scharpf, Fritz W. 2010. 'The Asymmetry of European Integration, or Why the EU Cannot Be a "Social Market Economy."' *Socio-Economic Review*, 8.2: 211–250.

Scobie, H. M., S. Mortali, S. Persaud and P. Docile. 1996. *The Italian Economy in the 1990s*. London: Routledge.

Slobodian, Quinn. 2018. *Globalists: The End of Empire and the Birth of Neoliberalism*. Cambridge, MA: Harvard University Press.

Stark, Jürgen. 2001. 'Genesis of a Pact.' In *The Stability and Growth Pact: The Architecture of Fiscal Policy in EMU*, edited by Anne Brunila, Marco Buti and Daniele Franco, 77–105. London: Palgrave Macmillan.

Tooze, Adam. 2018. 'The Bank that Nearly Broke Europe.' *Prospect*, 21 August 2018. https://www.prospectmagazine.co.uk/magazine/adam-tooze-European-central-bank.

Trichet, Jean-Claude. 2010. 'Interview with Libération.' Interview by Jean Quatremer. *Liberation*, 13 July 2010. *European Central Bank—Eurosystem*. https://www.ecb.Europa.eu/press/inter/date/2010/html/sp100713.en.html.

Chapter 10

Regional Variations and Crisis

Comparing European Union and Association of Southeast Asian Nations Integration Dynamics

Reuben Wong and Daniela Irrera

Regional integration has moved the locus of important decisions in functional and sensitive areas like trade, visa monitoring, counterterrorism and anti-piracy activities into international arenas, where states have to adapt their preferences and performances. This process – reactive rather than purposeful, short-term rather than teleological or conscious – has taken place in both the European Union (EU) and the Association of Southeast Asian Nations (ASEAN) since the 1990s. This is in spite of heightened anti-supranational sentiments in many states in Europe and the foundational norm of intergovernmental decision-making in Southeast Asia. Following Alberta Sbragia and others (Sbragia 2008; Warleigh-Lack and Van Langenhove 2010; Acharya 2012), this chapter suggests a need to look beyond Europe in comparative regionalism studies, including what the EU can learn from other regions.

Scholars have already explained the process through the impact of 'crisis'. Therefore, the EU was born and made progress after 1945 and into the 1950s when confronted with crises ranging from the collapse of European colonial empires and economic rehabilitation. West European nation states responded consciously and purposefully to the loss of national power by building European institutions in a bid to shore up national institutions which had lost capacity or legitimacy (Moravcsik 1998; Milward 2000; Kühnhardt 2005).

Similar arguments have been used to analyse regional systems very different from the EU, taking into account that crisis may produce also regional variations (Brennan and Murray 2015; Wong 2015; Saurugger and Terpan 2016). This chapter then focuses on the notion of 'crisis' as the critical juncture framework for understanding how it can activate – or deactivate integration dynamics in the EU and in Southeast Asia. In doing so, we particularly focus on two main variables: first, power relations between member states and regional organisations and, second, institutional change in regional integration dynamics, focusing both on formal institutions and practices. We apply such variables to some specific policy domains, dealing with traditional and non-traditional security. We argue that crisis continues to be a major driver in the process of supranational integration, producing different outcomes, but that regional factors mediate the impact of crisis on integration outcomes in the EU and ASEAN.

The chapter is divided into three parts. First, the scholarship on crisis and its impact on the integration process is critically assessed. Second, the basic argument that, under certain conditions, crisis leads to greater integration rather than disintegration, is evaluated based on the setting up of new supranational institutions and the movement of more decisions and policy areas outside the control of the nation state. These criteria are then applied to the EU and ASEAN to understand regional variations in the impact of crisis on integration dynamics and their implications even in the most sensitive policy issues.

THE SCHOLARSHIP ON CRISIS

'Crisis' is a term frequently utilised loosely, in many instances largely because of the motivation to garner attention to a particular issue area, or to guide the current discourse away from its usual path. In order to better distinguish between events that are worthy of study from others it is imperative to streamline the definition of the concept of 'crisis', such that it is not only relevant to the theme of regional integration, but it can also be operationalised.

Previous scholars have noted that there may be incidences of what some researchers may identify to be a crisis that precipitate altered perceptions in the minds of key actors but have little to no effect on the subsequent actions between nations (McCormick 1978). McCormick uses the Siege of Berlin and the subsequent Berlin Airlift of 1958 as an example of such an occurrence in his paper *International Crisis: A Note on Definition*, what he calls a 'bureaucratic crisis'. There was certainly pressure put on the decision-making abilities of both Khrushchev and Eisenhower, but the empty threat and ultimately simple resolution did not escalate into a larger situation that changed East-West relations.

In contrast Raymond Cohen discusses, in his paper *Threat Perception in International Crisis*, the 1939 "Poland and the corridor crisis". Still described as a crisis, it is notably different to the Siege of Berlin in its role as a catalyst in strengthening the British-Polish alliance in preparation for potential German expansion (Cohen 1978).

Thus, it can be seen that there is an extensive debate in the literature on the notion of crises and although they may not all be the same but instead have some significant differences, we have chosen to focus on a definition which may be applied to broader and practical contexts. Generally, a 'crisis' can be agreed to be an event that marks a phase of disorder in the seemingly 'normal' development of a system (Boin et al. 2005; Saurugger and Terpan 2016). Janice Bially Mattern's conception of 'crisis' agrees with this general conception, defining crisis as "socially unsettled times", wherein "order is imposed upon disorder" (Mattern 2005). A workable conception of crisis that can be operationalised then combines these two definitions, producing a definition that will distinguish a crisis from any regular threats:

(1) it is an immediate and ongoing situation of disorder which threatens the high-priority goals of more than one member of a regional integration project;
(2) where the amount of time available for an urgent response is highly restricted;
(3) where its occurrence is previously unanticipated and therefore surprises the members of the integration project. (Hermann 1963; Boin et al. 2005; Jones 2012)

Where crises are largely situations of high complexity and ambiguity, both with regard to the problem encountered and with regard to the solutions – together with their expected consequences – envisaged, crises usually call for action with a certain degree of innovation, however limited, on the part of the actors affected (Hall 1993; Saurugger and Terpan 2016).

For the purposes of this chapter, two main features of crisis should be stressed. Crises can take several forms and affect different dimensions, in a given context. However, its spatial dimension is rarely limited to a single domain or issue. Scholars have stressed the notion of 'transboundary crisis' to label a problem which plays out across one or many types of boundaries. Therefore, the effects of such crises usually affect multiple sectors, groups or countries (Boin, Ekengren and Rhinard 2013).

This brings us to the second feature: as per our definition of crises as associated with a high degree of uncertainty, responding to crises normally requires controversial attempts to develop innovative solutions beyond the routine set of practices institutions and governments are familiar with (Boin et al., 2005). Therefore, crises also imply a political dimension, since policy-makers are expected to reduce uncertainty and develop norms and practices capable of resettling a new *status quo*. However, this process may be complicated by the fact that, in the case of very complex crises, it may be not clear which policy-makers are responsible and should intervene.

THE RELATIONSHIP BETWEEN CRISES
AND INTEGRATION

There is no direct causal relationship between crises and integration. Rather, crises indicate a potential change to relatively stable institutions. The Punctuated Equilibrium Theory proposed by Baumgartner and Jones (1993) explores how crises are critical junctures – which essentially introduce periods of uncertainty into longer periods of stability – that will open up opportunities for change. Depending on the agents that seize these opportunities, and in the context of regional integration, integration may occur alongside the alternative possibility of disintegration.

According to the Punctuated Equilibrium Theory, crises will suspend the equilibrium in relatively stable structures for two reasons: first, a crisis relaxes the structural constraints that keep institutions in place by highlighting previously unnoticed vulnerabilities, thereby allowing agents to exercise relative freedom of manoeuvre to develop unconventionally risky policy options and, second, the routine cognitive framework for action becomes discredited, and alternatives are seen as necessary to regain legitimacy (Baumgartner and Jones 1993; Baumgartner, Green-Pedersen and Jones 2006; Saurugger and Terpan 2016).

If institutions are normally highly resistant to change, and in the case of regional integration, if member states and their citizens are generally highly reluctant to commit towards greater supranational integration, then crises as critical junctures open up opportunities for the alternative to be considered as viable and/or attractive – driving the process of supranational integration forward (Katznelson 2003; Duina 2007; Genieys and Hassenteufel 2012; Saurugger and Terpan 2016).

CHANGE IN THE FORM OF SUPRANATIONAL
INTEGRATION

Crises – for its threat to member states' high-priority goals – demand responses to be made within a critically short time frame (see definition). As such, responses to crises usually prioritise short-term considerations rather than a conscious long-term vision. And to the extent that crises expose the inadequacy of national responses as in the case of the Asian Financial Crisis (AFC) in 1997, one response to the loss of national power and control over specific issue areas is to build supranational institutions in order to shore up the capacity and legitimacy of national institutions (Rüland 2010; Wong 2015). Nonetheless, in the case of ASEAN, one still wonders how much member states are willing to move towards greater integration, given that sovereignty, and thus the value of *non-interference,* has always been a defining attribute of the institution from its creation in 1967 (Wong 2015; Narine 2016). In fact, Shaun Narine argues that ASEAN's functional level of regional integration will remain low, regardless of the number of crises Southeast Asia as a region is to be hit by, so long as ASEAN's member states continue to perceive sovereignty as paramount to their survival as viable states (Narine 2016).

At the same time, as Fabbrini and Putter (2016) state, more integration does not necessarily imply more supranationalism. Tackling a crisis may bring greater awareness among member states towards the need to develop a more coordinated policy but may result in a stronger intergovernmentalism rather than putting emphasis on EU institutions. A paradigmatic example of the fact that not all crises are the same, in the case of the EU, is represented by the ongoing migrants and refugees crisis. The *external migration policy* has been established – and labelled – by the Commission as a regime aiming at controlling the influx of immigrants into the EU by actions and programmes implemented beyond the EU borders and in collaboration with external actors. This policy has been at the core of the *Global Approach to Migration and Mobility*, a communication presented by the Commission, and more commonly known as GAMM. The Council approved the communication in 2011 as a comprehensive long-term strategy capable of tackling the implications of the migratory flows in the regions around Europe. The concept of migration was complemented with the concept of mobility. In doing so, the Commission created a balance between EU solidarity and the member states' preferences towards the restrictions to permit migrants to stay in the EU countries only as employed workers. Therefore, mobility became a set of mechanisms allowing foreign nationals to work and stay temporarily in the EU (Attinà 2016).

Even though GAMM was expected to provide a long-term strategy, institutions have been dominated by the member states' fears and attempts to close borders. This has produced a series of short-term responses, aimed at managing the humanitarian dimension of the emergency and then regulating access to people, according to their status. The EU created a regime for managing migration outside its own borders and avoiding irregular migration inflows into Europe.

STUMBLING TOWARDS GREATER SUPRANATIONAL INTEGRATION

As established earlier, crises provide *windows of opportunity* for institutional change, which can mean either integration or disintegration. That is to say, neither the crises by themselves will definitively lead to closer integration nor would the actors concerned be able to exercise full autonomous agency in deciding how integrated or disintegrated the institution should be. What is likely to result in *response* to a regional crisis is, therefore, an exercise of member states' agency *within* a decision-making space constrained – both time- and choice-wise – by the crisis (Saurugger and Terpan 2016)

Here, we want to explore the idea of member states *stumbling* towards greater supranational integration – even more so for the regional integration in ASEAN that emerged in the aftermath of or during crises. In other words, crises function as a motor of supranational integration by nudging member states towards greater policy coordination, however involuntary. Moreover, the frequently transnational character of crises meant that they can only be meaningfully overcome through working collectively and in so doing, unexpectedly move member states towards closer integration.

Consequently, our position builds on Kelly Gerard's criticism of current studies of ASEAN which are focused on the assumption of a zero-sum relationship between state and regional governance. Gerard argues that the significance of state borders as an indicator of a boundary for political power should not be erroneously amplified to the extent of neglecting factors that states do not really have complete control over (Gerard 2016). Where states are not always able to 'stand above and do things to their societies and engage in relations with other states in a relatively autonomous fashion' – especially in times of crises and in dealing with the resulting unpredictability – they may be nudged towards a course that they did not initially consciously plan for (Hameiri and Jayasuriya 2012; Jones 2012; Gerard 2016).

Defining Integration

Contrary to traditional definitions, our conception of supranational integration does not have to manifest in a hierarchical order, where supranational institutions definitively stand above member states. In fact, although some sovereignty is required to be ceded to the supranational body with authority over particular issue areas, member states retain the ultimate sovereignty (Wong 2015). For instance, these supranational institutions may either only move the locus of important decisions in some functional areas like trade and visa-monitoring, counterterrorism and anti-piracy activities away from states and into regional bodies outside the state or new bodies would be created under existing regional arrangements to deal only with selected and focused issue areas (Wong 2015).

Barnett and Finnemore's Theory on Institutional Resilience

Where crises highlight member states' inadequacy to respond individually, regional supranational institutions are invested with *pooled* sovereignty and mandated with missions that member states are neither willing nor able to perform, in a bid to arrest the declining legitimacy of the member states in the eyes of their citizens (Barnett and Finnemore 2004; Wong 2015).

Typically, however, organisations adapt to the changing international political climate and the emergence of new exigencies in unexpected ways, adopting new practices that are not formally or unanimously approved by member states. Through their ability to collect and strategically deploy information with a bird's eye view, and in a way meaningful to creating new social realities and orienting action, member states – though themselves the creator of the institution – are inclined to acknowledge the authority of the supranational organisations (Barnett and Finnemore 2004).

In the EU, especially, regional institutions are more likely to take on the momentum as explained by Barnett and Finnemore and encourage increasing alignment of member states' interests in the name of the EU. In the context of EU economic integration, for example, the European Court of Justice (ECJ) has a substantial role in overcoming national differences in order to allow for the Single Market to be realised. In the face of novel cases, the ECJ, nevertheless, is persistent in delivering and reviewing issues according to its original mandate; coupled by the EU's tendency towards "continual implementation and subsequent reassessment until they are resolved and approved", it is difficult to, therefore, expect the EU to abandon integration initiatives halfway through (Allison 2015).

In contrast, the preference of ASEAN member states for informality gives the organisation and the member states substantial freedom in deciding the extent of regional integration they are willing to accept. While ASEAN does devise initiatives, they would be abandoned in favour of new proposals when these initiatives are found to be too difficult to ensure compliance. ASEAN's approach of first trialling the proposals before deciding on whether to formalise or reject these initiatives later therefore hints at a more proactive approach in deciding the pace of regionalism (Allison 2015).

CRISIS AND INTEGRATION IN THE EU

The EU still offers a paradigmatic case of such dynamics and, particularly in respect to more recent crises, it provides room for further theoretical reflections on the ways they impact regional integration. By taking into account our main variable, we focus on two major crises which have produced – and are still producing – controversial impacts on the EU and within member states: migration and counterterrorism. In both policy domains, we briefly analyse and respond to three main aspects of our overarching research question:

- How were these policy domains shaped by recent events?
- What is the balance between national and supranational competence?
- How have the implications of the crisis increase integration?

Crisis and Integration in the EU: Migrants and Refugees

Taking the recent refugee crisis into account, issues pertaining to refugees and migration clearly constitute a transboundary crisis, given that they affect all EU member states collectively, and that the situation also require a series of measures across policy areas such as welfare, culture, labour and education. The more recent events occurring in the Mediterranean as well as in the Balkan region demonstrate that Europe is undoubtedly a region of immigration, and this imposes on the states the need to accept and manage the political consequences of this increasing phenomenon. Therefore, it is clear that the issue of external migration represents a political test for the EU and its values, particularly the welfare and security of the citizens of the European states and also the integrity of the states and societies (Marin 2011; Attinà, 2018).

As a result of such considerations, migrants and refugees are at the core of public debates, and policy-makers' speeches, academic reflections, as well as the security paradigm, which appears to be dominant. Next to a traditional policy approach which emphasises asylum as a human rights question and which proposes human rights instruments as responses, migrants are more frequently framed as a security problem, in terms of the lives or refugees to rescue, to protect, to manage, and ultimately to integrate into European societies.

This crisis clearly represents an elevated degree of urgency and uncertainty and requires a set of adequate responses from several actors. However, the main problem is that state leaders and EU policy-makers have different views on the uncertainty and urgency, and have developed different preferences towards the appropriate response.

Scholars have extensively analysed the EU mode of governance in the field of migration. It has followed a path of intense political reforms, within the pillar of Justice and Home Affairs. In parallel with the increased relevance of EU agencies such as Frontex, this has produced a mode of governance which has been defined by the majority of scholars as neither predominantly intergovernmental nor supranational. Deeper analyses have focused on the different actors involved in such process. Sandra Lavenex (2015, 368) has used the label *transgovernmentalism* to describe the combination of elements from both traditional 'communitarisation' and intergovernmentalism. This context is marked by a (often asymmetric) balance between having suprana-tional European institutions taking the lead and member states influencing decisions through their preferences.

Frictions and divisions significantly impair the capability and efficiency of collective crisis management by the EU leaders and also reduce the possibil-ity of reaching the required coordination among member states.

The weak EU migration governance is one of the paradigmatic examples of the EU's disappointing performance at both the internal (EU-wide) and international levels. In 2017–18, the EU has been criticised for controver-sial summits, inefficient deployment of search and rescue operations in the Mediterranean by different actors, insufficient attempts to save people along the Balkan route and the emergence of radical views of the governments of member and non-member states in the region.

At the same time, the mitigating of the quantitative effect of the next arrivals, tackling human trafficking, respecting international standards of human rights, playing the providing role of peace and stability in the neigh-bourhood and lowering the member states' radical views and temptation to close the borders are not easy tasks; they seriously challenge functional integration.

Despite a series of political and technical shortfalls (including the agree-ment with Turkey), the crisis is currently shaping EU performance by push-ing member states and communitarian institutions to find a collective solution and an extremely slow and asymmetrical process of adaption is currently advancing. It remains to be seen in the long term if the test – as expected of the EU – could be passed with greater progress in regional integration or if the process of further regionalism is to be resisted.

Crisis and Integration in the EU: Counterterrorism

Terrorist attacks are usually unpredictable, typically marked by uncertainty. Scholars have extensively studied the implications terrorism is likely to pro-duce on national, regional and global security, stressing the fact that, in the end, no prevention plan can be absolutely efficient.

Analyses on the organisational dimension (why terrorists start and con-tinue) as well as on the terrorists' instrumental behaviour (how terrorists behave and which strategy they adopt) have brought on similar conclusions. Counterterrorism policies are usually either based on prevention, deterrence, or a combination of the two. However, nothing can protect and resolve the unpreparedness of intelligence and governments in the face of the most sophisticated groups and the fallacy of their capacity to prevent attacks (Crenshaw 2010; Bakker 2011).

As such, terrorism represents a paradigmatic example of transboundary crisis, in terms of uncertainty, on the part of political actors who are expected to reduce the threat and provide a solution. Europe obviously represented a paradigmatic example of such processes. During the Cold War period, ideological tension, economic and social cleavages, and pending self-determination issues contributed to the birth and development of several phenomena all over the world. Europe, in particular, was marked by both left- and right-wing movements, which were, at the same time, part of global trends (Bosi and Della Porta 2012).

Until 11 September 2001, the security policies have been shaped by domestic preferences, particularly by countries that possess more expertise with regard to the fight against terrorism, like the United Kingdom, Italy and Germany. It was in the aftermath of the Twin Towers attacks that a European Security Strategy was formally developed, in which terrorism is listed as one of the major threats, together with organised crime and failed states. After 9/11, especially with the appearance and performances of Al-Qaida, terrorism started to be conceived as a mode of action. Therefore, analysts and policy-makers focused their attention on terrorist organisations' strategies and structure. The counterterrorism strategy, developed within the EU over the past decades, was characterised by the need to identify common definitions and actions. In practice, however, progress was constrained politically due to member states' preferences, as well as the lack of coordination among competent agencies.

The EU strategy – developed by the Council in 2005 – was introduced as a comprehensive framework mainly based on four pillars, namely prevention, protection, pursuit, and response. It was also a sophisticated articulated (and complicated) assemblage of norms, best practices, technical agencies and intelligence systems, in order to combine political agency with the need to coordinate responses and reduce the risk of attacks.

In reality, until the 2015 Paris attacks, the European territory had only been minimally affected by political violence and attacks. The rise of the Islamic State (a terrorist organisation active in Syria and North Africa, also known as 'ISIS' for short) and, in particular, the phenomenon of foreign fighters, had contributed to a change in perception of the crisis, animated the debates at the EU level and started to have an effect on integration in terms of policies and intelligence services.

In the case of ISIS, foreign fighters have been defined as those who regard it as their duty to participate in what they believe to be a jihad of the sword, a holy war against the regime of Syrian President Bashar al-Assad and its Shiite allies, and who join local or foreign groups with a jihadist political agenda (Bakker 2011). First, the existence of foreign fighters represent a social problem for EU integration, since the social models through which migrants have been integrated/assimilated in the European countries in the past decades proved ineffective in addressing the current needs of people and therefore require revisions accordingly. Second, they are a security threat. Even though police investigations have revealed that terrorists involved in all recent attacks in Europe were connected to ISIS and have travelled to Syria, there is still a significant lack of knowledge about the channels used to recruit people in Europe and their connections to the cells in Syria. At present, only estimates of the number of foreign fighters who have actually travelled to Syria, and who have returned to Europe, are available. More and detailed investigations on their actual presence in the country, the type of activities they undertook there and their accomplices and, finally, the dynamics of their return are required and essential to demarcate general trends of the phenomenon.

The need to strengthen the daily life security of European citizens without affecting their freedom of movement, one of the basic principles of EU democracy, remains a constant and irredeemable dilemma affecting the relations between member states and their different perceptions on how security should be strengthened.

CRISIS AND INTEGRATION IN ASEAN

Much more than the EU, narratives such as non-interference and sovereignty inform ASEAN's integration project. Such cautious narratives traditionally render considerations of integration in functional, both traditional and non-traditional, security areas – like human rights, environmental monitoring, counter-terrorism and anti-piracy activities – relatively sensitive and extremely tricky to raise. Yet new integration regimes dealing with issues in these security domains have risen in the aftermath of crises and have been shaped to differing degrees by them. Here, we study the advancement of a human rights regime as influenced by a situation of crisis, as well as the *idea* of the need for transboundary environmental cooperation in the wake of the 1997 environmental crisis (Wong 2016). In the former case, it was as a result of the AFC from 1997 to 1998 that member states – more specifically Indonesia – stumbled into the previously unfathomable area of regional human rights governance, leading to the counterintuitive formation of a human rights regime (Thio 1999; Tan 2011; Wong 2012; Wong 2016). In the case of the latter, disastrous economic and social consequences that affected the region as a whole with the advent of the haze crisis in the same period triggered the awareness of shared environmental concerns and the urgency to seek a common solution to the haze problem (Wong 2015, 2016).

Both the human rights and environmental regimes were shaped by crises that transcended the spatial boundaries of the states where the crises first originated, though the balance between national and supranational competence differs across both cases. This difference is reflected not just in the pace that charters and agreements were ratified but also that of the setting up of institutions to encourage compliance.

Crisis and Integration in ASEAN: The ASEAN Charter and the ASEAN Intergovernmental Commission on Human Rights

The AFC of 1997 not only tarnished the glow of the Asian economic miracle but also, and more importantly, exposed the institutional fault lines within ASEAN itself, hence triggering the need for an appropriate course of action to restore the legitimacy of the regional integration project (Wong 2015, 2016). The AFC had put the legitimacy of the entire ASEAN project at stake, for even though it originated in Thailand, the financial consequences had a domino effect on the economies of not just her Southeast Asian neighbours but also South Korea.

While Indonesia was not spared from having to suffer the disastrous consequences of the AFC economically as well, it was arguably the hardest hit, for the AFC, which exposed deep flaws in the country's national economy, resulted in the reverberation of the economic pain into the country's political domain. Former Indonesian president Suharto's authoritarian regime, which was in power at the time of the financial crisis, and whose approval was buoyed predominantly by its stellar economic achievements, quickly lost its political clout. Anti-governmental demonstrations, together with a loss of support from the military, ultimately forced Suharto out of office. The toppling of Suharto's authoritarian regime, formerly resistant towards any progress in the human rights realm, left a *window of opportunity* open for possible institutionalisation in the human rights domain. In addition, such a window of opportunity would and was – as conveyed by the Punctuated Equilibrium Theory – indeed exploited by different civil society groups and citizens to advance any agenda of human rights promotion.

The AFC indirectly led to the *fall* of Suharto's regime. This political revolution, however, unintentionally propelled Indonesia forward in developments in the human rights realm, as the recognition of the need to regain legitimacy led President Jusuf Habibie to relax media controls, release political prisoners, allow the establishment of new political parties and hold free elections in 1999 (Eldridge 2002; Wong 2016). In fact, in later administrations, the need for political legitimacy and accountability behoved Indonesian foreign minister Hassan Wirayuda to begin institutional reform of the

Indonesian Department of Foreign Affairs in order to make the department more responsive to feedback from the Indonesian civil society and citizens (Sukma 2011; Wong 2016). Crucially, to argue that the AFC caused Indonesia to *stumble* forward in terms of progress in human rights promotion both within the country itself and across ASEAN is to recognise that Indonesia's step towards human rights progression is an unforeseen, and to a certain degree, also an indirect and involuntary one. To attribute the crisis to the characteristic of a stumbling block that significantly constrained the freedom of political manoeuvre is significantly to acknowledge the impact of the crisis in spurring the development of unconventional policy options that detracted from the routine cognitive framework for action.

Moreover, the domestic flourishing of democracy and the respect of human rights after the demise of Suharto's regime has resulted in a spillover effect, region wide as well, given that Indonesia is considered ASEAN's biggest and most important member, as well as its active export of democratic norms, evident in Minister Wirayuda's declaration that Indonesia 'envision[s] an ASEAN that is democratic and that respects human rights' (Sukma 2011; Wong 2016).

Accordingly, the idea for a charter that would legally embody ASEAN norms and values was advanced during Indonesia's chairing of the 2003 ASEAN Summit in Bali and later incorporated in the ASEAN Security Community Plan of Action (Djani 2009; Wong 2016). Subsequently, the ASEAN Charter was adopted in Singapore in 2007, which also institutionalised shared human rights norms in the establishment of the ASEAN Intergovernmental Commission on Human Rights (AICHR) (ASEAN 2012; Wong 2015, 2016).

Evidently, the AFC, by undermining the performance legitimacy of most incumbent governments in Southeast Asia, indirectly and irrevocably strengthened the public movement for greater accountability and protection of civil and political rights. Even though one might argue that the effectiveness of both the ASEAN Charter and the AICHR is questionable as human rights violations in member states did not cease, we contend that this does not reflect the failure of integration in the human rights domain but rather, a delicate balance between what member states deem as national *interest* and common supranational *aspirations*—what member states are willing to negotiate and maybe agree on regarding a possible compromise in the future. As Ciorciari has posited, the ASEAN Charter and the AICHR, just by virtue of their creation, do crucially enshrine and codify human rights norms and – notwithstanding their current limitations – clearly mark an institutional landmark that has the potential to evolve and mature with time (Ciorciari 2012).

Crisis and Integration in ASEAN: The Transboundary Haze Agreement

The 'haze' – a phenomenon whereby blankets of smoke caused by slash-and-burn practices employed predominantly in the dense forests of Sumatra and Kalimantan, Indonesia, spread to and impact neighbouring countries – has been a perennial thorn in intra-ASEAN relations since the late 1990s (Wong 2015). The haze episode of 1997 was especially severe; it was indeed justifiably a crisis not simply because of severe disruptions to air traffic, tourism and public health in Southeast Asia (particularly serious in Kuala Lumpur, southern Thailand and Singapore) but also because of the scale of social and economic consequences triggered by the episode. In fact, to put the negative impact of the environmental crisis in figures: an estimated twenty to seventy million individuals across the ASEAN region were affected; and the Asian Development Bank placed estimates of economic losses at US$6.3 billion.

The advent of the 1997–1998 environmental crisis did direct the attention of ASEAN member states to the environmental domain and spurred the idea of a need for transboundary cooperation in the environmental domain, as later reflected in the creation of, and institutionalised through, the signing of the ASEAN Transboundary Haze Agreement in 2003. The window of opportunity opened by the serious haze crisis in 1997 further – as in the case of the AFC and ASEAN's human rights regime – allowed the entrance of environmental non-governmental organisations and an active citizenry to campaign for standards in environmental security.

Interestingly, despite the recognition of the scale of economic and social consequences triggered by the haze crisis, the Transboundary Agreement was only fully ratified in 2014 as a result of years of foot-dragging by Indonesia, where the haze crisis originated. Moreover, the haze continues to be almost an annual phenomenon that brings about substantial costs to neighbouring states in terms of public health, air quality, economic productivity and tourism (Wong 2016). In fact, persuading Indonesia to take action against errant companies responsible for slash-and-burn practices in Indonesian forests still proves to be a formidable task and what can be considered incremental progress in the area of environmental rights still requires much pushing by Indonesia's neighbours (Tay 2008; Wong 2015).

In comparison with the AFC and the resulting formation of a human rights regime in AICHR, one wonders why the impact of both crises in terms of encouraging closer supranational integration could vary so significantly. Why would Indonesia counterintuitively spearhead the development and promotion of human rights norms, despite decades of authoritarianism and Suharto's regime and the little respect of human rights; why, on the contrary, is Indonesia so reluctant to do more in combating illegal slash-and-burn practices that is hazardous and equally economically consequential? Why is progress on regional integration in the human rights domain much more conspicuous than agreement on environmental protection, which is moving at a glacial pace?

Here we consider that the environmental crisis did not lead directly to urgent questions of legitimacy (and the threat of non-legitimacy) in Indonesia, or that even if it did, Indonesia remains hardly bothered and shockingly naive about them, due to the Indonesian bureaucracy's vested interests in the forestry industry (Tay 2008; Weatherbee 2005). While the haze highlighted the Indonesian state's inability to deal with illegal logging practices, it did not expose the deep *structural* economic flaws (unlike the AFC which did). Compared to the AFC, the environmental crisis, therefore, proved to be a much smaller stumbling block in terms of the need for regional integration, or at least Indonesia did not see the pressing need to, hence giving the country relatively more political leeway to *choose* not to submit to pressures for a regional solution.

Nonetheless, the Transboundary Haze Agreement remains a legally binding document that is a significant improvement from past efforts with its institutionalisation of an ASEAN Coordinating Center for Transboundary Pollution Control and an ASEAN Transboundary Haze Pollution Control Fund. This means that the Haze Agreement now binds Indonesia to a legal framework, allowing it to "voluntarily accept responsibility . . . and cooperatively, with its neighbors, clean regional skies" (Tay 2008; Wong 2016). It is indeed much too pessimistic to assume inefficiency and ineffectiveness when it comes to regional integration in the environmental domain, for the Haze Agreement was only recently fully ratified. Besides, other member states, such as Singapore, have instituted national legislation in 2014 to bring to court and punish companies found to be responsible for the haze, which is a highly positive sign that no stone will be left unturned on Singapore's or any ASEAN member states' part for that matter in assisting Indonesia's ongoing attempts to resolve the haze problem (Wong 2016).

EXPLAINING VARIATIONS

What Are the Variations between Western Europe and Southeast Asia and Why?

Both the EU and ASEAN are regional integration projects, and both consider regional integration as a means to an end (Allison 2015). In the words of article 2 of the Treaty Establishing the European Community (TEEC),

> The Community shall have as its task, by establishing a common market and progressively approximating the economic policies of Member States, to promote throughout the Community a harmonious development of economic activities, a continuous and balanced expansion, an increase in stability, an accelerated raising of the standard of living and closer relations between the states belonging to it. (TEEC 1957)

On a similar note, ASEAN aspires to

> establish a firm foundation for common action to promote regional cooperation in Southeast Asia in the spirit of equality and partnership and thereby contribute towards peace, progress and prosperity in the region. (ASEAN 1967)

As Allison argues, both the EU and ASEAN share the view that integration is a *process* that may lead to the end goal of peace and stability in their respective regions, rather than integration being the end goal in itself (Allison 2015). Nonetheless, beneath this deceptively simple similarity, lies complex differences that can neither be easily compared nor, in some circumstances, reconciled.

The EU

If the history of the EU can be understood as ever-closer neofunctional integration in response to crises (Schmitter 2004), then how do we make sense of the apparent lack of coordination and trust between member states in the EU's response to the refugee and counterterrorism crises of 2015? Are the factors in these domains deemed highly securitised and thus ill-suited to supranational integration?

As recently as 2011, Schengen was being touted as an intergovernmental agreement that was fast developing – indeed morphing – into a supranational area of cooperation within the EU (Zaiotti 2011). But perhaps this was a more innocent time when Schengen was perceived as a project to promote economic integration and free movement for EU citizens, before the crisis of mass terrorism that hit Paris and Brussels in November 2015 and February 2016.

At the same time, the EU project has been also explained in different terms, as a civilian power (Duchene 1972) and as a security community (Attinà 2010), that is to say as a bigger political project aimed at building a community of actors which recognise the same values and a supranational idea. The making of Common Security and Defence Policy (CSDP) is the most evident (and difficult) attempt to create an international role for a unique actor. The EU foreign policy put more emphasis on conflict prevention than on management, through political commitment and constructive dialogue. Even though military action is seen as a measure of last resort, the EU developed a structure of crises management and conflict resolution, which is coherent with global trends on humanitarian intervention and also with its own commercial, economic, cooperative and diplomatic policy.

Nevertheless, the factor which played a major role in explaining such processes is the political will of member states and their level of adaptation to crises and their management. The propensity of member states to cooperate and to negotiate has passed through various phases and has been shaped by endogenous and exogenous factors. The features of crises themselves and the effects on the level of risks they cause combined with the expectations of European citizens have resulted in a reduction of the uncertainty. But at the same time, EU integration has also been marked by the changes occurring in the global system and the duties derived by multilateral and international cooperation.

ASEAN

The focus of the regional integration project in ASEAN lies predominantly in smoothing political difficulties among its member states, rather than the explicit promotion of any full-fledged economic, political or security integration (Narine 2016). As sovereignty continues to be regarded by an ASEAN scarred by differing colonial experiences as key to the survival of viable states, the principle of non-interference remains the defining attribute that governs the relationships among the ASEAN member states. The familiar structure – an intergovernmental one – of ASEAN's regional project thus frequently results in the commitment of regional citizens and elites in the ASEAN community being diluted by their own commitment "to more parochial identities and interests" (Narine 2016).

The expectation of a pooling of sovereignty necessary to building supranational institutions as part of the regionalisation project is, therefore, largely inconceivable to the ASEAN member states, and where crises which mandate closer cooperation in search of a regional solution do emerge, effective supranationalism is likely to move at of arduous, glacial pace.

Scholars of international relations have extensively investigated variations among regions and their impact on their performances in sensitive policy fields. In particular, it has been observed that they assure, to some extent, a degree of political and economic distinctiveness in the international system (Pekkanen, Ravenhill and Foot 2014).

In the specific relationship between the EU and ASEAN, which is at the core of this chapter, scholars have reached different assumptions. On the one hand, ASEAN would be influenced by the EU and its potential of power model (Zielonka 2008; Jetschke 2009); on the other hand, the EU would represent a point of reference but not a real model (Wong 2012).

In any case, a deeper investigation of the ways through which variations in the relationship between crisis and integration can significantly contribute to theoretical debates and produce effects in terms of policy prescriptions is needed.

Understanding how regional institutions develop crisis management capabilities and tools, how these norms and practices are 'allowed' by states and how such tools reduce the degree of uncertainty in an effective way is essential not only to test the performance of regional organisations in times of crisis but also to test their relevance to the stability and security of the international system.

CONCLUSION

As described in this chapter, regional integration has given rise to new bodies demanding more decision-making prerogatives. They have moved the locus of important decisions in functional and sensitive areas dealing with traditional and non-traditional security issues away from states and into international arenas outside the state. This process – reactive rather than purposeful, short term rather than teleological or conscious – has taken place in both the EU and ASEAN since the 1990s. The EU was born and made progress after 1945 and into the 1950s when confronted with crises ranging from the collapse of European colonial empires' economic rehabilitation. West European nation states responded consciously and purposefully to the loss of national power by building European institutions. Very similar political phenomena have been reproduced in regional systems very different from the EU, taking into account that crisis may also produce regional variations.

This chapter was mainly based on the notion of 'crisis' as the critical juncture framework for understanding how it can activate – or deactivate – integration dynamics in the EU and in Southeast Asia. We particularly focused on two main variables: first, power relations between member states and regional organisations; second, institutional change in regional integration dynamics, focusing both on formal institutions and practices. We argue that crisis continues to be a major driver in the process of supranational integration, but that regional factors mediate the impact of crisis on integration outcomes in the EU and ASEAN and are the cause of different outcomes.

We have tried to define crisis in a broader way, particularly focusing on the transboundary dimension and analysed why similar crisis, like economic ones (the 1997 AFC and the 2008 Euro crisis) or political ones (terrorism), which are expected to produce a response from competent political actors, may have instead a different implication on integration.

As it has been observed, particularly in the case of the migrants and refugees crisis in the EU, more integration does not necessarily imply more supranationalism. Tackling a crisis may bring greater awareness among member states towards the need to develop a more coordinated policy but may result in a stronger intergovernmentalism, rather than putting emphasis on EU institutions.

Any explanation results from the combination of endogenous and exogenous factors. As for the first ones, the impact of existing agreements and institutions played as a powerful constraint, even though regional norms, cultures and practices were more dominant. In the case of ASEAN, norms of sovereignty and non-interference and the lack of a supranational body (unlike the Commission, EP, or ECB in the EU) precluded any region-wide agreement to raise confidence and combat speculative attacks on the weaker economies (Thailand, Indonesia, Malaysia).

In the EU, the rigid nature of treaties was balanced by various mechanisms which assured the member states the satisfaction of certain preferences. At the same time, the existence and the successive consolidation of a European security culture allowed the creation of more ambitious ideas (CSDP) or agencies (Frontex), which have no equal in other regions and certainly not in ASEAN.

All these processes are particularly visible in the most recent and pervasive crises, that is to say, migration and counterterrorism. They are both typical examples of transboundary crisis, characterised by a high degree of urgency and uncertainty. The abovementioned factors played a relevant role in the development of the necessary responses and crisis management capabilities. Overall, the need to strengthen the daily life security of millions of citizens without affecting their freedom of movement and the principle of sovereignty remains a constant and irredeemable dilemma.

BIBLIOGRAPHY

Acharya, Amitav. 2012. 'Comparative Regionalism: A Field Whose Time Has Come?' *The International Spectator*, 47, no. 1: 3–15.

Allison, Laura. 2015. *The EU, ASEAN and Interregionalism: Regionalism Support and Norm Diffusion between the EU and ASEAN* (The European Union in International Affairs series). London: Palgrave Macmillan.

ASEAN.org. 1967. 'The ASEAN Declaration (Bangkok Declaration). Conclusion date 8 August 1967. *ASEAN.org*. Available at https://asean.org/the-asean-declaration-bangkok-declaration-bangkok-8-august-1967/.

ASEAN Human Rights Declaration, ASSOCIATION OF SOUTHEAST ASIAN NATIONS (Nov. 18, 2012), http://www.asean.org/news/asean-statement-communiques/item/asean-human-rights-declaration

Attinà, Fulvio. 2010. 'European Propensity to Peacekeeping and Minilateralism: A Quantitative Analysis of Four EU Countries and ESDP Operations.' In *Multilateral Security and ESDP operations*, edited by Fulvio Attinà and Daniela Irrera, 105–124. Farnham, UK: Ashgate Publishing Limited.

Attinà, Fulvio. 2016. 'Migration Drivers, the EU External Migration Policy and Crisis Management.' *Romanian Journal of European Affairs,* 16, no. 4:15–31.

Attinà, Fulvio. 2018. 'Tackling the Migrant Wave: EU as a Source and a Manager of Crisis.' *Revista Española de Derecho Internacional*, 70, no. 2: 49–70.

Bakker, Edwin. 2011. 'Characteristics of Jihadi Terrorists in Europe (2001–2009).' In *Jihadi Terrorism and the Radicalisation Challenge: European and American Experiences*, edited by Rik Coolsaet, 131–144. Farnham, UK: Ashgate Publishing Limited, 2nd edition.

Barnett, Michael and Martha Finnemore. 2004. *Rules for the World: International Organizations in Global Politics*. Ithaca, NY: Cornell University Press.

Baumgartner, Frank R. and Bryan D. Jones. 1993. Agendas and Instability in American Politics. Chicago, IL: University of Chicago Press.

Baumgartner, Frank R., Christoffer Green-Pedersen and Bryan D. Jones. 2006. 'Comparative Studies of Policy Agendas.' *Journal of European Public Policy*, 13, no. 7: 959–974. doi: 10.1080/13501760600923805.

Boin, Arjen, Magnus Ekengren and Mark Rhinard. 2013. *The European Union as Crisis Manager: Patterns and Prospects*. Cambridge: Cambridge University Press.

Boin, Arjen, Paul't Hart, Eric Stern and Bengt Sundelius. 2005. *The Politics of Crisis Management: Public Leadership under Pressure*. Cambridge: Cambridge University Press.

Bosi, Lorenzo and Donatella Della Porta. 2012 'Micro-Mobilization into Armed Groups: Ideological, Instrumental and Solidaristic Paths.' *Qualitative Sociology*, 35, no. 4: 361–383.

Brennan, Louis and Philomena Murray, eds. 2015. *Drivers of Integration and Regionalism in Europe and Asia: Comparative Perspectives*. London: Routledge. Routledge Research in Comparative Politics series.

Ciorciari, John. 2012 'Institutionalizing Human Rights in Southeast Asia.' Human Rights Quarterly, 34, no. 3: 695–725.

Cohen, Raymond. 1978. 'Threat Perception in International Crisis.' *Political Science Quarterly*, 93, no. 1: 93–107. doi:10.2307/2149052.

Crenshaw, Martha, ed. 2010. *The Consequences of Counterterrorism*. New York: Russell Sage Foundation.

Djani, Dian T. 2009. 'A Long Journey.' In *The Making of the ASEAN Charter*, edited by Tommy Koh, Rosario G. Manalo and Walter Woon, 137–150. Hackensack, NJ: World Scientific Publishing Co. Pte. Ltd.

Duina, Francesco. 2007. *The Social Construction of Free Trade: The European Union, NAFTA, and Mercosur*. Princeton, NJ: Princeton University Press.

Eldridge, Philip J. 2002. *The Politics of Human Rights in Southeast Asia*. London: Routledge.

Fabbrini, Sergio and Uwe Puetter. 2016. 'Integration without Supranationalisation: Studying the Lead Roles of the European Council and the Council in Post-Lisbon EU politics.' *Journal of European Integration*, 38, no. 5: 481–495.

Genieys, William and Patrick Hassenteufel. 2012. 'Qui gouverne les politiques publiques?' *Gouvernement et action publique*, 2012/2, no. 2: 89–115.

Gerard, Kelly. 2016. 'Crises, Civil Society and Regionalism in Southeast Asia.' In *Crisis and Institutional Change in Regional Integration*, edited by Sabine Saurugger and Fabien Terpan, 192–208. London: Routledge.

Hall, Peter A. 1993. 'Policy Paradigms, Social Learning and the State: The Case of Economic Policymaking in Britain.' *Comparative Politics*, 35, no. 3: 275–96.

Hameiri, Shahar and Kanishka Jayasuriya. 2012. 'Regulatory Regionalism in Asia.' In *Routledge Handbook of Asian Regionalism*, edited by Mark Beeson and Richard Stubbs, 177–185. London: Routledge.

Hermann, Charles F. 1963. 'Some Consequences of Crisis which Limit the Viability of Organizations.' *Administrative Science Quarterly*, 8, no. 1: 61–82. doi: 10.2307/2390887.

Hsien-Li, Tan. 2011. *The ASEAN Intergovernmental Commission on Human Rights: Institutionalising Human Rights in Southeast Asia*. Cambridge: Cambridge University Press.

Jones, Lee. 2012. *ASEAN, Sovereignty and Intervention in Southeast Asia*. New York: Palgrave Macmillan.

Lavenex, Sandra. 2015. 'Justice and Home Affairs: Communitarization with Hesitation.' In *Policy-Making in the European Union*, edited by Helen Wallace, Mark A. Pollack and Alasdair R. Young, 367–387. New York: Oxford University Press, 7th edition.

Katznelson, Ira. 2003. 'Periodization and Preferences: Reflections on Purposive Action in Comparative Historical Social Science.' In *Comparative Historical Analysis in the Social Sciences*, edited by James Mahoney and Dietrich Rueschemeyer, 270–304. Cambridge: Cambridge University Press.

Kühnhardt, Ludger. 2010. 'Introduction.' In *Region-Building: Volume 1: The Global Proliferation of Regional Integration*, edited by Ludger Kühnhardt, 1–8. New York: Berghahn Books.

Marin, Luisa. 2011. 'Policing EU's External Borders: A Challenge for the Rule of Law and Fundamental Rights in the Area of Freedom, Security and Justice? An Analysis of Frontex Joint Operations at the Southern Maritime Border.' *Journal of Contemporary European Research*, 7, no. 4: 468–487.

Mattern, Janice B. 2005. *Ordering International Politics: Identity, Crisis, and Representational Force*. New York: Routledge.

McCormick, James. 1978. 'International Crises: A Note on Definition.' *The Western Political Quarterly*, 31, no. 3: 352–358. doi:10.2307/447735.

Milward, Alan. 2000. *The European Rescue of the Nation State*. London: Routledge, 2nd edition.

Moravcsik, Andrew. 1998. *The Choice for Europe: Social Purpose & State Power from Messina to Maastricht*. London: Routledge.

Narine, Shaun. 2016. 'ASEAN and the Response to Regional Crisis.' In *Crisis and Institutional Change in Regional Integration*, edited by Sabine Saurugger and Fabien Terpan, 173–191. London: Routledge.

Pekkanen, Saadoa, John Ravenhill and Rosemary Foot, eds. 2014. *Oxford Handbook of the International Relations of Asia*. Oxford: Oxford University Press.

Rüland, Jürgen. 2010. 'ASEAN and the Asian Crisis: Theoretical Implications and Practical Consequences for Southeast Asian Regionalism.' *The Pacific Review*, 13, no. 3: 421–451. doi: 10.1080/09512740050147942.

Saurugger, Sabine and Fabien Terpan, eds. 2016. *Crisis and Institutional Change in Regional Integration*. London: Routledge.

Sbragia, Alberta M. 2008. 'Comparative regionalism: What Might It Be?' *JCMS: Journal of Common Market Studies*, 46, no. 1: 29–49.

Schmitter, Philippe C. 2004. 'Neo-Neofunctionalism' in Wiener, Antje and Thomas Diez (eds.) *European Integration Theory*. Oxford: Oxford University Press, 45–74.

Sukma, Rizal. 2011. 'Soft Power and Public Diplomacy: The Case of Indonesia.' In *Public Diplomacy and Soft Power in East Asia*, edited by Sook Jong Lee and Jan Melissen, 91–115. New York: Palgrave Macmillan.

Tan, Hsien-Li. 2001. *The ASEAN Intergovernmental Commission on Human Rights: Institutionalising Human Rights in Southeast Asia*. Cambridge: Cambridge University Press.

Tay, Simon. 2008. 'Blowing Smoke: Regional Cooperation, Indonesian Democracy, and the Haze.' In *Hard Choices: Security. Democracy, and Regionalism in Southeast Asia*, edited by Donald K. Emmerson, 219–240. Stanford, CA: Walter H. Shorenstein Asia-Pacific Research Center.

Thio, Li-ann. 1999. 'Implementing Human Rights in ASEAN Countries: "Promises to Keep and Miles to Go before I Sleep."' *Yale Human Rights & Development Journal*, 2, no. 1: 1–86.

Warleigh-Lack, Alex and Luk Van Langenhove. 2010. 'Rethinking EU Studies: The contribution of comparative Regionalism.' *Journal of European Integration*, 32, no. 6: 541–562.

Weatherbee, Donald E. 2005. *International Relations in Southeast Asia: The Struggle for Autonomy*. Lanham, MD: Rowman & Littlefield Publishers, 1st edition.

Wong, Reuben. 2012. 'Model Power or Reference Point? The EU and the ASEAN Charter', *Cambridge Review of International Affairs,* 25, no. 4: 669–682.

Wong, Reuben. 2015. 'Creeping Supranationalism: The EU and ASEAN Experiences.' In *Drivers of Integration and Regionalism in Europe and Asia Comparative Perspectives* (Routledge Research in Comparative Politics series), edited by Louis Brennan and Philomena Murray, 235–251. London: Routledge.

Wong, Reuben. 2016. 'Crisis and Regional Integration: Human Rights and Environmental Governance in ASEAN.' In *Crisis and Institutional Change in Regional Integration*, edited by Sabine Saurugger and Fabien Terpan, 155–172. London: Routledge.

Zaiotti, Ruben. 2011. *Cultures of Border Control: Schengen and the Evolution of European Frontiers*. Chicago: University of Chicago Press.

Chapter 11

The Governance of
the European Union

Which Role for National Governments?

Sergio Fabbrini

In her seminal 1992 work, *Thinking about the European Future: The Uses of Comparison*, Alberta Sbragia (Sbragia 1992, 257) noticed: "It is not accidental that the question of institutional reform has been perennially debated within the Community. . . . The evolution of institutions, the allocation of power among institutions, and the questions of legitimacy linked to such allocation are critical to the governance of the Community and its policy capacity." More specifically, Sbragia (ibid.) argued that any attempt of institutional reform would have to deal with the issue of "how much national governments should shape Community policy-making". The latter, one might argue, was her research question. The Community has become the European Union (EU), but its governance is still a central topic of debate, particularly after the multiple crises of the 2010s. During those crises, the role of national governments (coordinating in and through the European Council) has become predominant in policy-making – so predominant that the European Council has acquired the features of a proper political executive. However, the European Council's predominance has raised criticism for the lack of effectiveness and legitimacy of its decisions.

Making Sbragia's research question my own, the chapter investigates the problem of governance in the EU. The literature on governance is a growing industry, particularly in the field of EU studies (Borzel 2016; Piattoni 2010; Sabel and Zeitlin 2012). This literature has contributed to our understanding of how a multi-level and complex system, such as the EU, functions. Governance has been interpreted as "a way of governing that does not assume the presence of a traditional, hierarchical *government* at the helm of the polity" (Christiansen 2016, 97, italics in the original). In EU studies, governance's turn (since the 1990s) has led to an emphasis on the process of deliberation and decision, more than on the structure or the institutional form where that process takes place. For instance, according to Borzel (2016, 12), "The EU's governance has evolved over time developing different varieties of inter- and trans-governmental negotiation and regulatory competition in the shadow of supranational hierarchy." A 'processual' approach to EU governance, however, makes comparison with other multi-level systems uncertain or unlikely and justifying the assumption of the EU as an *ad hoc* system. As Sbragia (1992, 268) argued, "Although the Community is unique, analysis is more likely to suffer from studying it in isolation from other systems than from using the comparative method in less than ideal circumstances." My aim is to go beyond 'ad-hoc-ism' (Sartori 2009, chapter 1) and assumes that the EU is a political system in its own right, structured around institutions that incentivize regular patterns of decision-making and legitimacy (Fabbrini 2015b).

The chapter is organized as follows. First, it will develop a descriptive analysis of the basic structure of decision-making institutionalized within the EU, particularly after the 1992 Maastricht Treaty. In the EU, governance operates differently in different policy areas. EU governance exists in a differentiated intersection of decision-making regimes and policy issues, an intersection that defines different spaces for national governments' role and provides alternative modalities of EU legitimacy. The post-2008 crises brought decision-making differentiation to the fore, showing not only its resilience but also its contradictory implications, thus triggering a debate on the future of the EU as has never happened before (Fabbrini 2019). Second, the chapter considers the debate analysing the main official documents on the future of the EU. These documents focus exclusively on which policy regimes to activate and not on the governance structures to manage them. Looking for alternative models to the governance *status quo*, I identify two theoretical models. One is the club governance model that is derived from the interpretation of the EU as a quasi-international organization. The second is the state governance model that is derived from an interpretation of the EU as a quasi-state organization. Third, because the theoretical investigation has not answered persuasively my research question relative to the proper role of national governments in the EU, the chapter then considers the experience of comparative federalism for deriving useful concepts for understanding the future of the EU's governance. Distinguishing between federations by disaggregation (federal states) and federations by aggregation (federal unions), the chapter will show that the latter's governance model, defined as a multiple separation of powers system, is a useful reference point for conceptualizing a new role for national governments in the EU. The distinction between different federal models is as rare now as it was when Sbragia discussed the topic. As Sbragia (1992, 265) then remarked, "Federalization through integrative rather than deintegrative processes is so rare in the late twentieth century that scholars of contemporary federalism do not pay it much heed." Through a normative-deductive approach, the logic of the federal union's governance is thus applied to the EU, often considered a case of 'federalization through integrative processes', involving previously independent states that are both demographically asymmetric and with different national identities. The conclusion, finally, drives home the main argument, namely that the debate concerning the role that national governments should play in the EU would benefit from the experience of comparative federalism.

THE POST-MAASTRICHT DIFFERENTIATED GOVERNANCE OF THE EU

While the EU was a necessary response to the rivalry between the European states, there was never a 'constitutional moment' to define what form that response (at least until after the 1954 defeat of the European Defence Community project) should take. The institutional organization of the EU, either because it is the expression of incomplete contracts (Heritier 2007) or of interstate and inter-institutional compromises (Fabbrini 2015a), has solicited its own periodical redefinition. Incompleteness is inevitable as the institutional framework is derived from interstate and interinstitutional bargains taking place in the context of scarce information regarding other actors' preferences. This logic has accompanied the structuring of a differentiated governance regime since the 1992 Maastricht Treaty.

Following the historic turning point due at the end of the Cold War (1989–1991), the treaty celebrated a compromise between the intergovernmental governance managing new policies added to the European agenda (such as foreign affairs, defence, security, justice and home affairs, as well as the economic policy of the Economic and Monetary Union or EMU) and the supranational governance (which continued to govern the regulatory policies of the common market, becoming the single or internal market with the 1987 Single European Act). Certainly, between the two governance types, mixed governance models are set up for dealing with specific policy challenges. Heuristically, however, it can be said that the EU, since the Maastricht Treaty, has become differentiated between two main approaches for managing different policies. The regulatory policies of the Single Market are decided through a governance regime, usually termed the 'Community method', in which the Commission has the monopoly of legislative initiative. The Council of Ministers (subsequently only the Council) and the European Parliament (or EP) share co-decision-making power over the proposals put forward by the Commission, while the European Council, which consists of the heads of state and government, acts as the court of last resort to resolve disputes which would otherwise hinder the integration process if left unsettled (Dehousse 2011;

Devuyst 2018). Since Maastricht, with the new policies that have become part of the EU's agenda (and traditionally close to the core state powers, Genschel and Jachtenfuchs 2014), the governance regime has taken quite a different form. In these policies, the decision-making process has been circumscribed by the two intergovernmental bodies, the Council and, increasingly, the European Council (although the latter remained an informal institution until the 2009 Lisbon Treaty). The Commission now plays a technical role (a sort of secretariat) and the EP is marginalized (it is 'informed' of the decisions taken by national heads of government but does not have the significant power to sanction over those decisions) (Puetter 2014). While through the Single Market the integration process proceeds through legislative provisions, in new policy areas, it proceeds more through political decisions. In the former case, the European Court of Justice (ECJ) can verify the coherence of the laws approved with the Treaty's principles and dispositions, while in the latter case, its judicial supervisory role is necessarily limited. This differentiation of governance regimes results in the institutionalization of different roles for national governments in the policy-making process of the EU (Fabbrini and Puetter 2016).

The different roles for national governments are due to the different natures of the policies to be decided upon and the different perceptions of their domestic political salience. The new policy areas are traditionally close to the heart of national sovereignty. Once these policies were brought to Brussels, national governments, and not only the larger ones, sought to control their decision-making process. These policies are the key in political terms, with their inevitable impact on the electoral fortunes of the incumbent national governments. For this reason, the latter wants to control the decision-making process, especially during crises that affect the national level. The success or failure of migration policy, or the handling of the banking crisis, or the answer to security threats is destined to influence the electoral fortune of incumbent national leaders. For instance, the Commission's September 2016 proposal to distribute political refugees to the various member states of the EU on the basis of objective criteria was openly challenged by various national governments (particularly in Central and Eastern Europe, Krastev 2017) for precisely domestic political considerations. Much less internally divisive are the regulatory policies of the Single Market. The political externalities of market policies mainly impact private actors, while the political externalities of the new policies impact public actors (Genschel and Jachtenfuchs 2017). An example of this is the Commission's decision on 30 August 2016 ordering Apple to pay €13 billion to the Irish government, an amount equivalent to the taxes it would have paid since 2003 if it had not benefitted from an improper tax regime (given the European rules on competition). It affected a private multinational company, not a national government (indeed the Irish government is a beneficiary of the decision, although it opposed it fearing that it would reduce the country's fiscal attractiveness). Thus, the divisions between member states emerged in the new policies, those managed within and through the intergovernmental institutions and not in the regulatory policies of the Single Market. It should be added that those divisions have frequently been overcome through unilateral actions taken by government leaders of the strongest member states (Fabbrini 2016).

Since 1992, the question raised by Sbragia (1992, 257), concerning "how much national governments should shape Community policy-making" is answered namely by the setting up of different structures of governance to manage policies that have different domestic political impacts. Those structures of governance incentivize different roles for national governments and thus provide different answers to the democratic legitimacy needs of the EU decision-making process. The governance structure for Single Market policies derives its legitimacy from the indirect electoral legitimacy of the Council and the direct electoral legitimacy of the EP, with the Commission's role legitimized exclusively by the treaty provisions. At the same time, the Commission, the EP, and the Council check and balance each other, thus fulfilling the need for their institutional accountability. The increasing expansion of the EP's competences (through the growth of regulatory issues under the ordinary legislative procedures) is justified by the necessity to strengthen the legitimacy of the supranational governance regime. However, in policies with high domestic political salience, decision-making power is mainly controlled by national governmental leaders, coordinating within the Council and, above all, the European Council. In these policies, national governments accept to play a decision-making role on par with the EP, while leaving the power of legislative initiative to the Commission (as in supranational governance). The legitimacy of the intergovernmental governance has an indirect source. National leaders and ministers are legitimized through their participation in the Brussels' intergovernmental decision-making process and by individual accountability to their own national parliaments. Here the fusion (Wessels 1997) between the national and Brussels levels of government has reached its climax. Yet Brussels' intergovernmental institutions operate as collegial bodies and not as a sum of individual national leaders and ministers. Since it is unlikely that national parliaments, as single distinct legislatures, can check the action of the European Council or the Council as collegial institutions, it logically follows that intergovernmental decision-making takes place in a vacuum of both electoral and institutional accountability. If it is true what Sbragia argued in 1992 (1992, 258), namely that "the fate of national governments . . . will shape the Community's political future", then the post-1992 institutional solution found for the role of national governments has left our research question unanswered.

POST-CRISIS REFORM PROPOSALS

The limits of the differentiated governance structure of the EU were apparent during the multiple crises of the 2010s. Nevertheless, several proposals advanced by EU authorities did not deal with those limits. The Four Presidents' Report of June 2012 (Rompuy et al. 2012) proposes to move "towards a genuine Economic and Monetary Union" and to set up an integrated financial framework, an integrated budgetary framework, and an integrated economic policy framework. It finally considers the problem of democratic legitimacy and accountability of the EMU, to be resolved through "the involvement of the European Parliament as regards accountability for decisions taken at the European level, while maintaining the pivotal role of national parliaments, as appropriate". The predisposition to preserve the governance *status quo* seems evident in the proposal to institutionalize, and not to reform, intergovernmentalism. The Report says: "Some intergovernmental arrangements have been created as a result of the shortcoming of the previous architecture, but these would ultimately need to be integrated into the legal framework of the European Union". The Five Presidents' Report of June 2015 (Juncker et al. 2015) is even less courageous than the previous report. For "completing Europe's Economic and Monetary Union", the report proposes to move towards an economic union, a banking union, a fiscal union, and, finally, towards a more accountable union. The latter can be achieved through the strengthening of "the parliamentary oversight as part of the European Semester", a "new form of inter-parliamentary cooperation . . . to bring together European and national actors . . . in the European Parliamentary Week", and, finally, an "increasingly unified" external representation of the EMU via "a full-time presidency of the Euro-group".

The 'White Paper on the Future of Europe', which the then Commission president Jean-Claude Juncker presented to the EP on 1 March 2017, constitutes a further example of the predisposition for the *status quo* (in this case of the Commission) with regard to the governance of the EU. In the White Paper, five scenarios are imagined for the future of Europe. The first scenario envisioned is that of "carrying on" the current differentiated system, through a policy of muddling-through to adapt to crises. The second scenario, "nothing but the single market", nullifies what happened after Maastricht, advancing the proposition to return to the 1987 Single European Act. The third scenario is the idea of letting "those who want more do more" (giving rise to coalitions of the willing to pursue specific programs through forms of enhanced and structured cooperation), in accordance with the view termed multispeed Europe. The fourth scenario is "doing less more efficiently" and the fifth scenario is "doing much more together". The four scenarios specify the policies to be managed by each of them but are completely disinterested regarding how and who should manage those policies. For the White Paper as well, the current dual governance regime of the EU constitutes the natural order of things.

Alternative governance models for the EU are rarely discussed in the scientific literature. The mainstream theories deal more with the process of integration and not with the features of the latter's institutional outcome. One might plausibly derive alternative governance models from the explicit inter-pretation of the EU as a quasi-international organization or from the implicit assumption that the EU should evolve towards a quasi-state organization. In different ways, both theories presuppose the overcoming of the dual gover-nance regime of the current EU. The idea of the EU as quasi-international organization or association of states has been elaborated by Majone (2014) and is derived from James Buchanan's theory of organizations operating under conditions of internal complexity and external divergent pressures (Buchanan 1965). As Majone (2014) observed, the EU has become too com-plex of an organization because integration has gone too far. In this context, the EU should answer specific requests through a varied combination of states that are interested in participating in specific policies to satisfy those requests. Buchanan's theory of club of clubs offers a scientific basis for man-aging the inevitable growing internal differentiation of the EU. According to Majone (2014, 17), the "economic theory of clubs may be used to provide a robust conceptual basis for the analysis of integration *à la carte* and of other forms of functional integration." From a governance perspective, the EU *à la carte* would consist of transient combinations of clusters of states, deal-ing with specific problems, coordinating through and within the European Council, technically supported by the Commission but fully autonomous in their reciprocal negotiation, with the ECJ intervening only to resolve potentially destructive disputes. In the *club governance* model, thus, national governments are the only decision makers. Democratic accountability of the European Council is not an issue, as long as the latter's members are account-able to their national parliaments for the specific and *ad hoc* decisions they contribute to at the European level. However, it seems highly questionable for the EU to become a sort of service-provider organization based on dif-ferent clusters of national governments, disregarding altogether the need of guaranteeing a citizens' voice on its decisions.

The idea of the EU as a quasi-state organization has deep roots in European political culture. In recent literature, an implicit justification of the statist evo-lution of the EU can be found in Dani Rodrik's trilemma (2011, chapter 10), according to which "democracy, national sovereignty and global economic integration are mutually incompatible: we can combine any two of the three, but never have all three simultaneously and in full" (Rodrik, 2007). A higher level of one of them requires a lower level of the others, demonstrating a

zero⬚sum exercise. Deeper European integration implies less national sovereignty and weaker democratic control at the national level. One might
question the internal logic of Rodrick's paradigm which underestimates the
respective power of the states involved in the integration process. The management of the Euro crisis, for instance, increased rather than reduced the
national sovereignty and power of domestic democratic institutions in the
creditor states (in Germany, the *Bundestag* and the Federal Constitutional
Court or *Bundesverfassungsgericht*), while the opposite occurred in the
debtor member states (Matthijs 2017). The solution to Rodrik's trilemma
would imply a kind of centralization of the decision-making process as seen
in state organizations, blurring further the already opaque distinction between
national and European levels of government.

From a governance perspective, the quasi-state organization is compatible
with either intergovernmental (*state governance A*) or parliamentary (*state
governance B*) features. For *state governance A*, the European Council is the
inevitable centre of political authority. In this model, experienced mainly in
the EMU, the European Council is an executive institution (with a collegial
composition), whereas the supranational institutions' role is highly circumscribed. Specifically, the Commission plays a technical role, but not a political one, by supporting the European Council and Council deliberations. The
legitimacy of the European Council and Council are a by-product of the functioning of national democracies and not of a supranational democracy. This
governance model would necessarily imply, as proposed by the Four Presidents and Five Presidents' Reports, the formation of an inter-parliamentary
arena that connects the EP and national parliaments and allows for debates
on decisions taken up by national governments. An inter-parliamentary
debate makes public the decisions of the European Council but does not
render the latter accountable as a collegial institution. *State governance A*
underestimates how the Brussels-based intergovernmental institutions make
their collegial decisions, while their members (national government leaders
and ministers) can respond only individually to their legislature. Indeed,
the lack of a sanctioning power on the side of the EP makes the European
Council institutionally unaccountable. During the Euro crisis, this unchecked
and unbalanced decision-making role of national governments led to the formation of hierarchical relations between creditor and debtor member states
within the European Council and the Council of Economic and Financial
ministers or ECOFIN Council, relations incompatible with the principle of
equality between member states celebrated by all of the EU treaties (Fabbrini
F. 2016).

For *state governance*, the decision-making power instead moves towards
the EP, the institution representing European citizens, with national governments playing a co-legislative role (although subordinated to the popular

chamber regarding the formation of the parliamentary executive or Commission). In this governance model, experienced in the regulatory policies of the Single Market such as with competition, the EU should evolve towards a parliamentary state with the Commission as its executive. Parliamentary governance functions on the basis of competition among European-level political parties which seek to win control of the Commission (as the sole European government) through the electoral participation of citizens (as argued by Hix 2008, among others). The *spitzenkandidat* strategy pursued by the main European-level political parties in the 2014 EP elections (but called into question by the outcome of the 2019 EP elections) is an example of the attempt to move the EU in a parliamentary direction (Christiansen 2016). In this model, national governments are represented only in the second chamber without operating in any executive role. This strategy assumes the EU as being mainly a union of citizens rather than of states. As Sbragia (1992, 279, italics added) argued, "European federalists . . . tend(ed) to conceptualize a federal Europe without the institutionalization of *territorial politics*. In their view, a body representing a European electorate would constitute a strong political centre—and the representation of the member states' governments as governments would become tangential at best." *State governance B* underestimates not only the need to acknowledge the decision-making role of national governments but also the implications for parliamentary governance of citizens representing demographically asymmetric states with different national identities. A union of states, such as the EU, cannot squeeze its representational features into a single institution (the EP) that functions according to partisan (as opposed to territorial) cleavages (Fabbrini 2015a). Both perspectives of *state governance* leave unresolved the problem of how to balance the territorial/corporate representation of national governments with the individual representation of European voters. Is there an analytical alternative to the EU becoming either an association of states or a quasi-state?

BRINGING COMPARATIVE FEDERALISM BACK IN

A critical investigation of the experience of comparative federations might be useful to provide this analytical alternative (on the comparative federalism's literature, see Fossum and Jachtenfunchs 2017; Kelemen 2019). The research question raised by Sbragia (1992, 258) is still unanswered, namely "is it possible to 'federalize' the Community significantly while retaining a key policy-making role for national governments?" Although the debate on 'what does federalism mean' does not allow an unequivocal understanding of it, to consider "some relevant ideas about comparative federalism . . . may help in thinking about some of the critical issues in future institution building"

(Sbragia 1992, 258). A useful starting point is the distinction between a 'coming together federation' and a 'holding together federation' (Stepan 1999) or what Sbragia called an 'integrative and deintegrative processes' of federalization. Distinguishing between federations emerging from the disaggregation of previously unitary states and those that emerge from the aggregation of previously independent (demographically asymmetric and nationally differentiated) states can help us to understand the different governances' models adopted by the two federations. Indeed, the former federations (here conceptualized as *federal states*) have all adopted a fusion of powers model, whereas the latter federations (here conceptualized as *federal unions*) have all adopted a separation of powers model.

The United States and Germany are both federations, but their legal nature does not explain how the governance structure is institutionally organized in each. Distinguishing within the genus of federations between a federal state and a federal union helps to identify the latter as a federation with confederal features (because of its genetic formation). A federal union might be defined as a constitutionalized union of states formed through the aggregation of previously independent units with distinct national citizens. Federal unions include states that display substantial differences in both their demography and national identity (Fabbrini 2010). Empirically, in only two cases (the United States and Switzerland) has the aggregation ended up forming into a successful constitution-based federal union (in both cases, however, consolidation started after dramatic internal conflicts). Their constitutions formalize a pact between the elites of states or cantons to divide sovereignty vertically between levels of government and horizontally between governmental institutions. Horizontally, federal unions institutionalize confederal features through the upper chamber, respectively, the U.S. Senate and the Swiss Council of States, where the states are recognized by the same power of representation regardless of their population, a confederal feature that, in the case of the United States, also affects the state electoral colleges for the indirect election of the president. Because separation of powers also organizes the federated states' decision-making process, the latter cannot have national governments as unitary political subjects. Consequently, states or cantons are represented by representatives of their voters (or, in the pre-1916 United States, by representatives of their separated legislatures). Vertically, the states are separated from the centre through a delineation of the latter's competences. Historically, in fact, federal unions are characterized by enumerated powers at the centre, whose governmental institutions are in turn separated to prevent the centre's domination over the states. Indeed, since it was the states that started the aggregative process, they could both maintain local control over most public policies and guarantee their confederal representation at the federal centre.

Multiple separation of powers have triggered horizontal deliberative processes, without discarding the necessity to regulate them according to criteria of democratic legitimacy. The politicians involved in those policy-making processes represent, and are accountable to, separate constituencies and operate through different temporal mandates. At the same time, they are accountable to each other through the checks-and-balances mechanism. The constitution frames the context within which the dynamic interaction between the territorial units and the centre takes place for protecting or increasing their respective competences in the new contexts produced by social change. Comparative analysis of the United States and Switzerland tells us that the policies initially allocated to the federal centre were historically limited but with a general jurisdictional value in their application (i.e. they do not allow opt-outs to those who are part of their jurisdiction) (Kelemen 2014) and with autonomous (particularly fiscal) resources to manage them (although the acquisition of those resources highly varied across federated states/cantons, Wozniakowski 2017). Of course, separation is not written in stone. Parties and party systems play a crucial role in bridging both vertical and horizontal institutions. Indeed, when they are not able to do that (as in the 1861–1865 United States), the federal union moves towards a collapse.

The internal development and external projection of federal unions inevitably affected the vertical relations between levels of government and the horizontal relations between the centre's institutions, although much more in the United States than in Switzerland. In the latter, the limited size of the union and its decision to avoid any direct international role guaranteed a continuity in the relations between levels of government and a balance between horizontal institutions. In the United States, instead, the social complexity induced by industrialization, urbanization, and technological innovation, combined with the powerful international projection of the country since World War II (Hendrickson 2009; Katznelson and Shafter 2002) introduced formidable discontinuities in the power relations between levels of government, increasing the number of policies vertically controlled by the federal centre or managed through the cooperation between levels of government (Schutze 2010). In each case, these processes triggered the decision-making growth of the president, although checked by the legislature (and by, in particular, the Senate for policies crucial to the federated states, such as in foreign and security policy or justice affairs).

The governance structure of a federal union has, thus, had to solve a puzzle different from that of a federal state, that is a unitary state that has passed through a process of territorial decentralization of a previously unitary state or state-like dominion characterized by vertical decision-making centralization (as is the case in Europe of Germany, Austria, Belgium, or of highly decentralized countries such as Spain and the United Kingdom, and outside of Europe in Australia and to a limited extent Canada). If nation states have historically emerged from a process of cultural homogenization of citizens living within internationally recognized territorial boundaries, federal or federalized nation states could decentralize competences to the territorial units in a context of relative national/cultural homogeneity. The earlier federal or quasi-federal states have in fact adopted, in one form or another, the fusion of powers or parliamentary government (which centralizes political power in the executive or cabinet and in turn is dependent on the political confidence of the legislature's lower chamber, however, mitigated by the sectorial competences of the higher chamber representing the territorial units). The two federal unions considered have, however, adopted, in one form or another, the separation of powers model, although with a monocratic (the United States) or collegial (Switzerland) executive. Indeed, when the national homogeneity or common identity of the federal state is openly called into question by some of its territorial units (as in the case of Catalonia, Scotland, Flanders, or Quebec), then the parliamentary (or fusion of powers) governance of the federal state is no longer sustainable. It is implausible to integrate the claims for nationhood of those territorial units through the centralizing thrust of parliamentary government. Thus, it is true that in Germany the *Laenders'* governments are formally represented in the *Bundesrat* or in Canada the governments of the provinces are informally represented in the Conference of the First Ministers, but in both systems there is a chamber (the *Bundestag* in Germany and the House of Commons in Canada) giving legitimacy to the decision-making process (and holding the government expressed by that chamber accountable) (Fabbrini 2017a).

In conclusion, the federal union has an anti☐centralizing bias because it fragments the decision-making process between separate institutional entities rather than centralizing it into one single institution (the popular chamber that has the power to give or withdraw political confidence to the executive). Neither of the two federal unions offers a direct representation to state/canton governments at the federal level, although states or cantons are represented through their citizens. The federal union acknowledges the role of territorial politics (to use Sbragia's terms) at the federal level through the confederal representation of state's voters in the upper chamber of the legislature, but it would be implausible for it to give representation to governments, since states or cantons do not have parliamentary governments as unitary subjects (depending on the type of separation of powers). On the contrary, the federal state can accommodate the representation of a *Laender*'s or a province's parliamentary government (as in the German *Bundesrat*) or parliamentary leader (as in the Canadian Conference of Prime Ministers), but the latter does not have a voice in forming or dismissing the federal government (Scharpf 1988). This institutional property should be highlighted. It is true that the *Laender* governments are represented in the *Bundesrat* and it is also true that the *Bundesrat* plays a powerful role in policies of interest to the *Laender* (such as in budgetary policy). However, this representation does not make *Laender* governments the collegial executive of the *Deutsche Bundesrepublik* as in the intergovernmental governance of the EU. In Germany, the *Bundesrat* does not play any role in the formation or dismissal of the federal chancellor.

THE GOVERNANCE OF THE EU AS A FEDERAL UNION

If it is true what Sbragia observed (1992, 258, italics added), namely that "the future institutional design of the Community . . . is unlikely to submerge national governments into some kind of federation, *as conventionally defined*", then it might be useful to test the governance's logic of a federal union to evaluate whether it can provide an answer to Sbragia's observation regarding the EU. I will apply that logic through a normative-deductive approach (for a normative-inductive approach to the EU, see Nicolaidis 2013), assuming the EU to be, to use Sartori's concept (Sartori 2009, Chapter 1), the most similar case to a federation by aggregation (Fabbrini 2017b). How might we use the experience of federal unions to deal with the central topic of accommodating the decision-making role of national governments at the EU level? Only through a separation of powers strategy is it possible to find an answer to that question. Let us see why.

In the EU, the strategy of multiple separation of powers would imply different degrees of reform at both vertical and horizontal levels of government. On the vertical level, it would be necessary to separate supranational governance from the national institutions of government and to introduce a clear constitutional firewall between them. In the current governance system (specifically in the intergovernmental one, such as the European Council and the Council), national governments are thrust directly into the EU decision-making process. Not only does such a vertical fusion of powers confuse the responsibility between levels of government and tarnishes the role of European citizens, but it also allows the direct projection of an anti-EU national government at the EU level (making possible, for instance, the formation of a coalition of anti-EU national governments within the European Council and Council that would disrupt their functioning). After all, national leaders bring their domestic electoral needs to the highest executive institution (the European Council), and thus make the internal deliberation of the European Council potentially confrontational. In crises with redistributive effects and where heads of governments carry not only divergent policy preferences but also incompatible nationalist claims (as has happened in migration policy or in the banking union's reform), the European Council is inevitably exposed to a decision-making standstill. Unsurprisingly, leaders from the strongest national governments sought to overcome this decision-making stalemate through unilateral initiatives meant to manage those challenges which threatened their own domestic consensus. Certainly, it is undeniable that the European Council played a crucial role in promoting the integration process, particularly as a crisis manager or arbitrator on the most intractable issues (Bickerton, Hodson and Puetter 2015; Wessels 2016). Nevertheless, its role has raised collective action dilemmas that are not easily solvable (Fabbrini 2013). For instance, during the height of the financial crisis, its decisions arrived too little too late. To prevent such confusion, it is necessary to separate, through a constitutional act, those policies to be decided on both the national and the supranational levels.

On the horizontal level, in turn, it is necessary to introduce separations between the institutions that make up the centre's decision-making process. The centralization of decision-making (in either the European Council or the EP) is incompatible with the need to guarantee a representative equilibrium between states and citizens. Those institutions give decision-making pre-eminence to one or the other representative groups (states or citizens). Moreover, both intergovermentalization and parliamentarization imply the systemic domination of the largest over the smallest states, either in the European Council or in the EP. It is through the horizontal separation of executive and legislative powers that equilibrium is possible by making the EU executive power independent from both the EP and European Council and keeping reciprocal checks and balances on them. Separation of powers (if creatively implemented) combines the corporate/territorial representation of national governments and the individual representation of European citizens. Here there needs to be a compromise between the national governments of the European Council and the EP for a reformed governance system: the European Council recedes from playing an executive role at the EU level and the EP gives up the claim of forming the EU government.

Several institutional strategies might be considered for institutionalizing that compromise. Path dependency, however, would suggest rationalizing the current dual nature which the executive power has acquired in the EU (in the form of the European Council's and Commission's presidents). For this strategy, the president of the Commission would no longer be a *spitzenkandidat* but an official enjoying the 'advice and consent' of the EP (without thus becoming dependent on the latter's confidence), while the president of the Union (and no longer of the European Council) would be elected by the citizens of the member states (through electoral colleges and no longer by national governmental leaders). National governmental leaders would have the role to select a short list of candidates (preferably two) for the position of the Union's president, although it is the national electoral colleges to decide among themselves the winner. It is a popular (albeit not formally direct) election. In unions of demographically asymmetrical states, with distinct national identities, the direct election of an executive's leader is not advisable; otherwise, the larger states will be advantaged over the smaller ones. The state electoral college is a useful instrument for over-representing the smaller states compared to the larger ones. For instance, the allocation of the electoral votes to each member state's electoral college, the criterion of degressive proportionality as used for the election of the EP's members, could be adopted. In such an election, it is useful to remember that the latter would play no role. Once elected, the president would represent the Union, codirecting the executive (consisting of the commissioners) with the president of the Commission, which would be an expression of an agreement between the EP's majority and the newly elected president. She would be president of the Union and not of the European Council, because the European Council would withdraw from playing any executive role at the supranational level, although it would acquire a legislative role when crucial issues for the member states are at stake in the legislative process. The European Council as well as the Council would preserve their institutional identity of corporate (i.e. territorial) representation (as envisioned by Sbragia). Whereas the vote by the Council or European Council should always be through an absolute majority of its members, it may be agreed upon that, in specific and delimited issues and policies, the majority required should be qualified, thus guaranteeing the confederal features of the legislative chamber representing the member states.

The national governmental leaders of the European Council would have several reasons for accepting the change: first, because they would control the selection process of the candidates for the Union's presidency by shortlisting them; second, because the Commission's president would not depend on the EP's confidence; third, because the executive power would have two heads reflecting the views of states and citizens; fourth, because they would continue to enjoy indisputable power in approving or rejecting the executive's proposals on strategic issues (such as foreign and diplomatic affairs, defence matters, financial and taxation issues, composition of the supranational courts, *inter alia*). It might be established also that the members (commissioners) of the federal executive, as proposed by the two presidents, should receive the 'advice and consent' of the European Council (for those in charge of policy fields of importance for the member states) and of the EP (for the others). Besides the specific technicalities for setting up a proper executive power in the EU, what matters is that the latter must be separated not only from national executives but also from the supranational EP. Both the executive and the bicameral legislatures (the Council plus European Council representing member state governments and the EP representing European or member state citizens) must have the power of legislative initiative, although every legislative decision must emerge from a process of checks and balances involving both (and should be subjected to judicial supervision). The more the powers (executive and legislative) are separated, the more they have an incentive to carry out reciprocal checks. The more the legislature is internally separated, the more it has an incentive to ensure reciprocal balance between the two chambers. At the same time, the holders of executive power should be regularly accountable to the voters, directly or indirectly. Of course, it would be necessary to identify mechanisms to prevent separation of powers from turning into paralysing intra-institutional conflict (for the U.S. case, see Cain 2015 and Fukuyama 2014).

Differentiated governance is incompatible with the federal union's model. The policies allocated to the federal centre should be managed by the same governance system for making clear who is responsible for the decisions taken. Differentiation might confound accountability on those policy's decisions. Nor is policy differentiation compatible with the federal union's model, since all the members of the union are expected to be part of its shared government. In the EU, opt-outs have been the price to be paid for centralizing policies that one or the other member states would prefer to keep decentralized. However, in a federal union, the policies to share at the federal level should be limited (enumerated, but crucial), leaving to the states the power to differentiate all the other policies under their constitutional domain. Once the dividing line between self□government and shared government is established (Elazar 1987), a line separating the policies to be shared at the federal centre's level from those which must remain at the state/canton level, then differentiation can develop between the self-government of the states, but not within the shared government of the union. Differentiation should substantiate the peculiarity of each state and its democratic experimentation. This would likely require the relocation to the national self-government some of the policies now managed in Brussels and the transferring to shared government of those core state power's policies currently controlled by national governments through their Brussels intergovernmental institutions. As the experience of federal unions shows, that dividing line is an object of permanent negotiation between the states and the centre, thus generating a political dynamism (that in the U.S. case has taken the form of a pendulum between the centre and the states regarding the pre-eminence on deciding new policies, Beer 1993). A federal union is incompatible with a static equilibrium. In the EU's case, a permanent negotiating process between national government and supranational institution leaders would come to constitute the physiology and not the pathology of functioning as a federal union, although that negotiation would need to be regulated by constitutional criteria supervised by a supranational court (Fabbrini 2010). If the EU is no longer a centralizing organization that aims to bring to Brussels as many policies as possible (a process theoretically justified by the neofunctional spill-over effect), then the incentive on national governments to play an executive role in Brussels will also diminish. In this case, the national governments' role would be rather crucial for preventing centralization, thus preserving the dividing line between self-government and shared government.

CONCLUSION

With Sbragia 1992's contribution as a watermark, the chapter has discussed the EU's governance's question for assessing the current and future role of national governments. First, it has identified the differentiated governance regime which has emerged in the EU since the 1992 Maastricht Treaty, in order to clarify the different roles national governments are currently playing in those governance regimes. Because that differentiation has been dramatically challenged by the multiple crises of the 2010s, the chapter has considered, second, the main official EU proposals to meet those challenges. All of these proposals, however, focused on the policies to pursue for overcoming the crises and not on the governance's models for making their management more effective and accountable. In order to consider alternative governance models to the *status quo*, the chapter has thus moved to the literature, discussing the *club governance* and the *state governance* models. For the former, the governance question is reduced to the cooperation of different clusters of national governments regarding the policies of their interest. For the latter, the governance question is resolved through the institutional centralization of the decision-making process either in the European Council or in the EP. Because each of the two models is unable to accommodate a balanced representation of state and citizen interests, I have investigated an alternative perspective through an examination of the experience of comparative federalism. Third, that experience has helped to conceptualize the governance model of a federal union as a system of multiple separation of powers. In federal unions (such as the United States and Switzerland), separation of powers has offered an answer to the question of keeping on balance states' and citizens' interests. However, in none of those federal unions, do national governments play a political role as they do in the EU (whereas they are directly represented in a federal state like Germany, although without affecting the formation and functioning of the federal government). Fourth, the chapter has thus applied the analytical framework of the federal union to the EU, showing how it can help to solve the puzzle identified by Sbragia (1992, 4), namely the incorporation of "the governments of the Community's member states" without transforming the EU into an undemocratic federation of national executives. Regardless of specific technicalities, the puzzle can be solved through a compromise between the European Council and the EP for setting up a dual executive power separated and independent from both institutions. In conclusion, as Sbragia (1992, 267) argued, "a more systematic exploration of the institutional range of democratic federal systems help broaden the scope of analysis when one is thinking, either in scholarly or in political terms, about the future long-term shape of government within the Community." Thus adding (ibid.), "for scholars, the application of a comparative framework in analysing the Community can illuminate processes outside the Community as well as inside". What was then true for the European Community is even truer today for the EU.

BIBLIOGRAPHY

Beer, Samuel H. 1993. *To Make a Nation: The Rediscovery of American Federalism*. Cambridge, MA: Harvard University Press.
Bickerton, Christopher J., Dermot Hodson and Uwe Puetter, eds. 2015. *The New Intergovernmentalism: States and Supranational Actors in the Post-Maastricht Era*. Oxford: Oxford University Press.
Borzel, Tanja A. 2016. 'From EU Governance of Crisis to Crisis of EU Governance: Regulatory Failure, Redistributive Conflict and Eurosceptic Public.' *Journal of Common Market Studies*, 54, no. S1: 8–31.
Buchanan, James M. 1965. 'An Economic Theory of Clubs.' *Economica*, 32, no. 125: 1–14. doi:10.2307/2552442.
Cain, Bruce E. 2015. *Democracy More or Less: America's Political Reform Quandary*. New York: Cambridge University Press.
Christiansen, Thomas. 2016. 'After the *Spitzenkandidaten*: Fundamental Change in the EU's Political System?' *West European Politics*, 39, no. 5: 992–1010.
Dehousse, Renaud. 2011. *The 'Community Method': Obstinate or Obsolete?* New York: Palgrave Macmillan.
Devuyst, Youri. 2018. 'The European Union's Community Method.' *Oxford Research Encyclopedia of Politics*.
Elazar, Daniel J. 1987. *Exploring Federalism*. Tuscaloosa: The University of Alabama Press.
Fabbrini, Federico. 2016. *Economic Governance in Europe: Comparative Paradoxes and Constitutional Challenges*. Oxford: Oxford University Press.
Fabbrini, Sergio. 2010. *Compound Democracies: Why the United States and Europe Are Becoming Similar*. Oxford: Oxford University Press, 2nd edition.
Fabbrini, Sergio. 2013. 'Intergovernmentalism and Its Limits: Assessing the European Union's Answer to the Euro Crisis.' *Comparative Political Studies*, 46.9: 1003–1029.
Fabbrini, Sergio. 2015a. 'The European Union and the Puzzle of Parliamentary Government.' *Journal of European Integration*, 37, no. 5: 571–586.

Fabbrini, Sergio. 2015b. *Which European Union? Europe after the Euro Crisis*. Cambridge: Cambridge University Press.

Fabbrini, Sergio. 2016. 'From Consensus to Domination: The Intergovernmental Union.' *Journal of European Integration*, 38, no. 5: 587–599.

Fabbrini, Sergio. 2017a. 'Intergovernmentalism in the European Union. A Comparative Federalism Perspective.' *Journal of European Public Policy*, 24, no. 4: 580–597.

Fabbrini, Sergio. 2017b. 'Which Democracy for a Union of States? A Comparative Perspective of the European Union.' *Global Policy*, 8, no. 6: 14–22.

Fabbrini, Sergio. 2019. *Europe's Future: Decoupling and Reforming*. Cambridge: Cambridge University Press.

Fabbrini, Sergio and Uwe Puetter, eds. 2016. 'Integration without Supranationalisation: The Central Role of the European Council in Post-Lisbon EU Politics.' *Journal of European Integration*, 38, no. 5: 481–495.

Fossum, John E. and Markus Jachtenfuchs. 2017. 'Federal Challenges and Challenges to Federalism. Insights from the EU and Federal States.' *Journal of European Public Policy*, 24, no. 4: 467–485.

Fukuyama, Francis. 2014. *Political Order and Political Decay: From the Industrial Revolution to the Globalization of Democracy*. New York: Farrar, Straus and Giroux.

Genschel, Phillipp and Markus Jachtenfuchs, eds. 2014. *Beyond the Regulatory Polity? The European Integration of Core State Powers*. Oxford: Oxford University Press.

Genschel, Phillipp and Markus Jachtenfuchs. 2017. 'Different Crises, Similar Reactions: The Integration of Core State Powers in the Debt and Refugees Crises Compared.' Paper submitted at the ECPR General Conference, University of Oslo, Oslo, 6–9 September.

Hendrickson, David C. 2009. *Union, Nation, or Empire: The American Debate over International Relations, 1789–1941*. Lawrence: University Press of Kansas.

Heritier, Adrienne. 2007. *Explaining Institutional Change in Europe*. Oxford: Oxford University Press.

Hix, Simon. 2008. 'Why the EU Needs (Left-Right) Politics? Policy Reform and Accountability Are Impossible without It.' *Notre Europe: Etudes & Recherches* Policy Paper no. 19. http://personal.lse.ac.uk/hix/Working_Papers/NotreEurope_Hix%20_Bartolini.pdf.

Juncker, Jean-Claude, Donald Tusk, Jeroen Dijsselbloem, Mario Draghi and Martin Schulz. 2015. *Completing Europe's Economic and Monetary Union*. Brussels: European Commission.

Katznelson, Ira and Martin Shefter, eds. 2002. *Shaped by War and Trade. International Influences on American Political Development*. Princeton, NJ: Princeton University Press.

Kelemen, R. Daniel. 2014. 'Building the New European State? Federalism, Core State Powers, and European Integration.' In *Beyond the Regulatory Polity? The European Integration of Core State Powers*, edited by Phillipp Genschel and Markus Jachtenfuchs, 211–229. Oxford: Oxford University Press.

Kelemen, R. Daniel. 2019. 'Federalism and European Integration.' In *European Integration Theories*, edited by Antje Wiener, Tanja Borzel and Thomas Risse, 27–42. Oxford: Oxford University Press, 3rd edition.

Krastev, Ivan. 2017. *After Europe*. Philadelphia: University of Pennsylvania Press.

Majone, Giandomenico. 2014. *Rethinking the Union of Europe Post-Crisis: Has Integration Gone Too Far?* Cambridge: Cambridge University Press.

Matthijs, Matthias. 2017. 'Europe after Brexit: A Less Perfect Union.' *Foreign Affairs*, January–February. https://www.foreignaffairs.com/articles/Europe/2016-12-12/Europe-after-brexit.

Nicolaidis, Kalypso. 2013. 'European Democracy and Its Crisis.' *Journal of Common Market Studies*, 51, no. 2: 351–369.

Piattoni, Simona. 2010. *The Theory of Multi-Level Governance: Conceptual, Empirical and Normative Challenges*. Oxford: Oxford University Press.

Puetter, Uwe. 2014. *The European Council and the Council: New Intergovernmentalism and Institutional Change*. Oxford: Oxford University Press.

Rodrik, Dani. 2007. 'The Inescapable Trilemma of the World Economy.' Weblog. 27 June. https://rodrik.typepad.com/dani_rodriks_weblog/2007/06/the-inescapable.html. Accessed 9 August 2019.

Rodrik, Dani. 2011. *The Globalization Paradox: Democracy and the Future of World Economy*. New York: W. W. Norton and Company.

Rompuy, van Herman, et al. 2012. *Towards a Genuine Economic and Monetary Union*. Brussels: European Council.

Sabel, Charles and Jonathan Zeitlin. 2012. *Experimentalist Governance in the European Union. Towards a New Architecture*. Oxford: Oxford University Press, 2nd edition.

Sartori, Giovanni. 2009. 'Concept Misformation in Comparative Politics.' In *Concepts and Methods in Social Science: The Tradition of Giovanni Sartori*, edited by David Collier and John Gerring, 13–43. London: Routledge.

Sbragia, Alberta M. 1992. 'Thinking about the European Future: The Uses of Comparison.' In *Euro-Politics: Institutions and Policymaking in the 'New' European Community*, edited by Alberta M. Sbragia, 257–291. Washington, DC: Brookings Institution Press.

Scharpf, Fritz W. 1988. 'The Joint-Decision Trap: Lessons from German Federalism and European Integration.' *Public Administration*, 66, no. 3: 239–278.

Schutze, Robert. 2010. *From Dual to Cooperative Federalism*. Oxford: Oxford University Press.

Stepan, Alfred. 1999. 'Federalism and Democracy: Beyond the US Model.' *Journal of Democracy*, 10, no. 4: 19–34.

Wessels, Wolfgang. 1997. 'An Ever Closer Fusion? A Dynamic Macropolitical View on Integration Processes.' *Journal of Common Market Studies*, 35, no. 2: 267 299.

Wessels, Wolfgang. 2016. *The European Council*. New York: Palgrave.

Wozniakowski, Tomasz P. 2017. 'Why the Sovereign Debt Crisis Could Lead to a Federal Fiscal Union: The Paradoxical Origins of Fiscalization in the United States and Insights for the European Union.' *Journal of European Public Policy*, 25, no. 4: 630–649.

Conclusion

Jae-Jae Spoon and Nils Ringe

I do not need to emphasize that the European Union is in many ways *sui generis*. It is clearly unlike any of the national systems which social scientists study. Similarly, it is not necessary for me to point out that the European Union is unlike any other international or regional organization with which we are familiar. (Alberta Sbragia, Keynote at the European Community Studies Association Biennial Conference, Montreal, Canada, 2004)

Alberta Sbragia has been a scholar ahead of her time. Recognizing its unique attributes, she examined the European Union (EU) and its institutions through a comparative multi-level many of the debates among scholars of international relations and comparative politics regarding the EU (e.g., Sandholtz and Zysman 1989; Moravcsik 1993; Hix 1994; Moravcsik 1998; Sandholtz and Stone Sweet 1998), she recognized the limitations and contributions of the different theoretical approaches—all with the goal of providing a carefully nuanced view of what the EU is as an institution and as an organization and how and why this matters for policy-making and policy outcomes.

George Ross's chapter (chapter 1) opened this volume by situating Alberta Sbragia's research and analysis in the broader context of the historical trajectory of the European integration process and the evolution of the field of EU studies. Many of the themes he highlights reemerged throughout the remaining chapters. Shared rule, in particular, runs as a common thread through the volume, discussed in the context of either comparative federalism or multi-level governance. Another is comparison, either implicitly in the recognition that the EU is not *sui generis* or explicitly in several chapters that compare the EU with other political entities. The role of the member states and national political institutions in EU governance and the increasingly important interconnections between national and EU politics are two other recurrent themes in Sbragia's work and throughout this book.

The chapters in this volume have demonstrated that the big questions posed by Sbragia continue to matter. As the contributors show, we are still working to understand the complexities of the EU and how this matters for policy outcomes. Throughout the contributions, it is apparent that her thinking continues to inform scholars' investigations, analyses, and commentary on the EU. While some of the chapters engage directly with Sbragia's big questions, others apply her ideas to more specific empirical questions. Collectively, they address three important themes present throughout Sbragia's work: multi-level governance and comparative federalism; the complexity of the institutions of the EU; and the policy choices and outcomes inherent in EU membership. We can summarize these three themes and the related chapters with the following takeaways.

First, national institutions cannot be ignored. In her writing, Sbragia was often focused on the role of national institutions in the EU, asking "how much national government should shape Community policy-making" (1992, 257). Starting with this underlying premise, Peters, Perez, and Daniel demonstrate how governance in the EU is closely intertwined with governance (actors, institutions, and traditions) at the national level. These chapters illustrate that, to really understand European governance, one must not dismiss its constituent parts. Fabbrini then challenges the very relationship between the member states and the EU established through the institutions, proposing a significant reform of the EU executive that distinguishes between the national and the supranational institutions.

Second, focusing on shared governance enables comparison of the EU. "Shared rule is shared rule," Sbragia (2004) declared in an address to the European Community Studies Association. It can be achieved through either supranational or confederal arrangements. In their chapters, Maas and Brand, thus, argue that considering the EU as a federal entity—as an organization that embodies shared governance—allows scholars to compare policy outcomes and frameworks as diverse as private international law and citizenship laws in the EU with federations such as the United States and Canada. Wong and Irrera then implore us to consider the policy processes and outcomes of the EU and how they compare to those of another regional organization, the Association of Southeast Asian Nations.

Third, policy-making in the EU is interdependent. Jacoby and Jevtic-Somlai demonstrate by examining Germany's impact on immigration and macroeconomic policy in the Visegrád states that the horizontal interdependence of policy-making in the EU between rich and powerful states and states which are poor and less influential is one of "the tradeoffs intrinsic to enlargement" (Sbragia 2000, 321). Piattoni and Notermans then illustrate the vertical interdependence of policy-making by exploring the impact of policies imposed on Italy by the EU as a result of the Euro crisis. Examining a different aspect of the interdependence of policy-making, Salazar-Morales and Hallerberg explore trade policies of the EU and the United States toward third parties, most importantly China as an increasingly important international actor, through Sbragia's (2010) lens of "competitive interdependence."

In summary, the discussions and findings of these chapters have demonstrated the continued ability of Sbragia's scholarship to inspire research and analysis on and about the EU. Although she did not explicitly discuss the increasing politicization of the EU and the increasing salience of the EU in national politics, analyses that focus on these—as do several of the chapters in the volume—directly follow from her research agenda. Furthermore, more recent events, such as challenges to the common currency, immigration, and the rise of populism, can all be analyzed through the frameworks established by Sbragia.

Importantly, many questions still remain as the EU is confronted by new and continuing challenges from Brexit to democratic backsliding by the governments of some member states, to growing Euroscepticism and the reform of the now defunct *spitzenkandidat* process. We hope that, by revisiting many of the questions and ideas that Sbragia posed and developed in her scholarship, this volume has inspired students and scholars to continue on her career-long quest to understand what the EU is (and what it is not). After all, "being a pioneer is not for the faint of heart" (Sbragia 2007, 7).

BIBLIOGRAPHY

Hix, Simon. 1994. "The Study of the European Community: The Challenge to Comparative Politics." *West European Politics*, 17, no. 1: 1–30.

Moravcsik, Andrew. 1993. "Preferences and Power in the European Community: A Liberal Intergovernmental Approach." *Journal of Common Market Studies*, 31, no. 4: 473–524.

Moravcsik, Andrew. 1998. *The Choice for Europe: Social Purpose and State Power from Messina to Maastricht*. Ithaca, NY: Cornell University Press.

Sandholtz, Wayne and Alec Stone Sweet, eds. 1998. *European Integration and Supranational Governance*. Oxford: Oxford University Press.

Sandholtz, Wayne and John Zysman. 1989. "Recasting the European Bargain." *World Politics*, 41, no. 1: 45–78.

Sbragia, Alberta M. 1992. "Thinking about the European Future: The Uses of Comparison." In *Euro-Politics: Institutions and Policymaking in the "New" European Community*, ed. Alberta M. Sbragia, 257–291. Washington, DC: The Brookings Institution.

Sbragia, Alberta M. 2000. "'Trade-Offs Rather Than Bargains in Europe?' Symposium on Governing in Europe: Effective and Democratic?" *Journal of European Public Policy*, 7, no. 2: 316–321.

Sbragia, Alberta M. 2004. "The Future of Federalism in the European Union." Keynote Address delivered at the European Community Studies Association Canada Biennial Conference, Montreal, Canada.

Sbragia, Alberta M. 2007 "An American Perspective on the EU's Constitutional Treaty." *Politics*, 27, no. 1: 2–7.

Sbragia, Alberta M. 2010. "The EU, the US, and Trade Policy: Competitive Interdependence in the Management of Globalization." *Journal of European Public Policy*, 17, no. 3: 368–382.

Index

Note: Page references for figures are italicized.

About the Contributors

Ronald A. Brand is Chancellor Mark A. Nordenberg University Professor and Academic Director of the Center for International Legal Education at the University of Pittsburgh School of Law. He has been a member of the U.S. delegation in treaty negotiations at the Hague Conference on Private International Law for more than twenty-five years.

William T. Daniel is Assistant Professor in Comparative Politics in the School of Politics and International Relations at the University of Nottingham. His research interests are primarily focused on party politics and legislatures in the European Union (EU), with a specific focus on the European Parliament. His research has been published by Oxford University Press, *European Union Politics*, *Journal of Common Market Studies*, *Politics and Gender*, and *The Journal of European Public Policy*.

Sergio Fabbrini is Dean of the Political Science Department and Professor of Political Science and International Relations at the LUISS Guido Carli University in Rome. He holds a Jean Monnet Chair in European Institutions and Politics. His publications include *Europe's Future: Decoupling and Reforming* (2019) and *Which European Union? Europe after the Euro Crisis* (2015). He received the Pierre Keller Visiting Professorship at the Harvard Kennedy School of Government for the 2019–2020 academic year.

Mark Hallerberg is Dean of Research and Faculty and Professor of Public Management and Political Economy at the Hertie School of Governance. His research focuses on fiscal governance, tax competition, financial crises, and EU politics. He previously held academic positions at Emory University, University of Pittsburgh, and the Georgia Institute of Technology.

Daniela Irrera is Associate Professor of Political Science in the Department of Political and Social Sciences at the University of Catania, where she serves as Deputy Dean for Internationalisation and Research. She is Secretary General of the Italian Political Science Association, Convenor of the ECPR Standing Group on International Relations, member of the ISA Governing Council, and review coeditor for the *Journal of Contemporary European Studies*.

Wade Jacoby is Mary Lou Fulton Professor of Political Science at Brigham Young University. He is author of *Imitation and Politics: Redesigning Modern Germany* and *The Enlargement of the EU and NATO: Ordering from the Menu in Central Europe*. He received the DAAD Prize for his scholarship on Germany and the EU and was a Braudel fellow at the European University Institute.

Elizabeta Jevtic-Somlai is Faculty Adviser and Coordinator for the Model European Union course at Brigham Young University. From 2015 to 2017, she worked as Visiting Assistant Professor in the Political Science Department at Brigham Young University and previously worked in the field of international security with the United Nations for a decade. Her research focuses on the dichotomy between the protection of human rights and international security. She holds a PhD from the University of Kent.

Willem Maas is Professor and Jean Monnet Chair at York University, where he chairs the Glendon Political Science Department. His works include *Creating European Citizens*, *Democratic Citizenship and the Free Movement of People* (ed.), *Sixty-Five Years of European Governance* (co-ed.), *Multilevel Citizenship* (ed.), and several journal special issues.

Ton Notermans is Senior Lecturer of Political Economy at the Tallinn University of Technology (Estonia). He has taught at the Universities of Trento (Italy), Innsbruck (Austria), Pusan National University (Korea), and the Azerbaijan Diplomatic Academy. His research interests focus mainly on the history and political economy of monetary unions. He received his PhD from MIT.

Lauren K. Perez is Assistant Professor of Political Science at Francis Marion University. She earned her PhD from the University of Pittsburgh, and then became a Harper-Schmidt fellow at the University of Chicago. She studies legislative politics in multi-level settings, such as the EU, in order to better understand how factors from one level affect the legislative process at other levels.

B. Guy Peters is Maurice Falk Professor of Government at the University of Pittsburgh and founding president of the International Public Policy Association. He is also currently the editor of the *International Review of Public Policy* and associate editor of the *Journal of Comparative Public Policy*. His most recent publications include *Policy Problems and Policy Design* and *Institutional Theory in Political Science*, 4th edition.

Simona Piattoni is Professor of Political Science at the University of Trento (Italy). She has taught at the Universities of Tromsø and Agder (Norway) and Innsbruck (Austria). Her research interests include economic development, clientelism, cohesion policy, multi-level governance, and democracy. She received her PhD from MIT.

Nils Ringe is Professor of Political Science and Director of the Center for European Studies at the University of Wisconsin–Madison. He holds a Jean Monnet Chair. His research has been published by the University of Michigan Press, Oxford University Press, *American Journal of Political Science, British Journal of Political Science, European Union Politics, and European Journal of Political Research*.

George Ross is Professor Emeritus at Brandeis University and *ad personam* Jean Monnet Chair at the University of Montreal. He served as the president for the Council for European Studies (1990–1997) and the European Union Studies Association (2003–2005). His book *The European Union and Its Crises: Through the Eyes of the Brussels' Elite* won the 2012 Neal Prize for Excellence in EU Scholarship from the European Union Center of the University of Illinois. He received the 2017 Lifetime Achievement in European Studies Award from the European Union Studies Association.

Diego A. Salazar-Morales is a research associate at the Dahrendorf Forum. He has previously held research positions at the Hertie School of Governance where he is also a doctoral candidate. His research interests include global politics, policy instruments, and implementation. Diego holds an MSc in public policy and administration from the London School of Economics and Political Science.

Alberta M. Sbragia is Professor Emerita of Political Science and *ad personam* Jean Monnet Chair at the University of Pittsburgh. She founded the West European Studies Center in 1984 and the European Union Center of Excellence in 1998, serving as directors of both until 2010. Her book *Euro-Politics* (1992) was one of the first to examine the European Union through the lens of comparative politics. She is the recipient of the 2013 Lifetime Achievement in European Studies Award from the European Union Studies Association.

Jae-Jae Spoon is Professor of Political Science and Director of the European Studies Center at the University of Pittsburgh. She is the coeditor of the *Journal of Elections, Public Opinion and Parties* and *Research & Politics*. Her research has been published by the University of Michigan Press, the *British Journal of Political Science*, the *Journal of Politics*, *Comparative Political Studies*, the *European Journal of Political Research*, *European Union Politics*, and *Party Politics*.

Reuben Wong is Academic Director at the Global Relations Office and Associate Professor in the Political Science Department at the National University of Singapore. He held the first Jean Monnet Chair in Singapore and is also an associate fellow at the EU Centre Singapore, and Senior Research Affiliate at the College of Europe in Bruges, Belgium.

www.ingramcontent.com/pod-product-compliance
Lightning Source LLC
Chambersburg PA
CBHW022350280326
41935CB00007B/145